STUDENT'S BOOK
AND WORKBOOK **2**
with Digital Pack
COMBO A | CEFR **B1**

TH!NK

SECOND EDITION

Herbert Puchta,
Jeff Stranks &
Peter Lewis-Jones

CAMBRIDGE
UNIVERSITY PRESS

CONTENTS

Welcome p 4
- **A** Introducing yourself; Asking questions; The weather; Families
- **B** Meeting people; Irregular past participles; Losing things; Furniture
- **C** Buying and talking about food; In a restaurant; Shops; Things you have to do
- **D** Plans and arrangements; Sports and sport verbs; Travel plans

	FUNCTIONS & SPEAKING	GRAMMAR	VOCABULARY
Unit 1 **Incredible people** p 12	Talking about things you have and haven't done Developing Speaking: Offering encouragement	Present perfect with *just*, *already* and *yet* ▶ Present perfect vs. past simple	Personality adjectives Collocations **WordWise:** Phrases with *just*
Unit 2 **A good education** p 20	Asking and giving / refusing permission to do something Role play: Asking permission	▶ Present perfect with *for* and *since* *a*, *an*, *the* or no article	School subjects Verbs about thinking

Life competencies: Recognising others' good work ▶, **Culture:** Schools with a difference ▶, Review

	FUNCTIONS & SPEAKING	GRAMMAR	VOCABULARY
Unit 3 **On the screen** p 30	Comparing things and actions Developing Speaking: Asking for and offering help	Comparative and superlative adjectives (review) (*not*) *as … as* comparatives ▶ Making a comparison stronger or weaker Adverbs and comparative adverbs	Types of films **WordWise:** Expressions with *get* Types of TV programmes
Unit 4 **Online life** p 38	Giving advice	Indefinite pronouns (*everyone*, *no one*, *someone*, etc.) *all* / *some* / *none* / *any of them* ▶ *should(n't)*, *had better*, *ought to*	IT terms Language for giving advice

Life competencies: Achieving your goals ▶, **Culture:** From caves to Kindles – how reading has changed ▶, Review

	FUNCTIONS & SPEAKING	GRAMMAR	VOCABULARY
Unit 5 **Music to my ears** p 48	Role play: Helpful suggestions Developing Speaking: Asking about feelings	Present perfect continuous ▶ Present perfect simple vs. present perfect continuous	Making music Musical instruments **WordWise:** Phrasal verbs with *out*
Unit 6 **No planet B** p 56	Expressing surprise and enthusiasm	*will* (*not*), *may* (*not*), *might* (*not*) for prediction ▶ First conditional *unless* in first conditional sentences	The environment Verbs to talk about energy

Life competencies: Managing your money ▶, **Culture:** Green solutions around the world ▶, Review

PRONUNCIATION	THINK!	SKILLS
Intonation and sentence stress	**Values:** Human qualities	**Reading** Online survey responses: Who do you admire most? Article: Human moles **Writing** A short passage about someone you admire **Listening** Guessing game
Word stress	**Values:** Learning for life **Train to THINK** Learning about texts	**Reading** Article: The loneliest schoolboy in Britain Article: The power of 'yet' **Writing** An email describing your school routine **Listening** Conversation about a summer activity list

B1 Preliminary for Schools Exam practice

PRONUNCIATION	THINK!	SKILLS
Words ending in /ə/	**Values:** Preconceived ideas	**Reading** Article: A new kind of superhero Article: The history of watching TV **Writing** A paragraph about your TV habits **Listening** Interview with a teenage filmmaker
The short /ʌ/ vowel sound	**Values:** Responsible online behaviour **Train to THINK** Logical sequencing	**Reading** Article: Leaving footprints Short texts: Different types of messages **Writing** A web page giving advice **Listening** Conversation about falling for online scams

B1 Preliminary for Schools Exam practice

PRONUNCIATION	THINK!	SKILLS
been: strong /biːn/ and weak /bɪn/	**Values:** Following your dreams	**Reading** Magazine article: A bright star Article: The future of live music **Writing** The story of your favourite band **Listening** Interviews about music
/f/, /v/, /b/ consonant sounds	**Values:** Caring for the world **Train to THINK** Different perspectives	**Reading** Magazine article: Hot topic: saving the Earth Leaflet: Energy matters **Writing** An article for the school magazine **Listening** Interview about a town project

B1 Preliminary for Schools Exam practice

Pronunciation page 120

Get it right! pages 122–123

Speaking activities pages 127–128

WELCOME

A GETTING TO KNOW YOU
Introducing yourself

1 Read the email quickly. Write the names under the photos.

Alex
alex@mymail.com
Hi Patricia!

Hi Patricia,
My name's Alex and I'd like to be your e-pen pal.
I got your name and email address from my teacher, Mr Goodall. He lived in Peru for three years, and he's a good friend of your father's.
So, what would you like to know about me? I'm 15 years old. I live in a small house in Birmingham with my mum and my two little brothers. They're OK, but they can be annoying sometimes. I go to Ashton High School. I quite like school, but my teachers always give us too much homework. I usually do it when I get home from school, but I'm not doing that today – that's because I'm writing to you!
I like listening to music and playing games on the computer. I also like playing the guitar. I play in a band with some of my friends. I like sport, too. I play basketball and tennis. I'm in the school basketball team. We usually play matches on Sunday mornings. That's a bit of a problem because I don't really like getting up early at the weekend.
But what about you? I hope you'll want to write to me. There are lots of questions I want to ask you. Things like: what's life like in Peru? Do you like your school? What's it like? What's the weather like in Lima? Have you got a big family? All that sort of stuff to help me get to know you. Mr Goodall says you like volleyball, but that's all I know about you.
So please email me. I'd love to have a Peruvian friend.
Best,
Alex

2 Read the email and complete the information about Alex.

Name ⁰ _Alex_ Hometown ¹ _____
Age ² _____ Family ³ _____
Likes ⁴ _____
Dislikes ⁵ _____

Asking questions

3 Match the questions with the answers to make mini-dialogues.

1 What do you do? ☐
2 What are you doing? ☐
3 What do you like doing? ☐
4 Do you like studying English? ☐
5 Where are you from? ☐
6 Are you 14? ☐

a I'm watching TV.
b Yes, it's great.
c I'm from Italy.
d I'm a student.
e No, I'm 13.
f I love playing video games.

4 **SPEAKING** Work in pairs. Ask and answer the questions in Exercise 3. Give answers that are true for you.

5 Look at these sentences. Choose the next line for each of the mini-dialogues in Exercise 3.
1 What's your teacher's name?
2 Do you live in Rome?
3 What school do you go to?
4 When is your birthday?
5 Would you like to go out and do something with me?
6 Me, too. Do you want to come over and play the new Minecraft game?

6 **SPEAKING** Work in pairs. Think of an answer to each question from Exercise 5. Then practise your full dialogues.

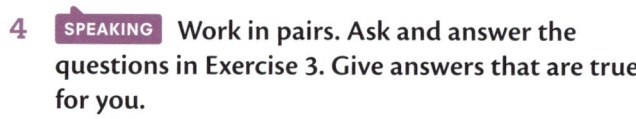

What do you do? — I'm a student.
What school do you go to? — Chester High School.

Cape Town

WELCOME
Paris

London

New York

Seville

The weather

7 What kind of weather do you love, like or hate? Draw a 😃, 🙂 or a 🙁 next to each one.

- ○ sunny ☐
- ○ wet ☐
- ○ cloudy ☐
- ○ warm ☐
- ○ cold ☐
- ○ windy ☐
- ○ humid ☐
- ○ rainy ☐
- ○ dry ☐
- ○ freezing ☐
- ○ hot ☐
- ○ foggy ☐

8 **SPEAKING** Work in pairs. Tell your partner.

I love rainy weather.

9 🔊 **W.01** Listen to the weather forecast for the UK. Tick (✓) the weather words in Exercise 7 that you hear.

10 🔊 **W.01** Listen again. What is the weather going to be like in Manchester, Birmingham and London?

11 **SPEAKING** Work in pairs. Look at the pictures. Ask and answer questions.

What's the weather like in New York?

It's freezing!

Families

12 Look at the family words. Complete the pairs.

1 mother and _____
2 brother and _____
3 aunt and _____
4 grandma and _____
5 husband and _____
6 niece and _____

13 🔊 **W.02** Listen to Alex talking to Patricia on Skype. How are these people related to Alex?

1 Peter _____
2 Lawrence _____
3 Lynne _____
4 Steve _____
5 Tony _____
6 Mary _____
7 Hemi _____
8 Claire _____
9 Becca _____
10 Harry _____

14 **SPEAKING** Work in pairs. Ask each other about your families.

Have you got any cousins?

Yes! I've got ten cousins.

B EXPERIENCES
Meeting people

1 **Put the parts of the dialogue in order. Write 1–10 in the boxes.**

- [ ] A Really! Where? When?
- [ ] A What book was it?
- [ ] A Did she give you one?
- [1] A Have you ever met a famous person?
- [ ] A Did you say anything to her?
- [ ] B It was my English course book, believe it or not. I had it with me to help me with my English.
- [ ] B Well, I realised that I didn't have my phone with me, so she signed a book that I was carrying.
- [ ] B It was last summer. We were on holiday in LA. We were walking out of a restaurant when she walked in.
- [ ] B Yes, I did. I asked her for a selfie.
- [ ] B Yes, I have. Millie Bobby Brown.

2 🔊 **W.03** Listen and check your answers.

3 **SPEAKING** Work with a partner. Practise the conversation. Change names, places and other details.

4 **Find examples of the following tenses in Exercise 1.**
1 A past simple positive statement.
2 A past simple negative statement.
3 A past simple question.
4 A past simple short answer.
5 A past continuous statement.
6 A present perfect question with *ever*.
7 A present perfect short answer.

Irregular past participles

5 **Write the past participles of these irregular verbs.**

1 think	_____	7 eat	_____
2 drink	_____	8 make	_____
3 wear	_____	9 run	_____
4 see	_____	10 win	_____
5 lose	_____	11 read	_____
6 hear	_____	12 ride	_____

6 **Complete the questions with past participles from Exercise 5.**
0 Who's the most famous person you've ever _seen_ ?
1 What's the strangest food you've ever _____ ?
2 What's the best book you've ever _____ ?
3 What's the funniest joke you've ever _____ ?
4 What's the most expensive thing you've ever _____ and never found again?
5 What's the best prize you've ever _____ ?
6 What are the most embarrassing clothes you've ever _____ ?
7 What's the longest phone call you've ever _____ ?
8 What's the longest distance you've ever _____ ?

7 **Answer the questions in Exercise 6 with your own information.**

The most famous person I've ever seen is Usain Bolt.

8 **Work in groups. Each person takes one of the questions from Exercise 6 and thinks of two questions to add.**

Who's the most famous person you've ever seen?
Where did you see him/her?
Did you say anything to him/her?

9 **Ask the other students in your group your questions.**

10 **Report back to the class.**

The most famous person Giovanni has seen is Usain Bolt. He saw him outside a shop in London. He didn't say anything to him.

Losing things

11 Read Liam's story. What was in the wrong container?

People often complain about airline companies losing their suitcases when they fly. It's never happened to me, but something a lot worse happened to my family recently.

About ten years ago my mum got a job teaching at a university in Thailand. At first she only went for six months, but she really liked it and agreed to stay longer, so we all went to live with her. We had a great time, but last year my parents decided that they wanted to return to the UK. Because we'd been there so long, we had loads of things we wanted to take back with us – all the furniture from our house, in fact.

So Mum and Dad went to a shipping company and arranged to take everything back in one of those big containers that you see on ships. The company packed everything into it: the armchairs and sofas, the TV, wardrobes, desks, even all the rugs and curtains. Our whole house was inside that big green metal box.

We flew back to the UK and waited for the container to arrive. About ten weeks later, we were having breakfast one morning when a big lorry arrived outside our house. On the back was a big green metal box. We were so excited. The men opened the container and started to take out our things. But they weren't our things. The container was full of gym equipment. It was the wrong one. We were so upset. But the story has a happy ending. The men took the container and gym equipment away, and about two months ago our things finally arrived.

12 Read the story again and answer the questions. Use the word in brackets in your answer.
1. When did Liam's mum start her job in Thailand? (ago)
2. When did the family move to Thailand? (later)
3. How long did they stay there? (about)
4. When did they decide to move back to the UK? (last)
5. How long after they got back to the UK did the first container arrive? (about)
6. When did the correct container finally arrive? (ago)

13 WRITING Write a short story about something you lost. Use these questions to help you.
- When did it happen?
- What was it?
- Where did you lose it?
- What did you do?
- How did you feel?
- Did you find it? If so, when and where?

Furniture

14 Tick (✓) the items mentioned in the story.

15 SPEAKING Name the other items. Which of these do you think Liam's parents probably didn't put into the container?

They probably didn't put the toilet into the container.

16 SPEAKING Discuss in small groups.
Your family is moving to the other side of the world. What five items from your bedroom or house do you want to take with you?

C EATING AND DRINKING
Buying and talking about food

1 🔊 **W.04** Listen and complete each space with one word.

Assistant	Morning. Can I help you?
Customer	Yes, please. Um, I want ¹_____ onions.
Assistant	OK, how ²_____ ?
Customer	Two large ones, please. And can I have ³_____ mushrooms, too? About half a kilo?
Assistant	OK, sure. Anything else?
Customer	Oh, yes – tomatoes. A ⁴_____ of tomatoes, please. And some chillies.
Assistant	Sorry, we haven't got ⁵_____ chillies today. Maybe try the supermarket across the street.
Customer	OK, thanks.
Assistant	So, ⁶_____ are your tomatoes. Are you making something special tonight?
Customer	Yes, I'm going to make a vegetable curry. I had one in an Indian restaurant last week so I thought I'd try and make one, too.
Assistant	What about lemons? Lemon juice is ⁷_____ good in a curry.
Customer	That's a good ⁸_____ ! But I don't need any. I've ⁹_____ got lemons at home. So, how ¹⁰_____ is that?
Assistant	Let's see. That's £4.15, ¹¹_____ .
Customer	Here you are – £5.
Assistant	And 85p ¹²_____ . Thanks. Enjoy your dinner!

2 Complete each sentence with *some* or *any*. Then match the sentences with the pictures. Write the numbers 1–8.

1 There's _____ butter in the fridge.
2 There are _____ eggs in the kitchen.
3 There aren't _____ olives on the pizza.
4 I'd like _____ of those tomatoes, please.
5 Sorry, there aren't _____ eggs.
6 I'd like _____ water, please.
7 Oh, there isn't _____ milk.
8 No, I don't want _____ orange juice, thanks.

 A  E

 B  F

 C  G

 D 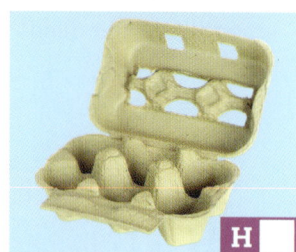 H

3 Which of these things would you always / never / sometimes use to make a sandwich? Write sentences.

> butter | bread | cheese | chicken
> coffee | eggs | milk | olives | onions
> pears | tomatoes | yoghurt

You always use bread to make a sandwich – but you never use ...

4 **ROLE PLAY** Work in pairs. Use your sentences from Exercise 3 to do a role play.

WELCOME

In a restaurant

5 🔊 W.05 Read the sentences. Mark them W (waitress) or C (customer). Listen and check.

1 Can we see the menu, please? ☐
2 Is everything OK? ☐
3 This soup is too cold! ☐
4 Can we have the bill, please? ☐
5 A table for two? This way, please. ☐
6 We'd like the soup to start. ☐
7 What soup have you got today? ☐
8 Are you ready to order? ☐

6 Complete each phrase with *much* or *many*.

1 too _____ butter
2 too _____ onions
3 too _____ things in your bag
4 too _____ milk
5 too _____ noise
6 too _____ cars

7 Complete the mini-dialogues with a phrase from Exercise 6.

1 A This coffee is horrible.
  B I know! There's _____ in it.
2 A Ugh! I can't eat this toast.
  B I know! There's _____ on it.
3 A This salad isn't very good.
  B I know! There are _____ in it!
4 A This restaurant is horrible. We can't talk.
  B I know! There is _____ here.
5 A It took me an hour to drive to work today.
  B I know! There are _____ on our roads.
6 A I can't carry this. It's too heavy.
  B There are _____ . Take something out of it.

Shops

8 Look at the shops below. What things can you buy in each place? Think of as many things as you can.

coffee shop ☐   phone shop ☐
chemist's ☐   post office ☐
bookshop ☐   supermarket ☐
clothes shop ☐ sports shop ☐

9 🔊 W.06 Listen. Which shop is each person in? Write the number of the dialogue next to the correct shop in Exercise 8. There are three shops you don't need.

10 🔊 W.06 Listen again. In which shop do you hear these sentences?

1 You don't have to wait in a queue. _____
2 You have to wear them two or three times. _____
3 You have to fill in this form. _____
4 You don't have to pay for the third one. _____

Things you have to do

11 Read the sentences below. For each one, think of possibilities for a) who said it and b) who to.

1 *You don't have to read it.*
2 *You have to give it to me before the lesson.*
3 *I don't have to do what you say!*
4 *I have to finish this tonight.*
5 *You don't have to throw it away.*
6 *It's fantastic! You have to see it!*

12 SPEAKING Work in pairs. Choose three of the sentences in Exercise 11. Act out a mini-dialogue for each sentence that you choose.

This book is really boring.

Well, you don't have to read it.

I do. I have to read it for school.

Oh. When do you need to finish it by?

Tomorrow!

D LOOKING AHEAD
Plans and arrangements

1 Read the email. Match the times and the events.

1 Saturday morning ☐
2 Saturday afternoon ☐
3 Saturday evening ☐
4 Sunday morning ☐
5 Sunday afternoon ☐
6 Sunday evening ☐

a sports events
b party for Katy's dad
c opening ceremony
d dancing
e charity run
f street party

2 Read the sentences. What do the underlined verbs express? Write A (arrangement) or I (intention).

1 A famous DJ <u>is playing</u> the music. ☐
2 <u>I'm running</u> in the race. ☐
3 <u>We're going to join</u> in. ☐
4 <u>I'm going to wear</u> my raincoat. ☐
5 <u>We're going to make</u> it a really special party. ☐
6 <u>We're having</u> a party at our place. ☐

3 Find other examples of the present continuous for arrangements in Katy's email.

4 **SPEAKING** Work in pairs. Ask and answer questions about plans you have for next weekend.

What are you doing on Saturday morning?

I'm going running. / I'm not doing anything.

Sports and sport verbs

5 Complete the table with the sports in the list.

| athletics | football | gymnastics | karate |
| rock climbing | running | skiing | tennis |

play	do	go

6 **SPEAKING** Work in pairs. Which sports do you often / sometimes / never do? Talk to your partner.

I often go running, but I never do karate.

WELCOME

Travel plans

7 🔊 **W.07** Put the parts of the dialogue in order. Then listen and check your answers.

☐ A Great idea. OK, see you soon. We're going to have a lot of fun this weekend!
☐ A Ah, OK. 3.15 is difficult for me. Is it OK if I don't meet you at the station?
☐ A Hey, Connor. What time are you arriving on Saturday?
☐ A Well, sometimes the train's late. If it's late, I'll meet you.
☐ B OK. As soon as the train leaves Liverpool, I'll send you a text message.
☐ B 3.15 – I'm going to catch the two o'clock train from Liverpool.
☐ B I know. It's going to be great!
☐ B Of course. I can walk. No problem.

8 Complete the sentences with the correct form of the verbs in brackets.

1 If I _____ (miss) the bus, I _____ (catch) the next one.
2 If the bus _____ (arrive) late, I _____ (take) a taxi.
3 If there _____ (not be) any taxis, I _____ (walk) to your place.
4 I'll send you a text message when I _____ (get) to the station.
5 As soon as I _____ (get) to your place, we _____ (start) having a good time.
6 If we _____ (not have) a good time, I _____ (not visit) you again!

9 Ellie travelled a lot last year. Complete the sentences with the past simple of the verbs in the list.

catch | drive | fly | miss | ride | ~~take~~

10 Complete the sentences with *be going to* and the verbs in the list.

buy | get up | not visit | take | try | visit

1 We don't like flying so we _____ a boat.
2 I want to go to Dublin. I _____ my ticket online.
3 My train leaves at 5.00, so I _____ very early tomorrow.
4 We'll only be in Madrid for one day, so we _____ any museums.
5 When we're in Birmingham, we _____ my cousins.
6 We love Italian food, so we _____ all the best restaurants in Rome!

11 Imagine you can go on a holiday to wherever you want, any time you want. Make notes about your plans:

• where you're going to go
• where you're going to stay
• how long your holiday is going to be
• what you're going to do
• who you're going to go with
• what you're going to eat
• what time of year you're going to go

12 **SPEAKING** Work in pairs. Ask and answer about the holiday you planned in Exercise 11.

Where are you going to go on holiday?

Thailand. And I'm going to stay in a hotel on the beach.

0 She _took_ a taxi in Paris.

1 She _____ the train in Vienna.

2 She _____ to Madrid.

3 She _____ the train in Berlin.

4 She _____ to Rome.

5 She _____ a bike in Athens.

1 INCREDIBLE PEOPLE

Get TH!NKING
Watch the video and think: what makes people incredible?

OBJECTIVES

FUNCTIONS:
talking about things you have and haven't done; offering encouragement

GRAMMAR:
present perfect with *just*, *already* and *yet*; present perfect vs. past simple

VOCABULARY:
personality adjectives; collocations; phrases with *just*

 READING

1 Look at the photos. What is your first impression of these people? What adjectives could you use to describe them?

> boring | caring | confident | cool | easy-going
> friendly | funny | happy | intelligent | serious

2 **SPEAKING** Discuss the photos in pairs.

> *He seems friendly.*
>
> *She looks like a happy person because she's smiling.*

3 **SPEAKING** Use the adjectives in Exercise 1 and other adjectives to describe people you know.

> *My brother is very easy-going.*
>
> *He doesn't get angry very often.*

4 Quickly read the responses to the survey question on the next page. Who do the respondents admire?

5 🔊 **1.01** Read and listen to the responses again. Mark the sentences T (true) or F (false).

1. Renata's got a daughter. _____
2. Renata works as a sports trainer. _____
3. Mr Ronay helps children to learn the piano. _____
4. Mr Ronay plays concerts all over the world. _____
5. Deming has never had lessons in painting. _____
6. Deming is very good at drawing pictures. _____
7. Anna's got a problem with her heart. _____
8. Anna never goes to school. _____

6 **SPEAKING** Work with a partner. Correct the false sentences in Exercise 5.

WHO DO YOU ADMIRE MOST?

INCREDIBLE PEOPLE   UNIT 1

VOCABULARY
Personality adjectives

1 My cousin Renata is an amazing person. She's 26 and she's got a little girl, Bruna, aged four. Her husband died three years ago, so she is bringing Bruna up on her own. Renata lives in São Paulo, where she works as a teacher. It's hard work, but she's always happy and smiling. Renata's a keen athlete, too – she's a very good runner and she trains a lot. She's already run two half-marathons, but she hasn't won a race yet. She hopes to run a marathon one day. Her life isn't easy, but she always stays **positive** about everything.
Juliana, 17

2 There's an elderly man who lives near us called Mr Ronay. He's very **charming** and I think he's just incredible. He's 85 and he has difficulty walking now, but that doesn't stop him being **active** and doing the thing he loves most: playing the piano. He has always been a very **talented** performer. When he was younger, he played concerts all over the world, but he can't do that any more. Now, he teaches the piano. He gives lessons at home, and he's just started to give free lessons to neighbourhood kids.
Urgun, 16

3 There's a boy at my school called Deming. He's 15 years old and he can be quiet and shy, but he's very interesting when you talk to him. He's also a wonderful artist with an amazing memory – he looks at a building for just a few minutes, then goes away and paints it exactly as it is in real life. He also paints things from his imagination. He's very **creative**. He has never studied art; he just knows how to draw and paint. He's already sold a lot of paintings, and he's just won a place at an art school in Beijing. But he's very **laid-back** about the success he's had.
Li Ju, 16

4 My best friend's sister, Anna, is amazing. She's 13 and she was born with a serious heart problem. She's already had about ten operations, but she is incredibly **brave**. She knows that there will be more operations, but she doesn't complain and always seems so **cheerful**. The problem makes her very weak, so she spends a lot of time in bed or in a wheelchair. But she goes to school when she can, and when she can't go to school, she studies in hospital or at home. She's just had another operation, but she's also just passed all her exams!
Luigi, 15

7 There are eight words in bold in the texts. Match the words with these meanings. Write the words.

- **0** is always doing things — *active*
- **1** is usually happy — _____
- **2** is very easy-going — _____
- **3** has very original ideas — _____
- **4** looks for the good in all situations — _____
- **5** is very good at doing something — _____
- **6** doesn't get scared easily — _____
- **7** is very easy to like — _____

8 Complete the sentences with the words from Exercise 7.

- **0** Why are you so *cheerful* today? Have you had some good news?
- **1** He stood up in the front of the whole school and read out his poem. He was really _____ .
- **2** She's very _____ and it's easy to see why she's got so many friends.
- **3** He's so _____ that some people think he's a bit lazy.
- **4** Have you seen him doing ballet? He really is a _____ dancer.
- **5** If you want to work in advertising, you need to be _____ and come up with really good ideas.
- **6** My dad is really _____ around the house. He's always cooking or fixing things or working in the garden.
- **7** He's had a really difficult life but he's really _____ about the future.

TH!NK values

Human qualities

9 Think about someone who is not famous but who you think is special.

- **a** Think of three adjectives to describe them.
- **b** Think about why you chose these adjectives. Make notes.

10 **SPEAKING** Tell your partner about the person you admire.

I really admire my sister. She's really confident in difficult situations.

13

GRAMMAR
Present perfect with *just*, *already* and *yet*

1. **Complete the sentences with *just*, *already* and *yet*. Then complete the rules.**
   1. She's _____ run two half-marathons but she hasn't won a race _____ .
   2. She's _____ had another operation.

   > **RULE:** In the present perfect, we often use
   > - ³_____ in negative sentences and questions to talk about something that hasn't happened but that we expect to happen soon. It comes at the end of the sentence.
   > - ⁴_____ to emphasise that something happened very recently. It goes before the past participle.
   > - ⁵_____ to show that something has been done or finished sooner than expected. It usually goes before the past participle.

2. **Match the pictures and the sentences. Write 1–3 in the boxes.**
   1. He's just woken up.
   2. He's already got out of bed.
   3. He hasn't woken up yet.

A

B

C

3. **Look at Jack's list of things to do for his party. Write sentences with *already* and *yet*.**

   Party list – things to do
   1. make cake
   2. send out invitations ✓
   3. organise music
   4. choose what to wear ✓
   5. decorate room
   6. buy drinks ✓

   1 He hasn't made the cake yet.

4. **Use your imagination to answer the questions. Use the present perfect and *just* in each one.**
   0. Why is Mum so angry?
      Because Dad's just crashed her car.
   1. Why is Jacob so sad?
   2. Why is your face so dirty?
   3. Why is Liam so scared?
   4. Why is Dana so excited?
   5. Why are you smiling?

5. **Tick (✓) the things you have already done.**

   EIGHT THINGS TO DO BEFORE YOU'RE 20:
   - ☐ start a vlog
   - ☐ meet a famous person
   - ☐ travel abroad
   - ☐ write a song
   - ☐ act on stage
   - ☐ learn to play a musical instrument
   - ☐ enter a competition
   - ☐ climb a mountain

6. **SPEAKING** Work in pairs. Ask each other questions.

   Have you started a vlog yet?

   Yes, I've already done that. Have you?

   No, I haven't done that yet.

   → workbook page 10

UNIT 1 INCREDIBLE PEOPLE

🎧 LISTENING

7 🔊 **1.02** Listen to three people: Jack, Sarah and Ella. They're going to play a game called *I've Never*. Complete the rules they describe.

Ella It's a game called *I've Never*. So, I think of something that I've ¹_____ done but I think both of you have done.

Jack Right.

Ella Then I say ²_____ . And you say if you've ever done the thing or not. If ³_____ say 'Yes, I've done that,' then I get ⁴_____ and another turn. But if ⁵_____ says 'No, I've never done that,' then I ⁶_____ a point and it's ⁷_____ .

8 🔊 **1.03** Listen to the rest of the conversation and the game. How many points does each person get?

9 🔊 **1.03** Listen again and choose the correct answer A, B or C.

1 How did Ella's family travel to Spain?

 A  B  C

2 What has Ella never worn?

 A  B  C

3 What kind of food has Ella never eaten?

 A  B  C

4 Who loses a turn of *I've Never* first?

 A  B  C
Ella   Jack   Sarah

10 Work in pairs. Answer the questions.
1 How do you win a point in the game?
2 When did Sarah travel by plane?
3 Why does Sarah think Ella has eaten Japanese food?
4 Why does Ella say she wants to stop playing the game? Do you think this is the real reason she wants to stop playing?

💬 SPEAKING

11 Work in small groups. Play *I've Never*.

> *OK, I've never travelled outside my country. And you?*

> *I have / I haven't.*

WordWise: Phrases with *just*

12 Look at the sentences from the unit so far. Choose the correct meaning of *just* in each one.
1 She's just had another operation. ☐
2 He looks at a building for just a few minutes, then goes away and paints it exactly as it is. ☐
3 I think he's just incredible. ☐

a only
b a short time ago
c really

13 What does *just* mean in these sentences? Write a, b or c.
1 Don't be angry. It's just a joke. ☐
2 I've just seen a fantastic film. ☐
3 It's cold today. The weather is just awful. ☐
4 No food, thanks – just a drink. ☐
5 She's just had some bad news. ☐

14 Match the questions and answers.
1 How many scoops of ice cream would you like? ☐
2 When did Paula get here? ☐
3 What do you think of Ariana Grande? ☐

a She's just arrived.
b She's just great.
c Just one, please.

→ workbook page 12

READING

1 **SPEAKING** What animal is this? How would you describe it? What special characteristics does it have? Discuss with a partner.

2 **SPEAKING** Work in pairs. Look at the photos and discuss the questions.
1 What do you think has happened?
2 What are the people doing?
3 How do you think they are similar to a mole?

3 **Read the article quickly. Name …**
1 the year Los Topos began: _____
2 three countries where they have worked: _____
3 how many of Los Topos have died: _____

4 🔊 1.04 Read and listen to the article again and answer the questions.
1 Where did Los Topos begin?
2 When did Los Topos first work in the US?
3 What did they say about their work in Indonesia?
4 Why don't they go to every disaster?
5 What kind of training do Los Topos offer?

HUMAN MOLES

Moles are small animals that live underground and dig tunnels, looking for food. Sometimes humans also need to be like moles, but for a different reason – to save lives.

In 1985, there was a powerful earthquake in Mexico City. As often happens in earthquakes, many people were buried under fallen buildings and needed help. However, there weren't enough people to go and help them. So a group of young people decided to form a volunteer group. They started to dig into the rubble to try to find people and get them out. The group, who called themselves *Los Topos* ('the moles' in Spanish), quickly became well known for their bravery, and they started to travel to help at disaster zones in other places.

Since 1985 Los Topos have helped in places all around the world. At first they only worked in Mexico, but over the years they have been to Nepal, Haiti and the Philippines. In 2001, after the attack on the World Trade Center in New York, they came to the United States for the first time. And they went to Banda Aceh, Indonesia, in 2004, after the terrible tsunami that killed tens of thousands of people. They say that this was the most difficult work they have ever done. In 2017, they helped in Mexico City again, after another serious earthquake. Altogether, they have been to more than twenty countries.

The group has also grown – people in the group come and go, but on average it has about 40 members. It is very professional and includes doctors and other specialists, such as psychologists and engineers, but they are not paid for their work. They go to disaster areas when local governments and rescue groups cannot manage alone, and they also offer courses for people who want to become rescue workers. Los Topos members themselves pay most of what they need to travel to disaster zones – when they get there, they eat whatever they can and sleep wherever they can.

So far, not one member of Los Topos has lost their life – let's hope that this continues.

GRAMMAR
Present perfect vs. past simple

5 Look at the article on page 16 again. Which of the following events do we know happened at a specific point in time? Then complete the rules.

1 Los Topos formed?
2 Los Topos went to Nepal, Haiti and the Philippines?
3 Los Topos went to Banda Aceh?
4 Los Topos grew into a bigger organisation?

> **RULE:** When we talk about a specific point in time in the past, we use the [5]_____ .
> When we don't refer to a specific point in time, we often use the [6]_____ .

6 Complete the pairs of sentences. Use the past simple and the present perfect form of the verbs.

0 visit
  a I _have visited_ Greece more than 20 times.
  b I first _visited_ Greece in 1998.
1 win
  a He _____ already _____ three gold medals, and he hopes to win more.
  b He _____ a gold medal in the 2020 Olympics.
2 meet
  a My mum _____ a lot of interesting people.
  b My mum _____ Prince Harry ten years ago.
3 record
  a They _____ their last album two years ago.
  b They _____ more than 20 albums so far.
4 live
  a We _____ in Samoa when I was young.
  b We're living in Austria now, but we _____ in many different countries.
5 sign
  a She _____ just _____ a contract with a new e-publishing company.
  b She _____ the contract for her first book on her 21st birthday.

→ workbook page 11

VOCABULARY
Collocations

7 For each collocation, choose the two correct answers.

1 Which of these can you make?
  a homework   b a mistake   c an appearance
2 Which of these things can you do?
  a your best   b a good time   c work
3 Which of these things can you get?
  a a bad day   b a job   c a reputation
4 Which of these things can you lose?
  a a race   b an idea   c your life
5 Which of these can you take?
  a a risk   b a house   c a photograph
6 Which of these can you form?
  a a group   b an opinion   c a lesson

8 What verbs can go before the six words you didn't choose in Exercise 7? Think of at least one verb for each word.

9 **SPEAKING** Talk to other people in the class. Ask and answer questions and complete the table.

Have you ever ... ? What happened?
Who did you ask?
What was the risk?
What did you lose?

Find someone who has ...	Who?	Details
made a big mistake.		
done some chores at home this week.		
got a job.		
lost something important.		
taken a big risk.		
formed a group.		

→ workbook page 12

WRITING
Someone you admire

10 Write a short passage about someone you have admired for some time. Include:
- how long you have known (about) them.
- what you admire about them.

DEVELOPING SPEAKING

1 🔊 **1.05** Look at the photos. What do you think the connection is between them? Listen and read to check.

Mike: You know our music teacher, Mr Grimes? He's leaving our school next month.
Emma: <u>Are you sure</u>? I haven't heard anything.
Mike: Yes, I'm sure. Steve said so. Mr Grimes told his class in yesterday's lesson.
Emma: That's a shame. He's a good teacher. His lessons are fun – jokes, games, smiles, <u>that sort of thing</u>.
Mike: I know. He's one of the best. But he's leaving, <u>and that's that</u>. Still, I was thinking – maybe we could do something to thank him. He's taught us such a lot. It would be nice to say thank you.
Emma: That's a good idea. What kind of thing?
Mike: Well, maybe a little concert? We could play or sing something for him.
Emma: No, <u>I don't think so</u>, Mike. A concert is too much. <u>Let's face it</u>, none of us are really good singers or musicians.
Mike: I know. But I want to do something.
Emma: Oh, you'll think of something. You always do!
Mike: Well, here's another idea. We could each make a recording – well, those who want to – and say something that we remember from his lessons. Then we could choose a bit of music …
Emma: … that he told us about! Yes! Mike, that's great. You've got to make it happen.
Mike: Well, I'll start by talking to the others, and find out what they think.
Emma: I'll help you if I can. <u>You know what</u>? I think everyone's going to love this, Mike. Really. Well done.

2 Read the dialogue again and answer the questions.
1. What is the news about Mr Grimes?
2. Why does Mike think it would be nice to say thank you to him?
3. What does Emma think of Mike's first idea?
4. What does Emma think of Mike's second idea?

3 SPEAKING Discuss the questions in pairs.
1. Is Mike right to want to say thank you to the teacher?
2. Do you think the recording is a better idea than the concert? Why or why not?

Phrases for fluency

4 Find the underlined expressions in the dialogue and use them to complete the conversations.
1. A That new girl, Sally – she likes you!
   B No, ¹_____ .
   A ²_____ ? I have a feeling she likes you a lot.
   B No. She never smiles at me. And she criticises me a lot, doesn't laugh at my jokes, ³_____ .
2. A Oh, you got it wrong again!
   B I know. ⁴_____ , I'm no good at computer games.
   A ⁵_____ ? We just need a rest. Let's go and watch some TV.
   B OK, but I don't want to play this game again, OK? I'm useless at it, ⁶_____ !

⚙ FUNCTIONS
Offering encouragement

KEY LANGUAGE
That's a great idea.   You've got to make it happen.
You should definitely do it.   I'll help you if you want.

5 Complete the mini-dialogues using the sentences from the Key Language box.
1. Jake   I'm not sure I can do this homework on my own.
   Paula   _____
2. Carmen   Do you think Steve would like to have a party for his birthday?
   Adrian   Yes, I do. _____
3. Millie   I've got an idea to get money for the school. I'd like to put on a play.
   Javier   Oh, yes, brilliant! _____
4. Seb   You know I'm learning the guitar? Do you think I should enter the talent show?
   Harry   Yes! _____

6 In pairs, write a new short dialogue, using the sentences from the Key Language box. Choose one of these ideas or your own idea.
- a surprise party for your mum
- an outing with your friends
- a present for someone in hospital

7 SPEAKING Act out your dialogue from Exercise 6.

PRONUNCIATION
Intonation and sentence stress   Go to page 120.

INCREDIBLE PEOPLE UNIT 1

LIFE COMPETENCIES

Everywhere you go, there are people who are doing great things that improve other people's lives. Saying thank you is a simple way to show you recognise (and appreciate) these great things.

Recognising others' good work

1. ▶ 03 Watch the video. What two small but important words does Anna talk about?

2. ▶ 03 Watch again and match the people with what they do.
   1. ☐ Anna's mum
   2. ☐ Anna's dad
   3. ☐ Mr Ward
   4. ☐ Dave

   a teaches Maths
   b plays for free at parties
   c listens well
   d makes breakfast in bed for Anna

3. Look at this poster. What does Quickshop supermarket want people to do?

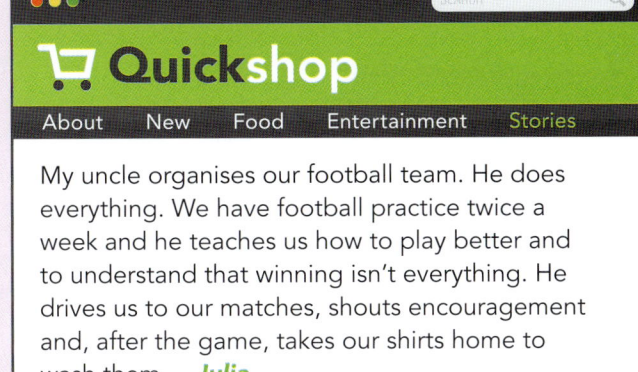

Quickshop
LOCAL HEROES!

Everybody knows a community hero: the teen next door who spends her summers helping at the hospital; the neighbour who helps out at the local school every day; the friend who picks up litter in the town centre.
Quickshop has just celebrated its 100th birthday, and to celebrate we want to give a special award to the people who work quietly to make our lives better.

Local Heroes are everywhere – we just need your help to find them!

4. **SPEAKING** Read these posts on the Quickshop website. Who do Julia and Milo think should win the award? Why? Discuss in pairs.

Quickshop
About New Food Entertainment Stories

My uncle organises our football team. He does everything. We have football practice twice a week and he teaches us how to play better and to understand that winning isn't everything. He drives us to our matches, shouts encouragement and, after the game, takes our shirts home to wash them. – *Julia*

Mrs Wilkins is the lollipop lady at the primary school. Every day, she helps the children cross the road because it's very dangerous. My mum says that Mrs Wilkins helped her cross the road when she was little, which was a long time ago! In the sun, wind and rain, Mrs Wilkins is always there, making sure everyone gets to school safely. – *Milo*

Me and my world

5. Think of somebody you know who should win a Local Hero award.
   - What do they do?
   - Why do they do it?
   - Is an award a good way to say thank you?
   - Can you think of another way to say thank you?

6. **SPEAKING** Tell the rest of your class about your Local Hero.

TIPS FOR RECOGNISING OTHERS' GOOD WORK

- Make a list of all the places you go to. Think of someone special who helps to run this place.
- It's nice to explain how the person helped you – 'Because of you, I can …'.
- Sometimes simply saying thank you with a smile is enough.

2 A GOOD EDUCATION

OBJECTIVES

FUNCTIONS:
asking and giving / refusing permission to do something

GRAMMAR:
present perfect with *for* and *since*;
a, *an*, *the* or no article

VOCABULARY:
school subjects; verbs about thinking

Get TH!NKING

Watch the video and think: how do you learn best?

READING

1 Look at the photos. Does your school have these rooms or places?

2 **SPEAKING** Write a list of all the things you think a school should offer as well as a good education. Then compare with a partner.

> *A school should offer students the chance to talk about any problems they might have in their lives.*

3 Look at the photos and the title on the next page. Why do you think this boy is the 'loneliest schoolboy in Britain'? Read the text quickly to check your ideas.

4 **2.01** Read and listen to the article again. Choose the correct answer to these questions.

1 What do we learn about the Out Skerries Islands from the text?
  A They are on the coast of Scotland.
  B There is a small airport.
  C It takes two and a half hours to get to the nearest town.
  D There is one shop on the island.

2 Why is Aron the only child at the school?
  A No other children live on the islands.
  B The government can't afford to send more children there.
  C The other children are taught by their parents.
  D The other children are too old for the school.

3 Why do some people complain about Aron's education?
  A They think it's not good for him to have no friends at the school.
  B They don't think he's learning the right things.
  C They think it costs too much.
  D They think he should be sent to private school.

4 How has the island changed over the last ten years?
  A There are more shops.
  B More families are coming to the island.
  C It's not as safe as it was.
  D There is less work there.

5 Think of three questions you would like to ask Aron and write them in your notebook.

> *What's the best part of your school day?*
> *Do you miss your brothers?*
> *Do you like always coming first in every test?*

6 **SPEAKING** Work in pairs. Take turns to be Aron. Ask and answer your questions from Exercise 5.

> *What's the best part of your school day?*
>
> *PE. I love being outside.*

A GOOD EDUCATION UNIT 2

THE LONELIEST SCHOOLBOY IN BRITAIN

Imagine a school where you are the only student – where you come first in every test. Welcome to the life of ten-year-old Aron Anderson, who goes to school in Out Skerries, a group of small, remote islands in Scotland. Aron has been the only boy at his school for two months.

The Out Skerries Islands, which are around 280 km from the coast of Scotland, are home to about 70 people. The nearest town is Lerwick on the Shetland Islands. You can only get there by boat and it takes two and a half hours. Apart from Aron's school, there are two shops, a church and a community hall on the islands.

Aron isn't the only child on the islands and he hasn't always been the only student at the school. Until July there were several other children there, including Aron's two brothers. But now they are older, so they go to the secondary school in Lerwick. They only go back to their homes at the weekend. Aron has been the only student since September.

The school is very small. It has two classrooms, an art room, a music room and a library. Each week Aron studies Maths, English, Science and Art with the same teacher. She also gives him PE lessons. This is usually an hour-long walk around the islands. He also has the school playground all to himself. Of course, there is one problem. He has no one to play with.

What's more, Aron's education isn't cheap. It costs the UK government £75,357 each year. That is twice the price it costs parents to send a child to Britain's most famous private school, Eton. Some people want to close down the school. They think it is too much money to spend on one child's education.

Aron has lived in Out Skerries since he was born and loves the outdoor life. He enjoys exploring the islands on his bike and diving into the sea from the pier. Like most boys his age, he also likes watching TV and playing on his games console.

But his mother, who works in one of the shops on the islands, is worried that Aron might get lonely. She would like to see more families with children coming to live there. A lot of people have moved away since the local salmon factory closed ten years ago. That's why there are so few children on the islands and why Aron has found himself being known as the loneliest schoolboy in Britain.

TH!NK values

Learning for life

7 Read the statements. Tick (✓) the things that you think Aron is probably not learning at his school.

1 Everyone is different and that's a good thing. ☐
2 Teamwork is important to achieve things in life. ☐
3 We need to learn to respect the natural world. ☐
4 It is important to be friendly and help others. ☐
5 It is important to know how to spend time on your own. ☐
6 It's good to learn how to get on with people of different ages. ☐

8 SPEAKING Compare your ideas with a partner.

I think he is learning how to get on with people of different ages.

Why?

Well, he has all that time with just his teacher.

Yes, I agree with you.

9 SPEAKING In small groups, discuss these questions.

1 Which of the things from the list in Exercise 7 do you think are important to learn?
2 What would you add to your personal list of important things to learn?

GRAMMAR
Present perfect with *for* and *since*

1 Look again at the article on page 21. Find all the sentences in the present perfect.

2 Complete the sentences below with *for* and *since*. Then complete the rules.

  1 Aron has lived in Out Skerries _____ he was born.
  2 Aron has been the only boy at his school _____ two months.

  > **RULE:** In the present perfect, we use:
  > • ³_____ to talk about a period of time.
  > • ⁴_____ to refer to the point in time when an action started.

3 When do we use *for* and when do we use *since*? Complete the chart.

  | ~~a month~~ | ~~last summer~~ | a long time | an hour
  a year | days | Friday | I phoned you | many years
  2014 | yesterday | your birthday |

for	_a month_	_____	_____
	_____	_____	_____
since	_last summer_	_____	_____
	_____	_____	_____

4 Complete the sentences. Use the present perfect form of the verbs and *for* or *since*.

  1 I _____ (be) at my new school _____ last December.
  2 Fatima _____ (not see) Michael _____ several weeks.
  3 They _____ (not write) us an email _____ three months.
  4 I _____ (have) this camera _____ I was ten.

5 Write sentences using the present perfect with *for* or *since* and the words in brackets.

  1 They are at the youth club. (three hours)
  2 Joanne and I are good friends. (primary school)
  3 She plays in the volleyball team. (two months)
  4 I ought to see a doctor. I'm sick. (a week)
  5 I don't hear a lot from Silvia. (last October)

  → workbook page 18

VOCABULARY
School subjects

6 🔊 2.02 Match the school subjects in the list with the photos. Write 1–12 in the boxes. Then listen and check.

 A ☐

 G ☐

 B ☐

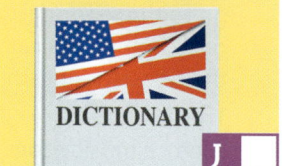 H ☐

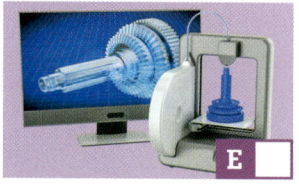 C ☐

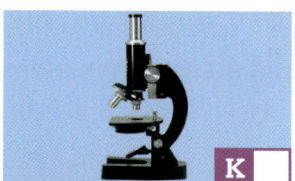 I ☐

 D ☐

 J ☐

E ☐   K ☐

F ☐   L ☐

> 1 Science (Physics, Biology and Chemistry)
> 2 Music | 3 Art Education | 4 Drama
> 5 Design and Technology | 6 Geography
> 7 English | 8 PE (Physical Education)
> 9 ICT (Information and Communication Technology)
> 10 Maths | 11 History | 12 Spanish

7 **SPEAKING** Answer the questions. Take notes. Then compare your answers with a partner.

  1 Which are your favourite subjects? Which don't you like? Why?
  2 Which of the subjects are you studying this year?
  3 How long have you studied each subject for?

  → workbook page 20

A GOOD EDUCATION UNIT 2

🎧 LISTENING

8 Read the list of ten things to do this summer. Match four of the activities with the pictures.

 A
 B
 C
 D

9 🔊 2.03 Listen to Tom talking to his mother.
1 Which things on the list does he want to do tomorrow?
2 What other things on the list does he mention?

TEN THINGS TO DO THIS SUMMER!

GET OFF YOUR PHONE AND GET OUTSIDE. THERE'S A WORLD OUT THERE. GO AND EXPLORE!

1 Climb a tree
2 Camp out in the wild
3 Run around in the rain
4 Eat an apple straight from a tree
5 Swing on a rope swing
6 Watch the sun rise
7 Climb a huge hill
8 Feed a bird from your hand
9 Swim in a river
10 Cook on a campfire

10 🔊 2.03 Listen again. Mark the sentences T (true) or F (false).
1 Tom's mum is surprised he wants her alarm clock. _____
2 Tom has less than two weeks to finish the challenge. _____
3 Tom found the list in a magazine. _____
4 Tom's mum thinks the challenge is a good idea. _____
5 Tom wants to climb the Malvern Hills with his friends. _____
6 Tom's mum isn't happy to take him to the Malvern Hills. _____

11 SPEAKING Have you done any of the things on the list? Tell your partner.

12 Think of more things you could put on the list.

⚙️ FUNCTIONS
Asking and giving / refusing permission

13 Put the dialogues in the correct order. Write the numbers 1–4.

1 ☐ Dad   Yes?
  ☐ Dad   I'm afraid I need to use it, too.
  ☐ Nick Will you let me use your laptop?
  ☐ Nick Dad?

2 ☐ Annie Can I watch the football match tonight?
  ☐ Annie Can I ask you something, Mum?
  ☐ Mum   Yes, of course you can.
  ☐ Mum   Go ahead.

14 Mark the sentences AP (asking permission), GP (giving permission) or RP (refusing permission).
1 Will you let me use your mobile? _____
  Yeah, sure. Of course I will. _____
2 Can I borrow your bike, please? _____
  No, sorry. I need it. _____
3 Can I use your laptop, please? _____
  Yes, you can, but I want it back tomorrow. _____
4 Is it OK if I borrow this necklace? _____
  Yeah, but be really careful with it, OK? _____

ROLE PLAY Work in pairs. Act out short conversations. Ask each other for permission. Use the ideas below, or come up with your own idea.

> borrow £20 | come with him/her
> copy his/her homework
> get some help with homework
> use his/her tablet

READING

1. **Look at the photos and answer the questions.**
   1. What do you think these people are thinking?
   2. What would you say to them?

THE POWER OF 'YET'

1 Does life sometimes seem to be full of impossible problems? How many times, for example, do you find yourself saying things like 'I really don't understand this maths problem', or 'I can't get into the school team'?

Well, maybe it's time to introduce yourself to the power of 'yet'. By adding this simple word, you can change everything. 'I really don't understand this maths problem *yet*.' 'I can't get into the school team *yet*.'

Suddenly, the impossible becomes possible. You can imagine those things happening.

2 I read about a school that has changed the way it marks its students' exams. The school recognised that the old pass/fail system wasn't helping student motivation. If you passed, then great, but those students who didn't pass often felt like failures. So now students who don't get the score they need to pass don't see a big red F for fail on their exam papers; they see a 'Not yet' instead. That way the students feel that they are on a journey. They haven't reached the end, but they know that they are going the right way.

3 This kind of thinking is part of what experts call 'having a growth mindset'. People with a growth mindset don't concentrate on failure. They aren't worried by not getting things right the first time and are happy to keep trying until they do. They enjoy the challenge and believe they can change. In contrast, people who just focus on the failure have what the experts call 'a fixed mindset'. These people are always worried about failure and are happy to give up when things don't go right. They don't think that they are able to change. Clearly, it is better to have a growth mindset than a fixed mindset.

4 But don't worry if you think that you have a fixed mindset. You can train yourself to develop a growth mindset. Remember that it all starts with questioning the things you believe about yourself. Stop believing that you can't or you haven't and realise that you just can't or haven't *yet*. Once you start doing this, you'll wonder why you didn't do it before. It's one small but very powerful word.

2 🔊 2.04 **Read and listen to the text and answer the questions.**
1. How does the word yet make a difference?
2. Why did the school change the way it graded exams?
3. How do people with a growth mindset behave?
4. How are people with fixed mindsets different?
5. What's the first step needed to change from a fixed to a growth mindset?

3 SPEAKING **Make a list of three things you would like to be better at. Work with a partner and discuss how you could achieve these things.**

> I'd like to be really good at the guitar.

> Find time to practise for an hour every day.

> Get lessons off the internet.

> Learn to play your favourite songs.

Train to TH!NK

Learning about texts

4 Choose the best description of this text.
- A an adventure story to entertain the reader
- B an ad to sell the reader something
- C a magazine article to give the reader information
- D a letter to persuade the reader to do something

5 Choose the title that best sums up the content of each paragraph. Write 1–4. There is one extra title.
- A ☐ A real-life example
- B ☐ You can change
- C ☐ The best advice is always free
- D ☐ It's all about 'yet'
- E ☐ Two ways of thinking

GRAMMAR
a, *an*, *the* or no article

6 Look at the sentences from the magazine article. Underline *a*, *an*, *the* and the nouns that come after these articles. Then go through the sentences again and circle the nouns with no article. Finally, complete the rules with *a*, *an*, *the*, – (no article).

Does life sometimes seem to be full of impossible problems?

I read about a school that has changed the way it marks its students' exams. The school recognised that the old pass/fail system wasn't helping.

The students feel that they are on a journey.

> **RULE:** We use ¹_____ or ²_____ + a singular countable noun when the listener/reader doesn't know exactly which thing we are talking about.
> *You can have **an apple** or **a banana**.*
> *We've got **a new car**.*
> ³_____ + noun when it is clear which thing(s) or person/people we are talking about.
> ***The apples** in this pie are from our garden.*
> ***The bananas** that I bought yesterday are horrible.*
> ⁴_____ + plural countable noun or + uncountable noun, when we are talking about things in general.
> ***Bananas** are sweeter than **apples**. **Chocolate** isn't good for you.*

7 Complete each sentence with *a*, *an*, *the* or – (no article).

0 She is __*a*__ good student.
1 She eats a lot of _____ fruit and _____ vegetables.
2 _____ book that you gave me was really good.
3 I have _____ idea. Let's watch _____ new Beyoncé video.
4 I never drink _____ coffee – I hate it.
5 I like lots of sports, but _____ sport I like most is _____ tennis.

8 Complete the text with *a*, *an*, *the* or –.

0 __–__ People need to drink. Of course ¹_____ orange juice and ²_____ apple juice are very popular, but they are not always ³_____ good choice. ⁴_____ Orange juice has got a lot of sugar in it, so don't drink too much of it. The best drink for your brain is ⁵_____ water. ⁶_____ glass of water is the best drink you can get, but ⁷_____ water that you drink needs to be fresh and clean.

→ workbook page 19

VOCABULARY
Verbs about thinking

9 Find these verbs in a dictionary and write their definitions in your notebook.

> believe | concentrate | guess
> imagine | realise | recognise
> remember | suppose | think | wonder

10 Choose the correct words.

1 The task was very difficult. I had to *remember / think* about it for a long time.
2 Come on, don't be silly. I don't *believe / realise* in ghosts!
3 Can you *imagine / concentrate* how great it must be to live at the beach?
4 When the teacher asked the question a different way, I *supposed / realised* that I knew the answer!
5 Did they really say they are moving to New York? I don't *suppose / believe* it!
6 I haven't seen her for six years. I don't think I would *realise / recognise* her.
7 I have no idea what the answer is. I'll just have to *recognise / guess*.
8 I was so tired that I found it hard to *think / concentrate* on the test.
9 Have you ever *wondered / believed* why I haven't phoned you for months?
10 If we want to get there faster, I *wonder / suppose* we should take a taxi.

> **PRONUNCIATION**
> Word stress Go to page 120.

11 **SPEAKING** Work in pairs. Ask and answer the questions.

1 Are there any places where you can think really well or not well at all?
2 Does music help you to concentrate or make it difficult for you to concentrate? Does it matter what kind of music it is?
3 In what situations can you imagine things really well? Do you find it difficult to use your imagination sometimes?
4 Do you find it difficult to remember things sometimes? What sort of things?
5 Have you ever tried meditation? Do you think meditating is useful?

→ workbook page 20

TH!NK
Schools with a difference

Culture

1 Look at the photo and the title. What do you think is different about this school?

2 🔊 2.07 Read and listen to the article. Which school is the oldest? Which school is the newest?

Schools with a difference

Every year Bangladesh is hit by heavy rains which cause large floods across the country. At these times life becomes difficult for millions of people who have no electricity or clean water. Many schools in these areas are forced to close. Shidhulai Swanirvar Sangstha is a charity which has provided education to more than 70,000 children with their floating schools since 2002. Each morning a school boat picks up children from nearby villages and when every child is on board, lessons can begin. In some of the lessons children learn about climate change and about protecting the environment. The charity has around 100 solar-powered boats and each one is fitted with a small library, a computer and internet access. The teachers also teach adults how to use the computers.

Each year more than 4,000 of India's poorest children get their education on the platforms of the country's railway stations. The idea for the Train Platform School came from a teacher called Inderjit Khurana. She wanted to do something for the children she met begging on the train she took to work each morning. She knew that without education, these children had no hope for their futures, and in 1985, she set up the first school and the school still exists today. Music and drama are among the methods used to teach the children how to read and write. When the children are ready, they can transfer to a full-time school. The schools also provide the children with food and medicine when it is needed.

You won't find any books at the West Philadelphia School of the Future in the US. Instead, all students have their own computers and learn on specially designed apps. Teachers don't use traditional whiteboards – they use hi-tech Smart Boards. When the school opened in 2006, both the teachers and the students found it difficult. They didn't know how to use all the technology. Since then the school has improved and these days students get high marks in Maths and reading, making it a very popular school with parents. The people who started the school hope that other schools will follow their example.

3 **SPEAKING** What makes your school different? Discuss in pairs. What could you change to make your school more unique?

A GOOD EDUCATION UNIT 2

4 **Read the article again. Complete the sentences with *Bangladesh*, *India* or *US*.**
1 The children here learn at stations. _____
2 This school uses the most modern technology. _____
3 The weather makes life difficult here sometimes. _____
4 This school uses solar power. _____
5 It's difficult to get a place at this school. _____
6 This school wants other schools to be like them. _____
7 Children here have 'floating' lessons. _____
8 The children get more than just an education. _____

5 **VOCABULARY** There are eight highlighted words in the article. Match the words with these meanings. Write the words.
1 of or from the sun _____
2 got better _____
3 usual, things as they have always been _____
4 when there is too much water on the land _____
5 staying above water _____
6 ways of doing something _____
7 asking people for money in the streets _____
8 an organisation which helps people, animals, the environment etc. _____

WRITING
An email describing your school routine

1 **INPUT** Read Ruby's email. Then answer the questions.
1 How does Ruby feel about her new class?
2 What does Ruby think of Nathan and why?
3 How does her work for school compare to last year?
4 What subject does she get a lot of homework for, and how does she feel about it?
5 Does Ruby think you've got less schoolwork than her?

2 **Find sentences in the email where Ruby writes about these things. What tense does she use in those sentences? Why does she use it?**
a asks how you feel about your new school
b talks about Nathan's mother
c compares school this year to last year
d talks about the amount of homework this year

3 **Put the words in the right order. Write the sentences. What tense are they in and why?**
1 new / too / class / kid / There's / a / my / in
_____
2 a week / at / three times / come home / 5.45 / I
_____
3 love / projects / I / class / But / the / do / this / in / we

4 **ANALYSE** Match the four paragraphs of Ruby's email with the content.

Paragraph 1   a Ruby's new class
Paragraph 2   b a request to write soon
Paragraph 3   c an introduction
Paragraph 4   d work this year compared to last

Ruby
ruby@yourmail.com

Hi!

Hi there!

I hope this finds you well. I haven't heard from you since the beginning of the holidays. Are you enjoying your new school?

I am, big time! I'm in a class with all my friends again – Rosa, Liz, Jacob and all the others. There's a new kid in my class, too. His name's Nathan and he's from Nantes in France. His mother is working in the UK for two years, and the whole family have come over. He's cool. We have lots of fun together.

But of course, it's not all fun. We've got important exams this year so there's a lot of work to do. I'm spending more time at school than last year, and I come home at 5.45 three times a week. We're also getting a lot more homework, especially for Art. But I love the projects we do in this class!

Well, I guess it's not so different for you. If you've got a bit of time, please let me know how things are going. I'd really like to know what life at school is like for you. And remember, please, you've got a friend in Brighton who would really like to get mail from you more often!

Write soon!

Ruby

5 **PLAN** Read Ruby's email again. Make notes with your own ideas on how:
a to answer the question in her introduction
b to describe your new class (new school? classmates?)
c to compare your work this year to last year's
d to say how you feel about your subjects (any subjects you particularly like/don't like? Why?)
e you could finish your email (what do you want to know from Ruby?)

6 **PRODUCE** Write an email to Ruby (about 200 words). Look at your notes from Exercise 5 and make sure you include all your ideas. Make sure you use the present simple when necessary.

27

B1 Preliminary for Schools

 **READING**
Part 6: Open cloze → workbook page 115

1   For each question, write the correct answer. Write one word for each gap.

The Tan-y-Bryn *Outdoor Adventure Centre*

The Tan-y-Bryn Outdoor Adventure Centre is on the island of Anglesey in North Wales. ¹_____ opening its doors in 1975, it has welcomed thousands of young people from all over the UK to enjoy fun, education and adventure in the beautiful Welsh countryside. Whether they are climbing up Mount Snowdon, swimming in the Menai Straits ²_____ birdwatching in the woodlands, visitors enjoy hands-on experiences they ³_____ never forget.

For school groups, youth clubs and families the Centre offers comfortable accommodation for ⁴_____ to 50 children and 10 adults. It also provides a full breakfast, lunch and dinner to make ⁵_____ no one goes hungry. Safety is a top priority – there ⁶_____ never been a serious accident at the Centre.

 LISTENING
Part 1: 3-option multiple choice → workbook page 17

2   🔊 2.08   For each question, choose the correct answer.

1   What did Sally buy at the shops?

 A    B    C

2   What time is it?

 A    B    C

3   How did Brian get to work?

 A    B    C

4   Which lesson did Fred enjoy most?

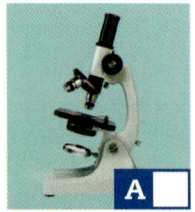 A   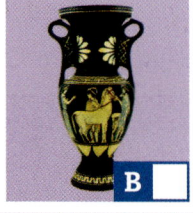 B    C

5   What month is Tom's brother's birthday?

 A    B    C

6   What's the score in the football match?

 A    B    C

7   Which man are the police looking for?

 A    B    C

TEST YOURSELF UNITS 1 & 2

VOCABULARY

1 Complete the sentences with the words in the list. There are two extra words.

> active | believe | brave | creative | formed | got | guess | lost | realise | recognise | take | wonder

1 I think I _____ the wrong opinion of her. She's actually really nice.
2 My grandmother's quite old, but she's still very _____ – she's always doing things!
3 He _____ the race by less than one second.
4 I didn't like the birthday cards in the shop, so I decided to be _____ and make one.
5 It's strange that Eve isn't here. I _____ where she is.
6 It's midday! Wow! I didn't _____ it was so late.
7 I didn't know the answer, so I had to _____ .
8 She didn't run away when the tiger was running towards her – she was very _____ .
9 I'm sure he saw me, but he didn't say hello. Maybe he didn't _____ me.
10 I've _____ a reputation for always being late. I don't think it's fair.

/10

GRAMMAR

2 Complete the sentences with the words in the list. You need to write the correct form of the verbs.

> bus | the bus | not open (x2) | not see (x2)

1 My best friend gave me my present this morning, but I _____ it yet.
2 I'm tired – I don't want to walk. Let's go by _____ .
3 She was at school today? Really? I _____ her there.
4 There was a sign on the gate that said 'No entry!', so I _____ it.
5 There's a new film on Netflix, but I _____ it yet.
6 We were late because _____ arrived 45 minutes late.

3 Find and correct the mistake in each sentence.

1 Can I have a glass of an orange juice, please?
2 I've travelled to already more than twenty capital cities.
3 We've lived here since ten months.
4 I've gone to the cinema last night.
5 This is my computer. I had it for two years.
6 It's important to drink a lot of the water if you want to be healthy.

/12

FUNCTIONAL LANGUAGE

4 Complete the mini-dialogues with the words in the list.

> afraid | Can | definitely | go | idea | Let's | OK | thinking

1 A _____ I use your pen, please?
  B Sorry, I'm _____ I'm using it right now.
2 A _____ go and see the new Marvel film tonight.
  B That's a great _____ !
3 A I'm _____ about doing a walk for charity. What do you think?
  B Yes, you should _____ do it.
4 A Is it _____ if I use your dictionary?
  B Yes, of course, _____ ahead.

/8

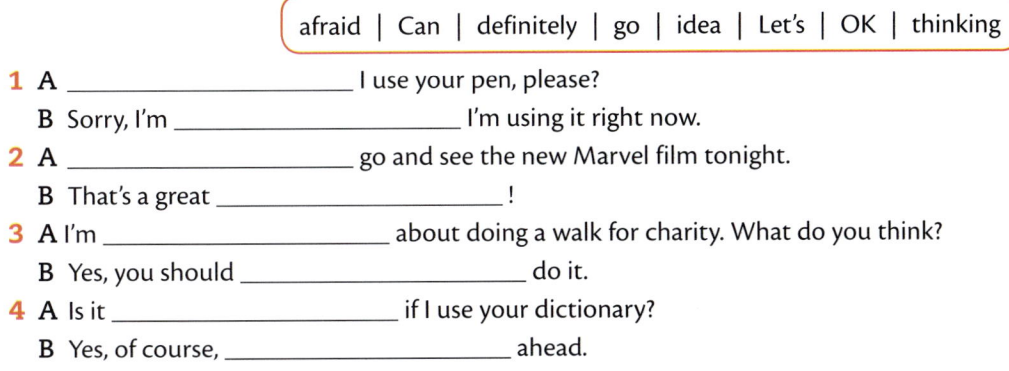

MY SCORE /30

22–30 10–21 0–9

3 ON THE SCREEN

OBJECTIVES

FUNCTIONS: comparing things and actions; asking for and offering help

GRAMMAR: comparative and superlative adjectives (review); (not) as … as; making a comparison stronger or weaker; adverbs

VOCABULARY: types of films; types of TV programmes; expressions with *get*

Get TH!NKING

Watch the video and think: what's your favourite form of entertainment?

A

B

C

D

E

F

READING

1 Match the words in the list with the photos. Write 1–6 in the boxes.

> 1 concert | 2 cinema | 3 play | 4 sports event
> 5 TV programme | 6 video game

2 **SPEAKING** Which of these kinds of entertainment do you like? Tell your partner.

3 **SPEAKING** Work in small groups. Talk about the things in Exercise 1. Say why people like or don't like them. Use the words in the list to help you.

> crowds | enjoyable | expensive
> friends | fun | interesting | relaxing

I think people enjoy going to the cinema because it is relaxing.

4 Look at the pictures and the title of the article on the next page. What do you think the article is about?

A a director
B an actor
C a type of film

5 🔊 3.01 Read and listen to the article and check your ideas.

6 Read the article again. Find:
1 two examples of things that influenced Tim Burton
2 the reason people were upset when Burton chose Michael Keaton for *Batman*
3 two examples of types of film that Burton has made
4 an example of creative work that Burton does apart from directing films

ON THE SCREEN UNIT 3

A new kind of SUPERHERO

Tim Burton is one of the most famous American film directors. His most popular films include: *Batman* (1989), *Edward Scissorhands* (1990), *Batman Returns* (1992) and *Dumbo* (2019). In 1990, he got a Daytime Emmy Award for his cartoon series *Beetlejuice* and in 1991 he got a Hugo Award for *Edward Scissorhands*.

Tim grew up watching horror films and cartoons. He read Edgar Allan Poe's horror stories and he loved drawing. He also made short films in his back garden. After leaving school, Burton studied animation. Then, he got a job at Walt Disney studios. He was a very good animator, but he didn't draw in the Disney style. So he left Disney and started to make his own films.

One of his most successful films is *Batman*. At first, people were upset when Tim Burton chose the comedy actor Michael Keaton to play Batman. Batman is a superhero who is taller and stronger than ordinary men, and Michael Keaton was too short. At 1.75 m, he was in fact the shortest actor ever to play Batman. However, the film was very successful and everybody loved Michael Keaton as Batman.

One of Tim Burton's most interesting characters is Edward Scissorhands. The idea for the character came from a drawing that Burton made in high school. Edward isn't human and he has got scissors instead of hands. In the film, Johnny Depp plays Edward. However, his character in the film is not as scary as Tim Burton's original drawing.

In one of his latest films, *Dumbo*, Dumbo the elephant has got bigger ears than the other elephants and they laugh at him. However, his big ears are an advantage. He can fly. This new film is more exciting than the old Disney film, but the CGI elephant is not as cute as the cartoon elephant in the 1941 film. There are some changes in the plot, but the new film is still as sad as the old one.

Tim Burton has directed many other films, including some of the best-loved children's stories like *Charlie and the Chocolate Factory* and *Alice in Wonderland*. He still produces films today, and sometimes he shows some of his drawings and cartoons at exhibitions around the world.

TH!NK values

Preconceived ideas

7 Read the sentences. How much do you agree with each one? Write a number: 1 (I agree), 2 (I'm not sure) or 3 (I don't agree).

1. If there is a film about a real-life famous person, the actor should look as much like that person as possible. ☐
2. I won't go to see a new film if there is an actor in it that I don't like. ☐
3. Cheap things are never worth buying. ☐
4. There are some shops where I would never buy clothes. ☐
5. It's crazy not to like someone because of the way they speak. ☐

8 SPEAKING Work in groups. Compare your ideas.

> *I don't agree with number 1. It's impossible to find actors who look the same.*

> *Do you think so? I agree with it. I think they should wear make-up to make them look very similar.*

31

GRAMMAR
Comparative and superlative adjectives (review)

1 **Complete these sentences from the article on page 31 with the correct form of the words in the list.**

> big | exciting | short | strong | tall

1 Batman is a superhero who is _____ and _____ than ordinary men.
2 At 1.75 m, he was in fact _____ actor to ever play Batman.
3 Dumbo the elephant has got _____ ears than the other elephants.
4 This new film is _____ the old Disney film.

(not) as … as comparatives

2 **Look at the examples of (not) as ... as to compare things. Answer the questions. Then complete the rule.**

His character in the film is not as scary as Tim Burton's original drawing.
The new film is still as sad as the old one.

1 Which is scarier: the original drawing or the character in the film?
2 Is the new film sadder than the old film?

> **RULE:** When we want to say that two things are (not) the same, we can use (not) ³_____ + adjective + ⁴_____ .

3 **Complete each sentence with your own ideas.**
1 a Football isn't as exciting as ___*skiing*___ .
  b Football is more exciting than ___*golf*___ .
2 a English is easier than _____ .
  b English isn't as easy as _____ .
3 a Watching TV isn't as good as _____ .
  b Watching TV is better than _____ .

4 **Complete the second sentence so it has the same meaning as the first. Use the word in brackets.**
0 Ben's sister is younger than him. (old)
  Ben's sister ___*isn't as old as*___ him.
1 Travelling by train is faster than travelling by bus. (slow)
  Travelling by train _____ travelling by bus.
2 Tom is 1.65 m. Sue is 1.65 m, too. (tall)
  Tom _____ Sue.
3 Dogs are noisier than cats. (quiet)
  Dogs _____ cats.
4 This mobile phone costs €225. And the bicycle costs €225, too. (expensive)
  The mobile phone _____ the bicycle.
5 Jo thinks Geography is easier than History. (difficult)
  Jo thinks Geography _____ History.
6 My room is tidier than yours. (untidy)
  My room _____ yours.

> **PRONUNCIATION**
> Words ending in /ə/ Go to page 120.

→ workbook page 28

VOCABULARY
Types of films

5 **Write the types of films in the list under the pictures.**

> action film | animated film | comedy | documentary | horror film
> romantic comedy (rom com) | science fiction (sci-fi) | thriller

6 **SPEAKING** Can you think of an example of each type of film? Are any of your examples more than one type?

Spies in Disguise is an action film.

1 _____

2 _____

3 _____

4 _____

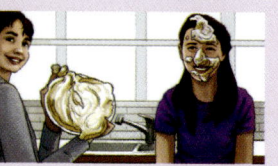
5 _____

6 _____

7 _____

8 _____

→ workbook page 30

🎧 LISTENING

7 🔊 **3.04** Listen to Part 1 of an interview. Why is Emma Harding a guest on the radio show?

8 🔊 **3.05** Listen to Part 2 of the interview. For each question, choose the correct answer.

1 Emma says that making a Lego film
   A takes a lot of time.
   B is far easier than you think.
   C requires lots of drawing.
2 When she was making the film, Emma
   A used her own camera.
   B didn't have any lights.
   C had some help from a friend.
3 Emma says that her film is
   A 10 seconds long.
   B 18 seconds long.
   C 20 seconds long.

Grammar rap! ▶08

GRAMMAR
Making a comparison stronger or weaker

9 Read the sentences. Choose the phrase that has a different meaning from the other two. Then complete the rule.

0 Eighteen photos look *a lot* / *much* / (*a little*) better than ten photos.
1 Together we made the script *a little* / *a lot* / *a bit* better.
2 I'm sure it's *a little* / *much* / *far* more difficult than it looks.

> **RULE:** Use ³_____ / ⁴_____ / *far* to make a comparative stronger.
> Use *a bit* / ⁵_____ to make a comparative weaker.

10 Rewrite these sentences using the words in brackets.
1 Sharks are more dangerous than dolphins. (a lot)
2 My brother is taller than me. (a bit)
3 My new phone's better than my old one. (far)
4 Her hair is longer than yours. (a little)
5 The film's more exciting than the book. (much)

11 Write sentences comparing these things. Use *much* / *far* / *a lot* or *a bit* / *a little*.

0 watching TV / reading a book (interesting / easy)
   I think watching TV is a lot more interesting than reading a book – and it's far easier, too.
1 gorillas / snakes (dangerous / beautiful)
2 English / Art (difficult / interesting)
3 my country / US (big / beautiful)

→ **workbook page 29**

WordWise: Expressions with *get*

12 Look at the sentences from the unit so far. Choose the correct meaning of *get* in each one.
1 Then you need to get yourself a camera.
2 He got a Daytime Emmy Award for his cartoon series *Beetlejuice*.
3 I couldn't wait to get home and tell my mum.
4 I still get emotional now when I think about it.

a become   c arrive
b received   d obtain, buy

13 Use a phrase from the list to complete each sentence.

> get a drink | get angry | get home
> got better | got bored | got there

1 The film was terrible – after 20 minutes, I _____ and fell asleep.
2 I was really late for school – when I _____ , it was already ten o'clock!
3 There's still a long way to go. I don't think we'll _____ before midnight.
4 He was ill for about a week, but then he _____ , I'm happy to say.
5 It was just a joke. Please don't _____ with me!
6 If you want, we can _____ in that café in the town centre.

14 Match the questions and answers.
1 Let's go and get a drink. ☐
2 When do you get angry with people? ☐
3 Do you ever get bored watching TV? ☐
4 What time do you get to school? ☐
5 Do you ever get a cold? ☐

a When they say things I don't like.
b Usually about eight o'clock.
c OK. The shop over there sells water.
d Sometimes – in winter, usually.
e Only when it's a programme I don't like.

→ **workbook page 30**

READING

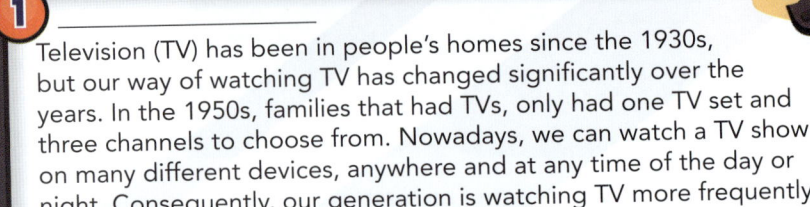

THE HISTORY OF watching TV

1 Read the article quickly. Write the titles in the correct spaces 1–4.
- **A** The rise in screen time
- **B** TV as a family activity
- **C** The changing world of TV
- **D** Non-stop drama

1 _____
Television (TV) has been in people's homes since the 1930s, but our way of watching TV has changed significantly over the years. In the 1950s, families that had TVs, only had one TV set and three channels to choose from. Nowadays, we can watch a TV show on many different devices, anywhere and at any time of the day or night. Consequently, our generation is watching TV more frequently than any other generation before.

2 _____
TVs were luxury items in the 1950s, and the families that did have one had to sit very close to it as the screens were very small.
Then in the 1960s, TVs became cheaper and more families owned one. Most people had a TV in their living room and families sat together and watched their favourite shows. Oh, and there was no 'Watch next episode' button. People had to wait patiently for a week to watch the next part of their favourite soap opera.

3 _____
Then, in the mid-2000s, TV broadcasters started to make programmes available via the internet. It was called on-demand TV and became very popular because people could choose when they wanted to watch a programme. Now, you could watch an episode of a sitcom straight away. Instead of watching one episode, people happily binge-watched six hours of their favourite TV series in one afternoon. Drama series became like one long film. And if you missed a documentary or an episode of your favourite reality show, you could easily watch it online later.
During this decade, far fewer people sat down with their families to watch a TV show. However, people still preferred to watch major sports events (such as the FIFA World Cup) live.

4 _____
In the 2010s, children and young adults began to watch much less broadcast TV than in the past. They watched their entertainment on smartphones, games consoles and via streaming services. This meant they could watch a show more easily at any time. Now, people spend more hours watching TV. In fact, the average person in Britain spends almost ten years of their life watching TV! As well as watching a show, they also need to read all the posts about it quickly, and tweet about it, too. This adds up to a lot more screen time.

2 🔊 3.06 Read and listen to the text again. Answer the questions.
1. Why did you sometimes have to wait seven days in the early years of TV to watch a programme?
2. How did 'on-demand' TV change the way people watch TV?
3. In the 2000s, which type of programme did people prefer to watch at the time it was broadcast?
4. What effect do social media have on the amount of time people spend looking at screens?

3 SPEAKING Which statements are true for you? In groups, compare your ideas.
1. I prefer to watch TV alone rather than with other people.
2. I sometimes binge-watch drama series.
3. I sometimes use social media to discuss TV programmes with friends.
4. I spend more time on a tablet or computer than I do in front of a TV.

GRAMMAR
Adverbs and comparative adverbs

4 Look at the sentences from the article. Complete them with the words in the list.

> cheaper | easily | long | patiently

1. TVs became _____ .
2. People had to wait _____ for a week to watch the next episode.
3. Drama series became like one _____ film.
4. You could _____ watch it online later.

5 Look again at the text on page 34 and find the adverbs. Then complete the rules with *adjective* and *adverb*.

> **RULE:** Use an ¹_____ to talk about a noun:
> *He's a slow runner.*
> Use an ²_____ to talk about a verb:
> *He runs slowly.*
> We usually form an ³_____ by adding *-ly* (or *-ily*) to the ⁴_____ , but some adverbs are irregular: *fast* ➡ *fast*, *good* ➡ *well*.

6 Write the adverbs.

0 quick   _quickly_   4 good   _____
1 careful _____   5 bad   _____
2 clever   _____   6 easy   _____
3 happy   _____   7 fast   _____

7 Look at the examples of comparative adverbs from the text on page 34. Then complete the rules.

1 This meant they could watch a show **more easily** at any time.
2 Our generation is watching TV **more frequently** than any other generation before.

> **RULE:** To form the comparative of most regular adverbs, add the word ³_____ before the adverb: *easily* ➡ *more easily.*
> If an adverb has one syllable, make the comparative by adding *-er*: *soon* ➡ *sooner*, *hard* ➡ *harder*, *fast* ➡ *faster*.
> • There are some irregular comparative adverbs: *badly* ➡ *worse*, *well* ➡ *better*.
> • Notice that the comparative of *early* is *earlier*.

8 Complete the sentences. Use the comparative adverb forms of the words in brackets.

0 Sue runs (fast) than me. _faster_
1 George writes _____ (clear) than me.
2 You need to do your homework _____ (careful) if you want to get good marks.
3 Sorry, I don't understand. Can you speak _____ (slow), please?
4 The party starts at ten o'clock, but you can come _____ (early) if you want to.
5 I only got 22% in the test, but you did even _____ (bad) than me!
6 Isabella always works _____ (hard) than the other kids.
7 Martina speaks English _____ (good) than I do.

➡ workbook page 29

VOCABULARY
Types of TV programmes

9 Look at the different types of TV programmes. Can you think of an example for each one?

cartoon

reality show

chat show

sitcom

drama series

soap (opera)

game show

sports programme

news

talent show

10 **SPEAKING** Work in pairs. Ask and answer the questions.

1 What kind(s) of programmes do you really like?
2 What kind(s) of programmes do you really NOT like?
3 What's your favourite programme at the moment? Why?
4 What's your least favourite programme at the moment? Why?
5 How do you watch TV programmes – on TV, on your phone, on a tablet …?

➡ workbook page 30

WRITING
A paragraph about your TV habits

11 Write a paragraph about your TV habits.

• Use your answers to the questions in Exercise 10 to help you.
• Try to use grammar and vocabulary from the unit (comparative adjectives, words for TV programmes, etc.).

DEVELOPING SPEAKING

1 🔊 3.07 Look at the photo. Why do you think the girl is tired? Listen and read to check.

Megan: Hi, Josh. Have you got a moment? I'd like some help with a Maths question.
Josh: Hey, Megan. Sure. How can I help? Is everything OK? <u>Looks like</u> you haven't slept for about a week!
Megan: Well, I didn't sleep much last night. Or the night before. <u>In fact</u>, I haven't slept well for three nights.
Josh: Why not?
Megan: It's that new drama – *The Big Show*. It came out last week. It's fantastic. And last night I watched it until … well, quite late.
Josh: How late?
Megan: Well, three o'clock in the morning. I watched all 20 episodes in three nights.
Josh: Wow! I'm not surprised you're tired and can't concentrate.
Megan: But it's so good! Last night there were only two more episodes to watch, I had to keep going. It's like running a long race – it starts to hurt but you have to carry on! My parents always tell me not to give up halfway through something.
Josh: But you shouldn't stay up all night.
Megan: I know. But it's brilliant. Anyway – could you help me with the Maths problem? Please?
Josh: Here, <u>have a look at this</u>.
Megan: A book!?
Josh: Yes, it explains everything. Just don't fall asleep while you're reading it, OK?
Megan: Oh <u>come on</u>, Josh! Please help me.
Josh: Sorry, I can't. I've got to go now. So, you'll have to do it yourself <u>after all</u>. Oh, and <u>guess what</u>? You've got ten minutes to do it before the lesson starts!

2 Read the dialogue again and answer the questions.
1 What does Megan want Josh's help with?
2 What has Megan done for the last three nights?
3 What does she compare watching the TV series to?
4 What does Josh tell her to do to understand the Maths problem?

3 SPEAKING Discuss the questions in pairs.
1 Is it OK for Megan to ask Josh to help her?
2 Is her comparison with running a good one?
3 Was Josh right not to help Megan?

Phrases for fluency

4 Find the underlined expressions in the dialogue and use them to complete the conversation.

Jim   Hi guys. ¹_____ ? I'm in the football team!
Mike You're joking!
Jim   No, I'm not. ²_____ . It's the team list.
Mike But you're not a good player, Jim. ³_____ , you're terrible!
Alice Oh, ⁴_____ , Mike! He's not so bad.
Susie That's right. And the school has picked him to play, so ⁵_____ you're wrong, Mike.
Mike Well, I guess so.
Jim   Yes. I'm good enough for the school team ⁶_____ !

FUNCTIONS
Asking for and offering help

KEY LANGUAGE
Could you … ?   Can you … ?
Can I … ?   Is everything OK / all right?

5 Look at these sentences. Are they asking for or offering help? Write A (asking) or O (offering).
1 Can you lend me a hand? ___
2 Can I help you at all? ___
3 Is everything OK? ___
4 Have you got a few minutes? ___

6 Complete the mini-dialogues using the expressions from the Key Language box.
1 Maisie   _____ help me with my homework please, Mum?
   Mum   Of course, Maisie, what subject is it?
2 Pablo   _____ give me a hand, Mr Terrence?
   Mr Terrence No problem. _____
3 Sofia   _____ have some ice cream, Grandma?
   Grandma   No, Sofia, dinner is almost ready.

7 SPEAKING Work in pairs. Use the questions in the Key Language box and in Exercise 5 to act out conversations in a shop, at home, at school and in other places.

ON THE SCREEN UNIT 3

LIFE COMPETENCIES

Everybody has got something they find really difficult. But just because it's hard doesn't mean we can't do it – whether it's getting better grades at school, improving at sport or even learning a new language. Commitment and determination can help us achieve our goals, no matter how large or small.

1 ▶09 Watch the video. How far did Kieran get in the 10 km race?

2 ▶09 Watch again and complete Kieran's notes.

Step 1: Identify goal	
Step 2: Best thing about achieving my goal	
Step 3: What may stop me	
Step 4: How to make sure those things DON'T stop me	

3 **SPEAKING** Work with a partner. What do you think of this advice? Are there any ideas you don't think are good?

How to achieve your goals:

1 Divide your main goal into smaller goals.
2 Make a weekly plan of action for each small goal.
3 Take the first step!
4 Expect some problems and be ready to solve them.
5 Ask friends and family for encouragement.
6 Review how well you're doing and make changes to your plan if necessary.
7 Stay focused!
8 Reward yourself!

4 Alex is shy, so people often think she's unfriendly. As a result, she doesn't have many friends. She'd like to make more friends, so she's going to follow the advice in Exercise 3. Complete her notes with your own ideas. Compare with a partner.

1 _____
2 _____
3 Start on Monday 12th.
4 _____
5 Tell Mum and my friend Katy about the plan. Update them every week.
6 Review the plan with Mum or Katy every Sunday.
7 Set calendar on mobile to remind me of plan every day.
8 _____

Me and my world

5 Choose one of the ideas from the list below that you would like to work on (or choose one of your own). Make notes like Alex's about how you're going to achieve your goal.

- Spend less time looking at screens
- Help more around the house
- Read more
- Eat more healthily

6 **SPEAKING** Tell your friends about your plans. Listen to each other and give ideas and advice.

TIPS FOR ACHIEVING YOUR GOALS

- Make a plan. It is a good way to ensure you have a clear idea of what you want to achieve.
- Be realistic when setting goals. Changing how you behave takes time.
- Reward yourself when you achieve something, but don't feel too bad and punish yourself if you don't.

4 ONLINE LIFE

Get TH!NKING

Watch the video and think: do you post too many things on social media?

OBJECTIVES

FUNCTIONS:
giving advice

GRAMMAR:
indefinite pronouns (*everyone, no one, someone,* etc.); *all / some / none / any of them; should(n't), had better, ought to*

VOCABULARY:
IT terms; language for giving advice

1

2

3

4

5

6

READING

1 **SPEAKING** Work in pairs. Answer the questions.
1 Which of these social networks do you know?
2 What do you think of them?
3 Do you know any other social networks?

2 **SPEAKING** Read these statements about using social networks. Which of them are true for you? Discuss them with a partner.
1 I've got a Facebook account but hardly ever use it.
2 I don't post many comments, but I like to read other people's posts.
3 I constantly check for updates on social media.
4 I sometimes post comments that I regret later.

3 Look at the photos on the next page. What do you think the article is about? Read the article quickly to check your ideas.

4 🔊 4.01 Read and listen to the article about online behaviour again. Mark the statements T (true) or F (false).
1 A digital footprint is like a footprint in sand because it disappears after time. _____
2 People who use the internet create an online history for themselves. _____
3 What you do online can lead to you receiving certain kinds of advertisements. _____
4 What you write online can be misunderstood by other people. _____
5 People should be careful about what personal information they include when they write online. _____
6 You can make life more difficult for thieves by not putting personal information online. _____
7 It's OK to put a credit card number in an email, but not a password. _____
8 It's possible not to leave a digital footprint if you go online. _____

5 **SPEAKING** Work in pairs. Correct the false statements in Exercise 4.

ONLINE LIFE | UNIT 4

LEAVING FOOTPRINTS

Imagine you are walking in the sand on a beach somewhere, or through deep snow on a mountain. As you walk, you leave footprints where you've been. Later, of course, the footprints disappear. But imagine if they didn't – if your footprints stayed there forever. And imagine, too, that you left footprints everywhere you walked, including in your home and in your town – so that someone could see everywhere you've been. How happy would you be about that?

Well, that's what happens when you use technology – computers, mobile phones, tablets. It's your digital footprint – a record of where you've been and what you've seen that you leave when you go online. Your comments on social media, your retweets, the apps you use, the emails you send, everything you've searched for – all of them are part of your digital footprint, and other people can see your footprint, or it can be tracked in a database.

Does this matter? Why would anyone be interested in what you write on Twitter or post on Instagram? Well, companies who sell things are interested, that's for sure – they want to send you adverts for things they want you to buy. But apart from businesses, there are other reasons why your digital footprint should matter to you.

1 HOW PEOPLE SEE YOU

Of course, you have nothing to hide, but if people get information about you, they might pick bits to make you look good – or bad. Perhaps one day you write something silly online. Maybe you make a bad joke. Years later, it's found by the university you're applying to, and they don't think it's funny. Then what? Maybe they decide you're not the 'right' kind of person for them.

2 YOUR PRIVATE INFORMATION

Everyone has information about themselves that they don't want everyone to know (for example, you might share your school reports with your parents but not friends), but the internet doesn't make the same decisions that you would.

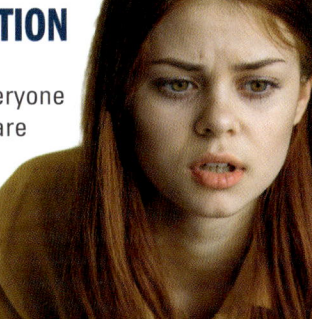

3 KEEPING YOUR MONEY SAFE

There are plenty of people looking at information about you, and some of them want to steal from you, but the less information you put out, the harder it is for them. Bank details, card numbers, passwords or PINs – none of them should be written in emails, text messages or anything else.

Overall, the message is: remember that you have a digital footprint, and think carefully before you click 'send' or 'post'. No one can go online and not leave a footprint – but with care, you can control it.

TH!NK values

Responsible online behaviour

6 Read the statements. Write them in two lists under *Do* and *Don't*.

1 Say bad things about other people online.
2 Talk to your teacher or another adult if you get bullied on social media.
3 Think carefully before you write a post about yourself or other people.
4 Write a post about someone when you are angry with them.
5 Write posts containing personal information about your family.
6 Think before you post a photo of yourself or someone else.

7 **SPEAKING** Work in pairs. Compare your lists. Think of at least two more statements for each list.

GRAMMAR
Indefinite pronouns (*everyone, no one, someone*, etc.)

1 **Complete these sentences from the article on page 39. Find other examples of indefinite pronouns in the article.**
   1 Imagine, too, that you left footprints _____ you walked.
   2 Perhaps one day you write _____ silly online.
   3 _____ can go online and not leave a footprint.

2 **Complete the table. Use the article on page 39 to help you. Then complete the rules with *some* / *any* / *no* / *every*.**

everything	¹_____	nothing	anything
everyone	someone	no one	³_____
everywhere	somewhere	²_____	anywhere

> **RULE:** The words beginning with
> • ⁴_____ mean 'all' (people / things / places).
> • ⁵_____ mean that we don't know exactly which (person / thing / place).
> • ⁶_____ mean that we don't care or it doesn't matter which (person / thing / place).
> • ⁷_____ mean 'not any' (person / thing / place).

3 **Complete the sentences with words from the table in Exercise 2.**
   1 Where's my pen? I've looked _____ , but I can't find it.
   2 Using social media can be a real problem. _____ should know that.
   3 The teacher asked a question, but _____ knew the answer.
   4 _____ has left a message for you at reception.
   5 Ouch! There's _____ in my eye!
   6 I've no idea where Sally is. She could be _____ .
   7 Do you want a place to relax on your holiday? There's _____ better than here!
   8 It's so noisy. Let's go _____ quieter.

4 **Complete these sentences so that they are true for you.**
   1 Everyone knows that I _____ .
   2 For my next holiday I'd like to go somewhere _____ .
   3 I don't like eating anything that has got _____ in it.
   4 I think anyone can learn to _____ .

→ *workbook page 36*

VOCABULARY
IT terms

5 **Match the phrases with the meanings. Write numbers 1–10.**

> 1 to key in your password | 2 to install a program
> 3 to attach a file | 4 to have network coverage
> 5 to upload a photo | 6 to delete a message
> 7 ~~to open an attachment~~ | 8 to buy an app
> 9 to activate flight mode | 10 to download a file

a to click on the icon of a file that comes with an email [7]
b to have a signal that lets you make phone calls, etc. [ ]
c to add a separate element (e.g. a photo, a document, a video) to an email [ ]
d to make an image available on the internet [ ]
e to pay for a program for your mobile or tablet [ ]
f to type a secret word that gives you access to a computer or a website [ ]
g to put a program on a computer [ ]
h to switch on a function on your mobile or tablet so you can't go online [ ]
i to remove a piece of text so it cannot be seen any more [ ]
j to copy information or a program from the internet onto your computer hard disk [ ]

6 **SPEAKING** Work in pairs. Ask and answer these questions.
   1 How many different ways do you have to go online?
   2 How often do you post something on social media?
   3 What kind of things do you usually post?
   4 What ways do you know of keeping passwords secure but remembering them?

7 **Draw spider diagrams for these verbs.**

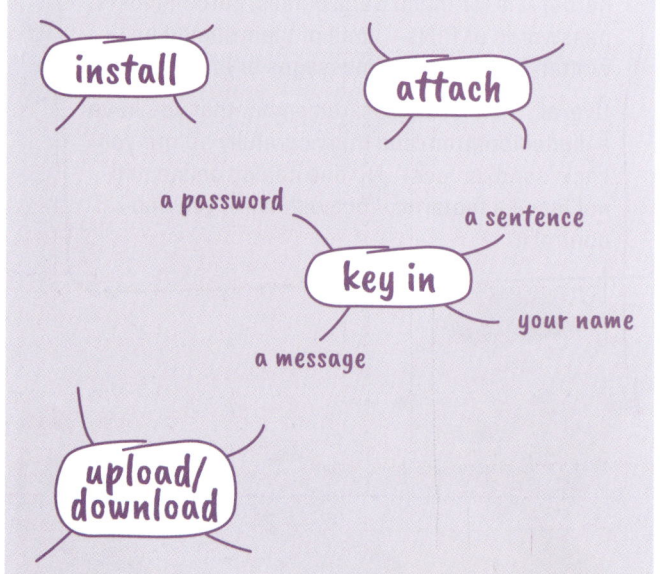

→ *workbook page 38*

ONLINE LIFE UNIT 4

GRAMMAR
all / some / none / any of them

12 Complete the sentences. Look back at the article on page 39 to check.

The apps you use, the emails you send, everything you've searched for – ⁰_____*all of them*_____ are part of your digital footprint

There are plenty of people looking at information about you, and ¹_____ want to steal from you.

Bank details, card numbers, passwords or PINs – ²_____ should be written in emails.

13 Complete the rule with *things / more / none*.

> RULE: We use the expressions *all / some / ¹_____ / any of them* to refer back to a group (of ²_____ or people) and say ³_____ about it.

14 Choose the correct words.

1 My friends had a great time at my birthday party. *All / None* of them wanted to leave!
2 Which of these pens is Carla's? They all look exactly the same, so *any / some* of them could be hers.
3 These bikes all look good, but I'm sure *some / any* of them are better than others.
4 These T-shirts are really cool. *None / Any* of them would be fine for me.
5 These caps weren't expensive. I got *all / none* of them for £12.
6 I tried on lots of different jeans, but *none / some* of them were the right size for me.
7 All the questions were really hard – I couldn't answer *none / any* of them!
8 Her songs are OK – I quite like *some / any* of them.

15 Complete the sentences with *all / some / none / any*. (There may be more than one possible answer.)

1 There are 32 students in Sarah's class. It's amazing that __*all*__ of them like music, but _____ of them listen to jazz.
2 I like most American TV shows, but _____ of them are terrible!
3 OK, he scored three goals – but _____ of them were lucky!
4 The cakes that I made were horrible – we couldn't eat _____ of them, so we threw them all away.
5 My three brothers like IT, but _____ of them is as good with computers as my sister.
6 Look at those cameras. _____ of them are very cheap, but others are very expensive.

→ workbook page 36

LISTENING

8 Match the words and phrases with the meanings. Write the numbers 1–6 in the boxes.

> 1 to fall for a scam | 2 personal data
> 3 phishing | 4 identity theft
> 5 a pop-up | 6 a PIN

a a secret number you use with your bank card
b information about you and your life
c a new window or message that appears on your computer screen
d when people try to get you to give information over the internet
e to not understand when someone tries to get money from you with lies
f to steal information about someone, then pretend to be them

9 SPEAKING Work in pairs. Answer the questions.

1 Which of the things in Exercise 8 did you already know about?
2 Do you know anyone who has had problems because they sent personal data to someone else?

10 4.02 Listen to Mark and his dad. Answer the questions.

1 Why is Mark's dad angry?
2 What does he want Mark not to do?

11 4.02 Listen again. Look at the six sentences. Mark them T (true) or F (false). Then correct the false ones.

1 Mark's grandfather didn't lose much money.
2 Mark doesn't think he will fall for a scam.
3 Identity theft is less of a problem now than before.
4 Mark got an email offering him a new laptop.
5 The brother of one of Mark's friends lost money.
6 Mark's dad thinks only teenagers are tricked online.

41

READING

1 Look at the messages. Match them with the types of communication in the list. Write a–e in the boxes.
1. email
2. message on a messaging app
3. post on an advertisement website
4. social media post
5. text message

2 🔊 4.03 Read and listen to the messages and choose the correct answers.

1. Why does Billy apologise to his brother Sam?
   A He wants to buy another guitar.
   B He has dreams that may not come true.
   C He won't be home in time to make dinner.
2. What's the purpose of Gemma's message (a)?
   A To invite Billy to her house on Sunday
   B To tell Billy she's not a good guitarist
   C To ask Billy if he can play a song
3. In her post (b), Gemma
   A says she learned something new.
   B tells people she had a good time with Billy.
   C says that Billy's a good guitar player.
4. In her post (c), Gemma says the guitar
   A is new and is in OK condition.
   B is an acoustic guitar.
   C comes in a case which costs extra.
5. Billy writes an email (d)
   A to suggest that he and Gemma play guitar together again.
   B to say he wants to buy her guitar.
   C to say he knows some good videos on YouTube.
6. In his message (e), Billy says that he
   A doesn't like Neil Young's music.
   B liked the guitar practice, but not the tea.
   C hopes they can play together again.

Train to TH!NK

Logical sequencing

3 Read the messages again. Work out a logical order. Write letters a–e in the right order.
1 3 5
2 4

4 SPEAKING Work in pairs. Compare your ideas and discuss any differences.

Hi Sam,
You know I want a better guitar. Well, my friend Jake told me that his friend is selling one, so I'm going to check it out this evening. I'm going to be really late back. So sorry – you'd better make your own dinner tonight. When your brother is a big star, he'll buy you dinner every night. 😊
— Billy Smith

a Hey Billy. I'm not doing anything on Sunday. Want to come round? I've been practising a song called *Heart of Gold* – do you know it? Maybe we could play together? To be honest, I'm not very good at the guitar. How about you? Gemma
— Gemma Black

b **Gemma Black**
Great fun yesterday. A new friend came round and we played guitar together. He's a beginner, but I'm not great, so we had fun. We watched a YouTube lesson for a song called *Heart of Gold* – it's not too difficult to play. We had tea together afterwards, too.

c Sign in | Post
Hi everyone, I've got an acoustic guitar that I want to sell. It's a two-year-old Yamaha, perfect condition, £250 with the case. Anyone interested? If not, tell your friends please!

d To: Gemma
From: billy@thinkmail.com
Hi!

Hi Gemma,
I've thought about the guitar. It's really nice but a bit more than I can really afford, so I'm going to stick with my old one for now.
But it was nice to talk. Thanks for the tip about the YouTube lessons – that guy is much better than the one I've been using. You know, we ought to practise together some time. What do you think?
Billy

e MESSAGES
Contacts

Hi G,
Thanks for last Sunday. It was fun playing the guitar with you and the tea was nice, too. I've listened to some more songs by Neil Young. Old guy, but cool tunes! We should do it again soon.
B
PS Love the photo on Instagram!

GRAMMAR
should(n't), had better, ought to

5 Complete these sentences from the messages on page 42. Then choose the correct words to complete the rules.

1 You _____ make your own dinner tonight.
2 We _____ do it again soon.
3 We _____ practise together some time.

> **RULE:** *Should*, *had better* and *ought to* are used to give ⁴**advice / information**.
> - *Should* and *ought to* mean more or less the same, but we usually don't use *ought to* in questions and negative statements.
> - The meaning of *had better* is often a little stronger. The speaker wants to say that there are ⁵**positive / negative** consequences if you ignore the advice.
>
> These verbs ⁶**do / don't** use an auxiliary verb in the negative: *shouldn't*, *oughtn't to*, *had better not*.

6 Match the questions to the answers. Write a–g in the boxes. Choose the correct word in each answer.

1 I've broken my friend's watch. What should I do?
2 I've got toothache. What should I do?
3 I didn't do very well in the test. What should I do?
4 I'd like to go climbing, but I've never done it before. What should I do?
5 I got an email from someone, asking me to send them money. Should I reply to it?
6 I'm angry with my brother. He said something I didn't like. What should I do?
7 This sweater my sister gave me looks terrible. I don't like it at all. What should I do?

a You *should / shouldn't* respond. It could be a scam.
b You *should / shouldn't* tell him. It's best to be honest with him.
c You'd *better / better not* return it to the shop. That would really hurt her feelings.
d You *shouldn't / ought to* go back and study everything again.
e You'd *better / shouldn't* get some training. It can be dangerous.
f You *ought to / shouldn't* see a dentist.
g You'd *better / shouldn't* say sorry the next time you see your friend.

7 Look at these pictures. Write short dialogues with (serious or funny) answers giving advice.

1 What should I do?
You should run after the man and give him his wallet.

→ workbook page 37

VOCABULARY
Language for giving advice

8 Look at the phrases below and answer the questions.

to give (bad / good / practical / useful) advice about [something]
to take / follow [someone's] advice
to ignore [someone's] advice
to advise [someone] [to do something]
to advise against [something]
to be advisable

a What's the difference between *advice* and *advise*?
b Which of the phrases mean(s)
  – not to listen to somebody's advice?
  – do what somebody has advised you to do?
c How do you say 'advisable' in your language?

9 Complete the sentences with phrases from Exercise 8. Use the correct verb forms.

1 I've told Peter he shouldn't post photos like that, but he has always _____ my _____ .
2 Should I buy a tablet or a laptop? Can you give me some _____ what's better?
3 He wants to become a web designer. His dad has _____ him to take a course. He should _____ that _____ .
4 My uncle has a heart problem. This web page _____ fatty foods.

FUNCTIONS
Giving advice

10 **SPEAKING** Ask and answer questions with a partner.

1 Imagine you meet somebody who has never used a computer. What advice would you give them about social networking?
2 Are you good at giving advice? Say why (not) and give examples.
3 When do you find it difficult to follow someone's advice?

TH!NK
The evolution of writing

Culture

1 Look at the photos. What do they show?

FROM CAVES TO KINDLES
– HOW READING HAS CHANGED

1 ☐

Cave paintings are the oldest pictures. Some of them, like the beautiful images in the caves of Altamira in the north of Spain, are almost 30,000 years old. Many of these paintings show animals or hunting scenes. The images do not have written words, but when we look at them, we get an idea of the emotions the people felt when drawing them. The paintings tell stories of hopes and fears. They are an early form of communication.

2 ☐

Sometime between 4000 and 3000 BCE, people in Egypt and Mesopotamia developed the skill of writing. They engraved text on stone tablets first. But it was impossible to carry stones from place to place. The invention of papyrus allowed documents to be moved easily. Writing on papyrus made it easier to correct mistakes, too. And do you know how they did that? When a scribe – the person who wrote the documents – made a mistake, they licked the ink off the papyrus before it got dry and made their corrections!

3 ☐

People made the first books from papyrus and from thin animal skins. Paper was invented in China as early as 105 CE. The quality of paper soon became very good. The world's oldest known printed book is from China, too. It was published on May 11, 868 CE. In Europe, books were written manually until the middle of the 15th century, when Johannes Gutenberg invented the printing press in Germany. Since that time, almost 140 million books have been published worldwide. For many people, one of life's greatest pleasures is spending a few hours in a bookshop browsing through the books.

4 ☐

Books will be around for many years, of course. But there are many other ways of reading books and magazines, such as e-books and apps on mobile phones, which allow you to buy and download reading material to carry around with you and read whenever and wherever you want to.

2 Read the article quickly. Match the paragraph headings with the paragraphs. Write the letters a–f. There are two headings you don't need.
   a The invention of books by Gutenberg
   b Early forms of written communication
   c Books in their most modern form
   d From stone tablets to the printing press
   e Communication without reading and writing
   f The history of bookmaking

3 🔊 **4.04** Read and listen to the article and check your answers in Exercise 2.

4 **SPEAKING** Work in pairs. Discuss the questions.
   1 How important are books for you? Give reasons.
   2 What book(s) have you read recently? Did you like it / them?
   3 Do you prefer printed books or e-books? Why?

PRONUNCIATION
The short /ʌ/ vowel sound Go to page 120.

ONLINE LIFE UNIT 4

5 **VOCABULARY** There are eight highlighted words in the article. Match the words with these meanings. Write the words.

0 a large hole in a cliff or mountain that goes inside — *cave*
1 paper made from plants — _____
2 looking through a book or magazine, without reading everything — _____
3 happiness, love and anger — _____
4 produced (and sold) a book — _____
5 moved the tongue across something — _____
6 words that are cut into stone — _____
7 a machine to make newspapers, books or magazines — _____

WRITING
A web page giving advice

1 **INPUT** Read this information and decide who it would be important for. Then answer the questions.

1 Where do people use public computers?
2 What other examples not mentioned in the text can you think of?
3 Why should you never save a password on a public computer?
4 What's the problem with just closing the browser when you want to finish a session?

2 Rewrite the sentences by putting the words in brackets in the right position.

1 Read our advice. (carefully)
   Read our advice carefully.
2 Click 'Yes.' (don't)
3 Make you do not simply close the browser. (sure)
4 You should log out. (always)
5 Ask them to go somewhere else. (politely)

3 Are the sentences above used to give advice or to give an opinion? Match each of them with one of the situations below. Write the numbers 1–5.

a when the system asks you 'Do you want to save the password?' ☐
b when you want to leave a site ☐
c to be smart and safe when using public computers ☐
d if someone looks over your shoulder and watches you ☐
e when you finish your session ☐

4 **ANALYSE** Match the content with the five sections of the text.

Introduction   a Don't leave important information on the screen.
Bullet point 1   b Log out properly.
Bullet point 2   c Don't let people watch you.
Bullet point 3   d What is the purpose of this text?
Bullet point 4   e Don't save information.

HOW TO USE A PUBLIC COMPUTER – SAFETY TIPS

There are times when you may want to use a public computer, for example in a hostel, a library or at an airport. That's when it's especially important to be smart and safe.

- **Don't save!** When you want to log into a social networking website or your email, the system will ask you, 'Do you want to save this password?' Don't click 'Yes' when you are working on a public computer.

- **Log out!** Make sure you do not simply close the browser when you want to leave a site. You should always log out of all sites when you finish your session.

- **Close windows!** If you need to walk away from the computer for any reason, you should close all the windows on the computer first. Don't leave any information on the screen that other people shouldn't see.

- **Watch out!** Be careful of people looking at the screen over your shoulder. Ask them politely to go somewhere else so you can use the computer in private.

5 **PLAN** What would be important advice for good online behaviour? Make notes.

Here are some ideas:
what (not) to share on social networks
creating secure passwords and how to keep them safe
what to do when you receive offensive comments on social networking websites
what you should know about uploading photos on social networks

6 **PRODUCE** Write your text for a web page giving advice on good online behaviour (about 200 words).

Use an introduction and bullet points to structure your text.

Use language from Exercises 2 and 3 to give advice, and make sure your readers understand what situations your advice refers to.

B1 Preliminary for Schools

READING
Part 2: Matching

→ workbook page 43

1 For each question, choose the correct answer. The young people below are looking for a film to watch. Look at the eight film reviews. Decide which film would be most suitable for the people below.

1 Dawn loves thinking about the future and how human society will be different. She's a fan of films that are set in a time many years from now but doesn't really enjoy films that are too frightening.

2 Paula's job is very boring so when she gets home she likes watching films with special effects, but she's not a fan of sci-fi. She also likes films with fast action.

3 Keith is a romantic guy who enjoys a good love story but it must have a happy ending. He doesn't like serious films very much, and likes to have a laugh, too.

4 Lisa's not really a fan of fiction and only watches films about real life. She's interested in anything from history to nature to science, as long as she learns something from it.

5 Graham likes many different kinds of films, but cartoons are his favourite. He especially likes them when they are based on a true story, especially on historical events.

HOT NEW FILMS

A THE INVISIBLE WORLD
Using the most advanced camera technology in the world, this documentary takes us to places that have never been filmed before. From deep under the sea to inside the human body, this film contains some of the most amazing images you will ever see.

B THE KING WHO NEVER WAS
In 1936 Edward VIII decided to give up being king after less than a year so he could be with the woman he loved. This film revisits one of the most popular 'royal stories' of all time and mixes fact and fiction to create an interesting drama. It will keep audiences entertained.

C IT COULD HAPPEN TO YOU
Imagine waking up in the future in a house that is not the house you went to sleep in. Imagine not recognising your children – even though they all seem to think you are their mum. This fascinating sci-fi takes us to a world where people buy and sell memories.

D WILL THEY? WON'T THEY?
Ever since school, Jack and Jill have been best friends. But now they are in their twenties, and their feelings are changing. Is either of them brave enough to see that they are falling in love? Will they do something about it? Of course, it is all OK in the end in this likeable rom com.

E JOAN OF ARC
The well-known story of the young French woman who fought and died for the freedom of her country, back in the 15th century. Her fantastic story is told in a very emotional way in this animated version, with the voices of many famous film stars. It is also a historically accurate account. Young children might find it disturbing.

F TOMORROW NOW
The year is 2080 and for the last ten years Earth has been in contact with aliens. Today is the day that we finally welcome them to our planet. How will they change our lives and are they really as friendly as they seem? One of the scariest films you will see this year.

G COUNTDOWN TO DISASTER
A speeding train is going to crash into a nuclear power station and no one can stop it. Or can they? Special agent Ryan has got an hour to stop the disaster, but there's a problem – he has a bomb tied around his waist. Car chases, explosions and amazing special effects – this thriller has got it all.

H OLIVER TWIST
This wonderful version of the famous Charles Dickens story will be enjoyed by everyone. An animated cartoon, it takes us back to Victorian London and wonderful characters like Oliver himself, The Artful Dodger and Fagin. There have not been many better animated fiction films in the past twenty years.

WRITING
Part 2: An article or story

→ workbook page 107

2 Choose one of these questions. Write your answer in about 100 words.

Question 1
- Your English teacher has asked you to write a story.
- Your story must begin with this sentence.
  I had tickets to see my favourite band and I was very excited.
- Write your **story**.

Question 2
- You see this notice in an international English-language magazine.
- Write your **article**.

ARTICLES WANTED!
USING LESS ENERGY

What things in your everyday life do you use energy to do?
What can you do to reduce the amount of energy you use?
Why is it important to save energy?
Tell us what you think.
Write an article about these questions and we will publish the most interesting in our magazine.

TEST YOURSELF — UNITS 3 & 4

 VOCABULARY

1 Complete the sentences with the words in the list. There are two extra words.

> advice | advise | attachment | comedy | documentary | download | ignore | key | mode | news | thriller | upload

1. If you're on a plane, don't forget to put your mobile phone in flight _____ .
2. There was a _____ programme on TV last night – I've never laughed so much in my life!
3. You need to fill in a form. You can _____ it from our website.
4. There was an interesting programme last night – a _____ about the history of my country.
5. Let me give you some _____ . Don't go to that new café, it's awful.
6. My father always watches the _____ on TV to see what's happening in the world.
7. I'm sure you think it's a good idea, but I'd _____ against it, to be honest.
8. I got your email but you forgot to send the _____ with it. Can you send it, please?
9. The first thing I do when I switch my computer on is _____ in my password.
10. He doesn't know what he's talking about, so you should just _____ his advice!

/10

GRAMMAR

2 Complete the sentences with the words in the list.

> best | better | everyone | no one | none | someone

1. I advertised my bike for sale, but _____ wanted it.
2. This place makes the _____ hamburgers I've ever eaten.
3. I've got a problem and I need to talk to _____ , please.
4. I asked all my friends, but _____ of them knew the answer.
5. I think her new film is _____ than her last one.
6. The school trip was wonderful. _____ had a really good time.

3 Find and correct the mistake in each sentence.

1. Grandad looks really tired. I think we ought go home now.
2. The film isn't as good than the book.
3. There were four football matches on TV last night, and all of them was brilliant!
4. It's the most bad party I've ever been to.
5. He talks more quiet than his brother.
6. She's really angry. We'd better to go and say sorry.

/12

FUNCTIONAL LANGUAGE

4 Complete the mini-dialogues with the words in the list.

> against | everything | hand | help | ought | should | with | would

1. A Is _____ OK?
   B Yes, thanks. But perhaps I _____ take an aspirin.
2. A Can I _____ you at all?
   B Well, yes, that _____ be great. Thanks!
3. A Could you help me _____ something? I want to send money to someone who wrote me an email.
   B Well, you know, that's not a good idea. I'd advise _____ it.
4. A Joe? This is heavy. Can you lend me a _____ ?
   B Hmm, it looks too heavy. You _____ to use a machine.

/8

MY SCORE /30

22–30 10–21 0–9

5 MUSIC TO MY EARS

OBJECTIVES

FUNCTIONS: asking about feelings; making helpful suggestions

GRAMMAR: present perfect continuous; present perfect simple vs. present perfect continuous

VOCABULARY: making music; musical instruments; phrases with *out*

Get TH!NKING

Watch the video and think: how do you listen to music?
▶13

1 _____

2 _____

3 _____

4 _____

5 _____

6 _____

READING

1  5.01 Listen. What type of music do you hear? Write the words under the pictures.

dance music | jazz | opera | pop | rap | rock

2 What other types of music can you think of?

3 **SPEAKING** Work in pairs. What kind of music do you like? Ask and answer questions.

Do you like ... ?
I love/like/can't stand ...
I've never listened to ...

4 Look at the photos on the next page and answer the questions.
1 Who are the people?
2 What do you think the connection between the photos is?

5 Read the article quickly and check your ideas.

6 🔊 5.02 Read and listen to the article again and answer the questions.
1 What type of music did Sheku play at the royal wedding?
2 How many people watched him play at the wedding?
3 When and where did Sheku first play in front of the prince?
4 How did Sheku announce he was playing at the wedding?
5 Where did Sheku study music?
6 Who did Sheku perform with on a talent show?
7 Why was he offered a record contract?
8 How successful was *Inspiration*?

A BRIGHT STAR

MUSIC TO MY EARS — UNIT 5

On Saturday May 19th 2018, millions of people around the world watched as Prince Harry married the American actress Meghan Markle at St George's Chapel in Windsor Castle, in front of 600 guests. As they signed the marriage register, a young cellist played three pieces of classical music.

It was a dream come true for 19-year-old Sheku Kanneh-Mason. It was the biggest performance of his short professional career so far, and a sign that he was quickly becoming one of the most admired classical musicians in the world.

This wasn't Sheku's first performance in front of the prince. A year earlier Harry was in the audience for a charity concert in London. Perhaps it was Sheku's performance at this concert that resulted in his royal invitation. The following April an excited Sheku announced on Twitter that Meghan had phoned him to see if he would like to play at the wedding.

Sheku has been playing the cello since he was six. He is one of seven children in an amazingly talented family from Nottingham in England. Sheku and his six brothers and sisters are all extremely talented classical musicians. His eldest sister, Isata, won a scholarship to the famous Royal Academy of Music in London to study the piano. A few years later, Sheku followed her when he gained a place at the same institution to study the cello. He was only nine years old. He has been performing with Isata and his older brother Braimah for many years. In 2015 they decided to enter the talent show *Britain's Got Talent* as the Kanneh-Masons. Their performances on the show were watched by several million people and they reached the semi-finals.

A year later Sheku entered the BBC Young Musician of the Year competition, which he won. He became the first black musician ever to win the award. He was just 17 years old. As a result of this success he also got a contract with the music publishing company Decca to record an album.

In 2018, he released his first album, *Inspiration*. The album spent four weeks in the UK top 40 charts and it contains many famous classical pieces. Sheku also includes classical versions of songs by Bob Marley and Leonard Cohen on the album. It has introduced a younger audience to classical music.

The future is looking bright for Sheku Kanneh-Mason!

TH!NK values

Following your dreams

7 Match these people with their dreams.
   1 Jessie is a really good artist. ☐
   2 Kylie loves acting. ☐
   3 David is great at football. ☐
   4 Lance has written a book. ☐

   a 'I want to get it published.'
   b 'I want to be in a play.'
   c 'I want to play professionally.'
   d 'I'd love to have an exhibition of my work.'

8 What should the people in Exercise 7 do to realise their dreams? Give advice. Make notes for each one.
   David / join club

9 SPEAKING Work in pairs. Compare your ideas.

10 SPEAKING Discuss these questions in small groups.
   1 What is your dream?
   2 What can you do to make it come true?

49

GRAMMAR
Present perfect continuous

1 **Complete the sentences with the correct form of the words in brackets. Check your answers in the article on page 49.**
   1 Sheku _____ (play) the cello since he was six.
   2 He _____ (perform) with Isata and his older brother Braimah for many years.

2 **Match the example sentences below with the rules. Write the numbers 1–3.**
   1 I've been learning the piano for two years.
   2 I've been practising the piano since 10 am.
   3 I've been playing the piano all day and I'm tired now.

   RULE: The present perfect continuous is used for actions happening over a period of time. We use it to:
   a emphasise how long an activity has been happening. The activity may or may not be complete. ☐
   b talk generally about situations or activities that started in the past and are still continuing now. ☐
   c talk about situations or activities that have stopped but have a result in the present. ☐

3 **Choose the correct words.**
   1 He's been *talking / talked* on the phone all morning.
   2 I've *being / been* playing this game for hours now.
   3 Jo *hasn't / haven't* been feeling well for a few days.
   4 They've *been / being* studying since ten o'clock.
   5 We *haven't / hasn't* been living here for very long.
   6 The dog's been *barked / barking* for half an hour.

4 **Complete the sentences. Use the correct form of the words and *for* or *since*.**
   1 We're tired because we _____ (run) _____ hours.
   2 I _____ (wait) for her _____ 40 minutes!
   3 He _____ (watch) TV _____ 9 am.
   4 She's red because she _____ (lie) in the sun _____ this morning.
   5 They _____ (walk) in the rain _____ an hour and they're really wet.
   6 Dad's exhausted because he _____ (work) in the garden _____ he got up.

5 **SPEAKING** Work in pairs. Find out how long your partner has been doing these things.
   1 living in their house
   2 learning English
   3 going to school
   4 talking

   How long have you been learning English?
   For two years.

   → workbook page 46

PRONUNCIATION
been: strong /biːn/ and weak /bɪn/
Go to page 120.

VOCABULARY
Making music

6 **Complete the story of Dymonde with the verbs in the list.**

   enter | entered | going | playing | record | released | start | streaming | won | writing

   Alana Bolan started out as a teacher, but she always wanted to be a musician and she always loved [1]_____ *music* and *lyrics* for songs. One day she decided to [2]_____ *a band,* so she put an advert online. She soon found the band mates she was looking for. They called themselves Dymonde. They practised hard and started [3]_____ *local gigs.* A few months ago they decided to [4]_____ *a talent show.* They [5]_____ *the competition,* and their prize was a day in a recording studio. They used it to [6]_____ *a single* called *New Love.* They [7]_____ the *single* a week ago, and loads of people have been [8]_____ it. It's already [9]_____ *the charts.* Radio stations have been playing it lots, too. Next month their album is coming out and they are [10]_____ *on tour* all over the country. Get your tickets fast! They are running out quickly.

   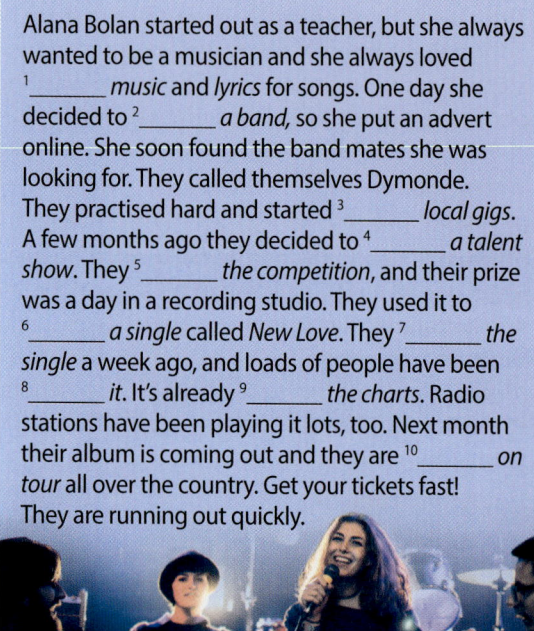

7 **SPEAKING** Work in pairs. Ask your partner about their favourite band. Use the expressions in Exercise 6.

   Who writes the songs?
   Have you been to any of their gigs?

   → workbook page 48

WRITING
The story of your favourite band

8 **Write the story of your favourite band.**
   Write about:
   • how they started.
   • how long they have been together.
   • how long you have liked them and why.

LISTENING

9 🔊 5.05 Listen to the interview with Dana. What is she talking about?

10 🔊 5.05 Listen again and answer the questions.
1 How important is music for Dana?
2 What instrument would Dana like to play?
3 What music does Dana listen to when she's studying?
4 What does Dana think about song lyrics?

11 🔊 5.06 Now listen to Ben answering the same questions. Write three things he has in common with Dana.
1 _____
2 _____
3 _____

💬 SPEAKING

12 Work in pairs. Do the quiz. Then discuss your answers to these questions.
- Do you agree or disagree with your score? Why?
- What music do you listen to when you are sad?
- What songs have special memories for you?
- What are your favourite song lyrics?
- How do you choose what music to listen to?
- What music do your friends like?

DOES MUSIC ROCK YOUR WORLD?
COULD YOU LIVE WITHOUT IT?
Take our quiz and find out just how important music is in your life.

For each question, choose the sentence that describes you best. Then work out your score and find out just how music mad you are.

1
A I only listen to music when I'm happy. ☐
B Music makes me feel better when I'm feeling down. ☐
C I listen to different music depending on how I feel. ☐

2
A I have loads of memories connected to different songs. ☐
B I never listen to music from when I was younger. ☐
C I get bored with songs quickly. ☐

3
A My musical taste influences the clothes I wear. ☐
B Music has nothing to do with fashion. ☐
C I don't really think about what I wear. ☐

WordWise: Phrasal verbs with *out*

13 Complete each of these sentences from the unit so far with a word from the list.

| coming | find | go | running | sort | started |

1 Alana Bolan _____ out as a teacher.
2 Next month their album is _____ out.
3 Hurry up and get your tickets. They are _____ out quickly.
4 When I've got a problem to _____ out, listening to classical music can help.
5 I'd never _____ out and buy any music.
6 _____ out just how music mad you are.

14 Match the phrases and the meanings.
1 to start out ___   4 to come out ___
2 to find out ___   5 to run out ___
3 to go out ___   6 to sort out ___

a to discover
b to begin your working life
c to leave your house
d to become available
e to find an answer or solution to a problem
f to finish, use or sell all of something, so that there is none left

15 Complete the sentences with the correct form of the verbs in Exercise 14.
1 John isn't here. He _____ about 20 minutes ago.
2 It's a really old film. I think it _____ in 2005.
3 We need to go to the supermarket – we _____ of milk.
4 The police are trying to _____ who started the trouble last night.
5 We had some problems with the computer, but we _____ them _____ yesterday.
6 She's a famous singer now, but she _____ as a dancer.

→ workbook page 48

4
A I have the same musical tastes as my best friends. ☐
B I like different music from most of my friends. ☐
C I always know if I'm going to be friends with someone when they tell me their taste in music. ☐

5
A I always listen to the lyrics in songs. ☐
B Melody is more important than lyrics. ☐
C Melody and lyrics are both really important in a song. ☐

GO TO PAGE 127 TO FIND OUT YOUR SCORE!

READING

1 **SPEAKING** Work in pairs. Make a list of advantages and disadvantages of listening to live music compared to listening to recorded music.

Advantages *Disadvantages*
More exciting It's expensive

2 Read the article quickly. Which band is thinking of using holograms on stage?

THE FUTURE OF LIVE MUSIC

Technology has always played an important part in the development of pop music – from the instruments that the bands play and the live shows that they perform to the way we listen to music in our homes or on the move. But advances in technology over the next few years are promising to bring even bigger changes.

HOLOGRAMS

For around 50 years, people of all ages have been enjoying ABBA's music. They have played almost 100 international concerts, but since 1982, when the band played their last show, fans have had little hope of ever seeing their favourite group live on stage again. That is now about to change as the band have announced plans for their first shows in nearly forty years. Bands from the 70s and 80s playing together again is nothing new, but it is no surprise that a band as big as ABBA are planning to do things a little bit differently. The four members of the band will not be on the stage together. Instead, they will appear as holograms. The holograms will show the band as they looked back in 1979, when ABBA were the biggest band in the world. And they won't be the only band to have returned to the stage via holograms. In 2018 Freddie Mercury appeared in hologram form alongside Queen in Las Vegas, even though he died more than 25 years ago.

VIRTUAL REALITY (VR)

VR technology has made lots of progress recently. You may soon be able to enjoy watching your favourite band live without even leaving your house. Developers have been making plans to launch a new app that will allow fans to watch live concerts that are being streamed directly to VR headsets. Not only will you be able to watch the band from the crowd, but you will also have the possibility of watching the show on stage with the band. And all of this will cost you about a tenth of the ticket price for the venue.

These advances in technology are very exciting, but do fans really want to watch a show knowing that their musical heroes aren't really there? And can watching through a VR headset ever really match up to the experience of actually being there? Is the latest technology really always the best? Perhaps we should look at the case of vinyl. Who would have thought that a format that was replaced by the CD, then downloading and, finally, streaming, would have made such a big return. Perhaps sometimes the old-fashioned ways of doing things might just be better.

3 🔊 5.07 Read and listen to the article again. Answer the questions.

1 Which sentence best describes ABBA's popularity?
   A They are mainly liked by older people.
   B They are more popular now than they were fifty years ago.
   C They have been successful for half a century.
   D They were forgotten for quite a few years.

2 How will ABBA's new shows be different?
   A The band won't be there on stage.
   B They will play mainly new songs.
   C They will all be a lot older.
   D The audiences will be mainly young people.

3 Why might watching a concert using Virtual Reality be considered better than going to a venue?
   A Most people already have the technology in their homes.
   B It allows you to watch from different places in the venue.
   C You can play with the band on stage.
   D It costs 50% less.

4 What is the writer's conclusion about technology and music at the end of the text?
   A Technology can be used to bring people what they want.
   B There's nothing we can do to stop new technology from taking over.
   C We should always be looking for better ways of doing things.
   D It might not always be true to say that new is better.

Grammar rap! ▶14

GRAMMAR
Present perfect simple vs. present perfect continuous

4 Look at the article on page 52 to complete the sentences. Then complete the rules and match them with the example sentences.

1 For around 50 years, people _____ enjoying ABBA's music.
2 They _____ almost 100 international concerts.

RULE:
- Use the present perfect ³_____ to talk about an action that is not finished. ☐
- Use the present perfect ⁴_____ to stress the *finished result* of a completed activity and the *amount* completed. ☐

5 Complete the sentences with the phrases in the list.

's been taking | 've been preparing | 've been watching
've eaten | hasn't taken | 've played
've been playing | 's been writing | 's written | 've made

1 Sarah _____ more than 200 poems.
  She _____ poems since she was eight.
2 He _____ piano lessons for three years.
  He _____ any piano exams yet.
3 I _____ football since I was five.
  I _____ for three different teams.
4 We _____ films all evening.
  We _____ three bags of popcorn.
5 I _____ more than 100 cakes.
  I _____ for the party all day.

6 Complete the sentences using the correct forms of the verbs in brackets.

1 He _____ autographs since he was ten.
  He _____ over 500. (collect)
2 Jade _____ at Netflix for five years.
  She _____ there since 2016. (work)
3 Mum _____ since 6 am.
  She _____ over 400 km. (drive)
4 We _____ for an hour.
  We _____ more than 2 km! (swim)
5 Tom _____ more than 2,000 children.
  He _____ since he was 22. (teach)
6 They _____ apples all day.
  They _____ hundreds! (pick)

→ workbook page 47

VOCABULARY
Musical instruments

7 Write the instruments in the list under the pictures.

bass guitar | drums | guitar | keyboard
piano | saxophone | trumpet | violin

1
_____

5
_____

2
_____

6
_____

3
_____

7
_____

4
_____

8
_____

8 🔊 5.08 Listen. Which instrument is playing?

1 *bass guitar*

→ workbook page 48

SPEAKING

9 Work in pairs. Answer the questions.

1 Do you play an instrument? If yes, how long have you been playing it? If no, would you like to learn to play one?
2 Which of the instruments in Exercise 7 do you really like? Which instruments don't you like?
3 What famous musicians can you think of? How long have they been playing music? Have you seen them playing live?

DEVELOPING SPEAKING

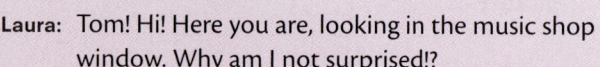

1 🔊 5.09 Look at the photos. Why does the boy look unhappy? Listen and read to check.

Laura: Tom! Hi! Here you are, looking in the music shop window. Why am I not surprised!?
Tom: Oh, hi Laura. You OK?
Laura: Well, I'm fine. But you don't look very happy. <u>What's up</u>?
Tom: Nothing.
Laura: Oh, come on. What's the matter?
Tom: Well, I'm just a bit upset. Look. There's that keyboard, the one I've always wanted, 25% off. Down to £240. And I still can't afford it.
Laura: Oh, I see. But you've been saving for ages, haven't you?
Tom: Yes, and I've saved £150. But it's not enough, is it? Even with 25% off, I still need another £90.
Laura: Can't you ask your parents to help? Can they lend you some money?
Tom: <u>No way</u>. They've just bought a car. They haven't got any spare money at the moment.
Laura: <u>Tell me about it</u>. I asked my parents to lend me some money the other day. They were nice about it, but they said no. They're saving to go to Canada to see my uncle.
Tom: OK, <u>there's no point in</u> standing here looking in the window. I'll just have to forget about it for now. Let's go.
Laura: Well, <u>if you say so</u>. What a shame.
Man: Hello! Looking at the keyboards? Come in and have a look. You can try one if you want.
Tom: Thanks, but no thanks. I can't afford the one I want. That black one, the Condor.
Man: That one? I've got another one in the shop. It's got a scratch on it, so I'm thinking of taking another £100 off the price. Interested?
Tom: Absolutely! <u>I can't wait</u> to see it!
Laura: Come on, Tom, let's go in!

2 Read the dialogue again and answer the questions.
1. How much money has Tom saved?
2. How much more does he need to buy the keyboard he wants?
3. Why won't Tom's parents be able to lend him any money?
4. Why is the shop-owner going to reduce the price of one keyboard by another £100?

3 🗣 SPEAKING Think of Tom's situation. Look at the statements below and discuss in pairs.
1. Would you save up for a more expensive keyboard model or buy a cheaper one with the money you have got?
2. Would you buy a damaged product if it is cheaper/reduced in price?

Phrases for fluency

4 Find the underlined expressions in the dialogue and use them to complete the conversations.

1. **A** Hey Mandy. ¹_____?
   B I'm tired! I had problems with the homework last night.
   A ²_____ ! I took four hours to finish it! And I think I got some things wrong.
   B Me, too. Oh well. ³_____ worrying about it. Let's give it to the teacher and see.

2. **A** The Cup Final's on TV tonight.
   ⁴_____!
   B I know. It's really exciting. Do you want to come and watch it with me at my house?
   A ⁵_____! Your television's terrible.
   B Well, ⁶_____. But I think our TV's really good.

⚙ FUNCTIONS
Asking about feelings

KEY LANGUAGE
1. What's up?
2. Is something the matter?
3. How are you feeling?
4. Are you OK?

5 Match these answers to the questions in the Key Language box.
a. Not great. ____
b. Yes, I'm fine. ____
c. Nothing. ____
d. I'm just a bit upset. ____

6 🗣 SPEAKING When you feel upset, what other things can people do to help you feel better? Discuss in pairs.

ROLE PLAY Helpful suggestions

Work in pairs. Student A: go to page 127. Student B: go to page 128. Look at the role cards and do the role play.

UNIT 5

LIFE COMPETENCIES

Learning to manage your money is an important skill to develop. By planning what you spend, you can buy the things you need and not waste your money on things that aren't important.

Managing your money

1 ▶ 15 Watch the video. Summarise Anna's advice about money in one sentence.

2 ▶ 15 Watch again and complete the sayings.
   1 _____ doesn't grow on _____ .
   2 You can't have your _____ and _____ it, too.
   3 A _____ and his _____ are easily parted.

3 You have £80 for the week. How will you spend it? For each question, choose an option. Add up your answers and make sure you have enough money!
   1 Computer games
      • Play the games you have – free
      • Buy a second-hand game – £20
      • Buy a brand-new game – £50
   2 Clothes
      • Wear what you have – free
      • Buy something second-hand – £20
      • Buy something new – £50
   3 Food
      • Eat at home – free
      • Buy some snacks at school – £10
      • Go for a meal with your friends – £20
   4 Mobile phone
      • Don't use any data or make any calls – free
      • Get a cheap plan with some data – £5
      • Get a plan with unlimited calls and data – £15
   5 Saving money
      • Don't save any money – £0
      • Save £10
      • Save £30

4 SPEAKING Compare your spending choices with a partner. Explain how you made your decisions.

5 Complete your choices again, but this time you have £40. Was it more difficult?

6 SPEAKING Discuss these questions with your partner.
   1 Are you saving money at the moment? What for?
   2 What do you do when you have no money?
   3 Do you have a spending plan?
   4 If you don't, do you think it might be useful to have one?

Me and my world

7 Look at the pie chart. What percentage of their money does this person save?

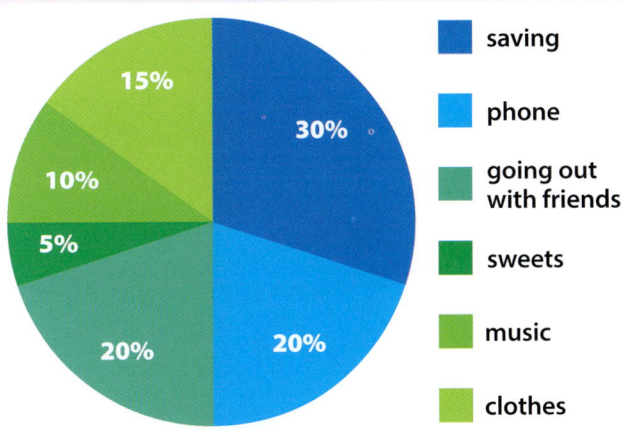

8 SPEAKING Draw a pie chart for how you spend your money. Then work with a partner and compare your pie charts. Are they similar or very different?

TIPS FOR MANAGING YOUR MONEY

• Keep a spending diary and write down what you've bought each week. Then you'll be able to see what you spend your money on.

• Try to save a little bit of money each week. And when you receive lots of money at once try to save half of it. That way, you'll always have money when you need it.

• Open a bank account. It's easier to know how much you have saved, and harder to waste money, if you don't have the cash on you.

6 NO PLANET B

Get TH!NKING

Watch the video and think: do you use a lot of plastic?

OBJECTIVES

FUNCTIONS: expressing surprise and enthusiasm

GRAMMAR: will (not), may (not), might (not) for prediction; first conditional; unless in first conditional sentences

VOCABULARY: the environment; verbs to talk about energy

A

B

C

D

E

F

READING

1 Match the words and phrases in the list with the photos. Write 1–6 in the boxes.

> 1 a beautiful beach | 2 a dirty beach
> 3 clean water | 4 an attractive landscape
> 5 an endangered species | 6 a polluted river

2 SPEAKING Work in pairs. Which of the above are easy / difficult / impossible to find in your town or country? Use the expressions below.

- There is / are lots of … in …
- I think 50 years ago there were more / fewer …
- It would be good to have more …

3 SPEAKING Tell your partner about places you have visited. Which of the things in Exercise 1 did you see?

Years ago I visited …

I was surprised / disappointed to see …

I saw lots of …

4 Look at the photo on the next page. What do you think the article is about? Read the text quickly to check your ideas.

5 🔊 6.01 Read and listen to the article again. Mark the sentences T (true) or F (false).

1 More people came to the meeting than Jackson Hinkle expected. ____
2 Team Zissou want more people to use plastic bottles. ____
3 JUST Water bottles are made of plants. ____
4 Brittany Trilford wrote a letter to world leaders. ____
5 Brittany thinks people her age are happy with world leaders. ____
6 Brittany believes that politicians should do more than they have. ____

6 SPEAKING Work with a partner. Correct the false information in the sentences in Exercise 5.

NO PLANET B — UNIT 6

HOT TOPIC: SAVING THE EARTH

Many young people today are very worried about the future of the planet. This week, we look at what two teen activists are doing in their fight to save the Earth. As always, we are curious to get our readers' reactions. So tell us what you think!

Jackson Hinkle, the US

American teenager Jackson Hinkle and his friends invited classmates to the first meeting of an adventure club on Instagram. They thought around 30 students might come to the meeting. In fact, 300 students turned up. The group decided to set up Team Zissou Environmental Organization, and it quickly became a national movement. Their main goal is to end single-use plastics in schools and communities. Team Zissou's first campaign took place on World Water Day and they made several important promises:

We will raise money for water fountains across the school district.

We will get local businesses to stop selling single-use plastic water bottles because they cause a lot of pollution.

We will sell JUST Water in our canteens.

Jackson has learned one very important thing from his campaigning: Never give up. You must keep trying.

JUST Water comes in a paper-based bottle and has a plant-based cap. The bottle is made from 82% renewable resources, so it won't damage the environment. If sales go well in the four schools, the district might get rid of plastic water bottles and sell JUST Water in all 64 schools.

Brittany Trilford, New Zealand

When she was just 17, Brittany Trilford, from Wellington in New Zealand, was invited to speak to world leaders at the United Nations Conference in Rio de Janeiro, Brazil. She spoke about climate change and the need to stop talking and to act now to make real change. Brittany wants to protect the beautiful environment she lives in – an environment that will be seriously affected by climate change. She wanted world leaders to know that young people feel angry – angry because world leaders are not doing enough to protect the environment for future generations.

Her message to governments around the world is that they need to act now and think of new and better laws that may help the serious situation. Young people don't want more promises, they want action. They want to see results. Promises won't be enough.

One thing we all know now – we ARE destroying our environment. There is no Planet B, so please, let's ALL look after this one. Brittany Trilford and Jackson Hinkle have done amazing things. It's OUR turn now.

TH!NK values

Caring for the world

7 Read and tick (✓) the values that are connected to the problems discussed in the article.

1 We have responsibilities towards future generations. ☐
2 People have a right to express their opinions freely. ☐
3 All people have a right to live in peace. ☐
4 Our behaviour can make a difference. ☐
5 Humans have a responsibility to use environmentally-friendly materials. ☐
6 We must change our behaviour towards our planet. ☐

8 SPEAKING Work in pairs. Say what you think about the values.

> I think number … is an important value.

> It says … and I agree that … . Do you agree?

> Yes. If we don't … , then future generations will/won't …

9 SPEAKING Work in pairs. What environmental issues are you worried about? What do you think you could do to help?

GRAMMAR
will (not), may (not), might (not) for prediction

1. **Complete the examples from the article on page 57. Underline other examples of will, won't, may (not) and might (not). Then complete the rule.**

   1. They thought around 30 students _____ to the meeting.
   2. We _____ JUST Water in our canteens.
   3. Promises _____ enough.

   > **RULE:** Use *will* or ⁴_____ to express future certainty, and ⁵_____ (*not*) or **might** (*not*) to express future possibility.

2. **Complete the sentences. Use *will* or *won't* and the verbs in brackets.**

   1. I'm not exactly sure, but I think she _____ (be) home by eight o'clock at the latest.
   2. I wonder if people _____ (live) on other planets in the future.
   3. I'm worried about him coming with us. I'm sure he _____ (like) any of the people at the party.
   4. Who do you think _____ (win) the next World Cup?
   5. It's getting cloudy. Do you think it _____ (start) raining soon?
   6. Oh, don't worry about my parents. I'm sure they _____ (be) angry.

3. **Read the sentences and choose the correct words.**

   1. Don't worry, I *will / might* pick you up at 7.
   2. The weather's a real problem. We *may / may not* be able to go for a walk.
   3. She's not feeling well at all. She *might / might not* have to stay at home.
   4. It *may / may not* be cold later, so take a jumper with you.
   5. It's my dad's birthday tomorrow. My wife and I are going to visit him, so we definitely *won't / might not* be here.
   6. I'd like to get up and watch the sunrise with you, but I *may / won't* just sleep instead.

4. **SPEAKING** Work in pairs. Think about next weekend. Talk about:
   - a sport you will / won't do
   - someone you may / may not see
   - a film you might / might not watch

   → workbook page 54

VOCABULARY
The environment

5. **Match the words with the meanings.**

   1. extinct   3. waste   5. flood
   2. laws   4. melt   6. pollution

   a. official rules that say what people are allowed and not allowed to do ☐
   b. change from solid to liquid (for example, from ice to water) ☐
   c. a large amount of water covering an area that is usually dry ☐
   d. not existing any more ☐
   e. things that make water, air and the ground unclean ☐
   f. material that people throw away ☐

6. **SPEAKING** Work in pairs. Ask and answer questions.
   1. Which animals do you know that are extinct or in danger of extinction?
   2. What laws to protect the environment are there in your country?
   3. What problems with waste are there where you live?
   4. What might happen if the ice around the North and South Poles melts?
   5. Are floods common in your country?
   6. Are the air and water very polluted in your area? What could your class do to help fight pollution?

7. 🔊 **6.02** Match the words in the list with the photos. Write 1–4 in the boxes. Then listen, check and repeat.

 A ☐
 B ☐
 C ☐
 D ☐

> 1 smog | 2 recycling | 3 litter | 4 rubbish

8. **Think about the environment in your country. Write notes.**

some rivers polluted   air pollution from factories

9 **SPEAKING** Work in pairs. Look at your notes from Exercise 8. Make predictions for the next 30 years. Which environmental issues concern you the most? Then report to the class.

> *Some of the rivers in our country are polluted, for example ... We think this will create big problems for the fish, and ...*

> *In some parts of the country, for example in ..., the air is polluted. We think this will change. There will be stricter laws so there won't be ...*

→ workbook page 56

🎧 LISTENING

10 Read the headlines in the online newspaper story and look at the images. Write down six words you might find in the article.

CARROTS IN THE CAR PARK
RADISHES ON THE ROUNDABOUT

The deliciously eccentric story of the town growing **ALL** its own vegetables.

11 🔊 6.03 Use the information from the newspaper headlines and your imagination to say what you think is special about the town of Todmorden. Then listen to the story and check your ideas.

12 🔊 6.03 Listen again and answer the questions.
1 What's the 'Incredible Edible' project all about?
2 Who takes part in the project?
3 Who had the idea?
4 Why did they decide to do something?
5 What was the reaction to their idea like?

13 Do you think the experiment will last? Why (not)? Would you like to see a similar experiment in your town or neighbourhood?

⚙️ FUNCTIONS
Expressing surprise and enthusiasm

14 🔊 6.03 Listen to the radio programme again. The phrases below can be used to express enthusiasm. Tick (✓) the ones that the reporter uses.
- ☐ Oh, really?
- ☐ Wow!
- ☐ That sounds wonderful!
- ☐ How exciting!
- ☐ That's amazing! (wonderful! etc.)
- ☐ What a brilliant idea!
- ☐ Incredible! (Cool! Fascinating! etc.)

15 Put the dialogue in order. Read it out with a partner.
- ☐ A He's offered me a role in his next film.
- ☐ A I'm only going to meet Steven Spielberg.
- ☐ A I'm going to California this summer.
- ☐ A Three hours.
- ☐ B Cool!
- ☐ B Oh, really? Only three hours. Why's that?
- ☐ B How exciting! What are you going to talk about?
- ☐ B Wow! That sounds exciting. How long are you going to stay there?

16 **SPEAKING** Practise dialogues with a partner. A says something surprising, B reacts, using one of the expressions from Exercise 14, and asks a question. A says something surprising again, etc. Use your own ideas, or the ones here.
- go to the moon
- meet Zendaya
- win a big prize
- see an alien
- only eat white food
- stay up all night

Train to TH!NK

Different perspectives

1 Read these different texts. Match them with the text types in the list. Write numbers 1–4. Give your reasons. There are two text types you don't need to use.

- [ ] note
- [ ] online article
- [ ] diary entry
- [ ] informative leaflet
- [ ] text message
- [ ] adventure story

2 **SPEAKING** Work in pairs. Discuss who the texts are for and what their purpose is.

> I think text 1 is probably for … I think somebody wrote it in order to …

1 This morning we took part in the Incredible Edible project. I was so proud when I saw that all of the students in my class had brought vegetable plants …

2 Meeting the guys who want to plant vegetables by the football field at 5… Hope to CUL8R. S.

3 … to buy OUR vegetables. They come from local farms. They are organic and fresh – and you don't have to pick them yourself. Prices are reasonable; the quality is high!

4 Our reporter has learned that the council will publish a list of spare land that can be used by the Incredible Edible project. It has been …

READING

3 🔊 6.04 Read and listen to the text. What type of text is it? Choose from the text types in Exercise 1. Who might this text be for?

ENERGY MATTERS

Unless we change our behaviour, our planet won't survive. To produce electricity, we burn coal and oil, known as fossil fuels, but creating energy in this way puts CO_2 into the air and causes air pollution and smog. As a result, we are destroying our Earth. What can we do to solve these problems? If we use renewable energy, it will provide us with cleaner air and water. So what is renewable energy? It is energy that doesn't use up the resource used to make it. Solar power, wind power and hydroelectric power are examples of renewable energy sources.

SOLAR POWER

Using the power of the sun produces very little pollution and it is also much cheaper than using fossil fuels. Morocco is now using solar power in a big way. When we say big, we mean big! They have the largest solar plant on Earth. Its wind and hydroelectric power plants will soon provide half of Morocco's electricity. Morocco might become the world's superpower in solar energy, producing enough electricity for one million homes.

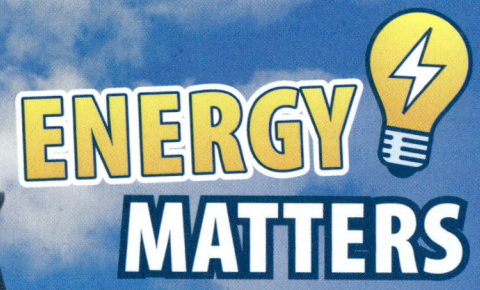

HYDROELECTRIC POWER AND WIND FARMS

In the past, Turkey relied on fossil fuels and natural gas to produce electricity. In recent years, it has increased its use of renewable energy. Private companies have built nine small hydroelectric power plants and they use river water stored in dams to produce electricity. They have also built six wind farms, and they have set up 20 other renewable energy projects. Wind power is another clean alternative to fossil fuels. It is everywhere! Wind farms use very little land and they don't use any water.

A SIMPLE WAY TO REDUCE ENERGY

Something simple that everyone could do to help save the environment: using energy-saving light bulbs. Mexico has given almost 23 million of them to families for free. Now, more than 5.5 million Mexican families use energy-saving light bulbs. If they use energy-saving light bulbs, they may save up to 18% on their electricity bill. This is a simple thing that YOU can do, too. You will use a tenth of the electricity if you use energy-saving light bulbs at home.

4 Work in pairs. Cover up the text and try to complete the sentences.
1 In order to survive, we will need to …
2 In the past, Turkey relied on …
3 In recent years, Turkey has …
4 Mexico has given away 23 million free …

5 Read the text again. Which of the ideas …
- do you think is best?
- has the most direct effect on people's lives?
- would be easy or difficult to do in your country?

GRAMMAR
First conditional; *unless* in first conditional sentences

6 Complete the sentences with the correct form of the verbs. Look at the leaflet on page 60 and check your answers. Then choose the right answers to make the rules.

1 If we use renewable energy, it _____ (provide) us with cleaner air and water.
2 Unless we change our behaviour, our planet _____ (not survive).
3 You _____ (use) a tenth of the electricity if you use energy-saving light bulbs at home.

> **RULE:** We use the first conditional to talk about the consequences of a ⁴*possible / impossible* future action.
> - Condition clause: *if* + present simple
> - Result clause: *will / won't* + main verb
> The condition clause can come before or after the result clause.
> *Unless* means ⁵*only if / if not*.

7 Match the parts of the sentences.

1 Unless someone lends me a bit of money, ☐
2 I'll only be able to go to the concert ☐
3 They won't pass the exam ☐
4 Won't she miss the train ☐

a if my dad drives me there.
b if she doesn't leave for the station now?
c I won't be able to take the bus home.
d unless they study hard.

8 Write first conditional sentences. Then decide in which of them you could use *unless*.

0 environment / suffer / if / we not recycle more
   The environment will suffer if we don't recycle more.
   The environment will suffer unless we recycle more.
1 if / I give this phone / charity / they find someone who needs it
2 if / this tap not stop dripping / how much water / we waste in a day?
3 situation / become worse / if they not change behaviour
4 Look – battery full! / if you not disconnect charger / you waste energy
5 if she read this book / she understand situation better
6 if / you not stop shouting / I not listen any more

9 Complete the questions. Use the correct form of the verbs.

0 What __will__ you __do__ if they __don't help__ you? (do / not help)
1 If you _____ , _____ you _____ good marks in your test? (not study / get)
2 Unless the weather _____ really bad on Sunday, we _____ to the beach. (be / go)
3 If she _____ you to her birthday party, _____ you _____ her a present? (invite / buy)
4 She _____ him unless he _____ her very nicely. (not help / ask)
5 If I _____ to visit you, _____ you _____ me around your town? (come / show)

10 SPEAKING Work in pairs. Ask and answer questions using the first conditional. Use your own ideas or the ones here.

1 What will you do if it rains all weekend?
2 What will you buy if you get some extra money this month?
3 What will you do tonight if you don't have any homework?

→ workbook page 55

VOCABULARY
Verbs to talk about energy

11 6.05 Match the verbs with their definitions. Write 1–8. Listen and check.

> 1 to reuse | 2 to throw away | 3 to recycle
> 4 to waste | 5 to charge | 6 to disconnect
> 7 to save | 8 to leave on standby

a to not switch an appliance off completely so it is ready to be used at any time ☐
b to collect and treat rubbish in order to produce useful materials that can be used again ☐
c to fill up an empty battery again ☐
d to get rid of something ☐
e to stop something from being wasted ☐
f to stop the connection between an electrical appliance and the power source ☐
g to use something again ☐
h to use too much of something or use it incorrectly ☐

12 SPEAKING Work in pairs. Discuss these questions.

1 Do you waste a lot of energy? What could you do to save energy?
2 What things do you reuse?
3 What things do you recycle? Do you think there is enough recycling done where you live? Why?

→ workbook page 56

TH!NK
Green solutions around the world

Culture

1 Look at the photos. Where do you think these places might be?

2 🔊 6.06 Read and listen to the article. Check your ideas.

GREEN SOLUTIONS AROUND THE WORLD

THE NETHERLANDS
Can a ban on cars help business?

In the mid-seventies, there was a problem in the city of Groningen, in the Netherlands. Lots of people used the motorway in the city centre and there were too many cars. This caused a lot of traffic jams. The city council decided to replace the motorway with green areas, pedestrian areas, cycleways and bus lanes. They stopped cars from parking in the market square and discouraged cars from entering the city centre.

At first, shop owners said they would lose customers. But they didn't, and soon businesses and shops which were not in the car-free zone wanted the council to expand it.

Today, 61% of trips taken in the city are done by bicycle. The city centre is full of places for bikes to park and most buildings have bicycle garages. As a result, today Groningen has got the cleanest air of any big Dutch city.

ECUADOR
Can a camera trap programme help save a nature park?

The Bigal River nature park is located between the Amazon forest and the Andes. It is a beautiful area, and is home to many different animals and birds. However, human activity has had a negative effect on the wildlife that lives there. Many animals and birds are endangered because of loss of habitat and hunting.

To show people how wonderful the nature park is, the Sumac Muyu Foundation set up camera traps around the park. These traps record a video whenever an animal enters a certain place in the park. It shows where they are in the park, and it studies changes in behaviour caused by humans.

The camera traps have been in the nature park since 2014. They have collected hundreds of hours of film showing wildlife, and the material is being used to help fight new building projects in the protected land.

MEXICO
Can a wood-burning stove really be environmentally friendly and still be efficient?

People in many countries still rely on open fires. Although the fires help people cook and stay warm, the smoke and gas can cause illnesses. They also use precious fuels such as wood or coal. The so-called Patsari stove uses less wood and so it improves both air quality in the home and family health.

The stove was developed in Mexico. It is made of sealed-together brick stones so no gas can come out from the stove. The stones heat up when somebody lights a fire underneath, and the back of the stove is attached to a chimney, which takes the smoke out of the home.

Health studies show that families with a Patsari stove get 30% fewer lung infections and 50% fewer eye infections.

3 **SPEAKING** Work in pairs. Read these things people say. Are they from the Netherlands, Mexico or Ecuador?

1 'People in our town feel much healthier now.'
2 'I hope those birds don't disappear.'
3 'I still get a lot of customers in my restaurant.'
4 'We're happy that they didn't build there – and the video certainly helped.'
5 'It's much nicer inside my house now.'
6 'I never have a problem – there's always somewhere to leave it.'

4 Do you know of any other towns, cities or countries where there has been an environmental project?

5 VOCABULARY
There are eight highlighted words in the article. Match the words with these meanings. Write the words.

0 an organ in the chest that you use to breathe — *lung*
1 the place where an animal or plant usually lives — _____
2 things that people or animals do, or the way they act — _____
3 of great value because of being rare, expensive or important — _____
4 the result of an action or other cause — _____
5 tried to prevent something from happening — _____
6 very tightly closed — _____
7 make something bigger — _____

PRONUNCIATION
/f/, /v/, /b/ consonant sounds
Go to page 120.

WRITING
An article for the school magazine

1 INPUT Read this article from a school magazine. Then answer the questions.
1 How has the river changed?
2 What are the main reasons for the problems?
3 What will happen if the situation doesn't change?
4 What should be done?

2 Put the words in the correct order to make sentences from the article. Then go through it and find the evidence the writer uses to support each of these statements.
1 so / the / beautiful / once / Quiller River / was
2 situation / alarming / is / the
3 the / riverbanks / and / look at / just

3 Match the sentence halves. Which of them talk about possible consequences? Which are suggestions? Which are predictions?
1 If politicians wake up and we all do something, ☐
2 We need stricter laws ☐
3 In a few years' time ☐
4 So I really think politicians ☐
5 The situation will be even worse in a few years ☐

a to protect our river.
b unless factories stop polluting the water.
c we might once again be able to enjoy the beauty of the river.
d should do something about it.
e all the fish may be dead.

4 ANALYSE The article has four paragraphs. Which of them …
a expresses the writer's hope that the situation will be better in the future?
b introduces the topic?
c describes problems and says what should be done?
d describes problems, says what will happen if nothing is done and what should be done?

Quiller River POLLUTION

The Quiller River was once so beautiful that there is even a song about it. And now?

The situation is alarming. There are lots of factories along the river. Newspapers have recently reported that the water in the river is totally polluted. There are hardly any fish left, and the water itself smells terrible. The situation will be even worse in a few years unless factories stop polluting the water. That is why I really think politicians should do something about it. We need stricter laws to protect our river.

And just look at the riverbanks. They are covered in litter. It seems that there are lots of people who throw their waste into the river. This must stop! We should all get together and help clean up the riverbanks.

In conclusion, if politicians wake up and we all do something, we might once again be able to enjoy the beauty of the river. Let's hope it's not too late.

5 PLAN Choose a local environmental problem and make notes about what the situation is now, possible consequences and what should be done.

6 PRODUCE Write an article for your school magazine raising awareness about the environmental issue you have chosen.
- Find a good title.
- Write an introduction that catches the reader's interest.
- Describe what the problems are, what you think the consequences might be and what should be done.

B1 Preliminary for Schools

 **READING**
Part 5: 4-option multiple-choice cloze    workbook page 79

1 For each question, choose the correct answer.

GLOBAL fishing crisis

A growing concern around the world is how the food production industry is being affected by changes in the environment. For example, millions of people around the world consider fish to be an important part of their ¹_____ diet. However, fishing to meet this demand has become a major environmental issue, along with animal extinction, air ²_____ and global warming.

Certain ³_____ of fish are in danger and are no longer found in their usual feeding areas, so fishing boats must travel further out to sea to catch fish. More fishermen are now choosing to catch rarer fish to sell at higher prices, which is affecting populations of less ⁴_____ fish.

Unfortunately, the problem of overfishing is getting worse and some fish populations could possibly ⁵_____ out if certain changes aren't put in place. Many people know that we need to ⁶_____ our oceans and sea life, so they are fighting for stricter fishing laws.

1 A regular   B frequent   C proper   D ordinary
2 A climate   B pollution   C condition   D damage
3 A collections   B numbers   C descriptions D species
4 A ordinary   B common   C usual   D typical
5 A blow   B carry   C run   D wear
6 A protect   B care   C prevent   D keep

 **LISTENING**
Part 2: 3-option multiple choice    workbook page 35

2 🔊 6.09 Listen to six short conversations. For each question, choose the correct answer.

1 You will hear a girl and her brother talking about the girl's night with her two friends.
   What does the girl say about the night out?
   A Everyone thought the film was incredibly funny.
   B The most enjoyable part of her night took place after the film.
   C She learned some surprising information about school from her friends.

2 Listen to a man and a woman talking about a tennis match.
   What does the man say about the match?
   A He disagrees with the coach's decision.
   B He thinks the match wasn't very exciting.
   C He doesn't understand the actions of the coach.

3 Listen to a boy and a girl talking about the boy's phone.
   What does the boy say about the phone?
   A Every time he has a conversation, the phone switches off.
   B When the battery is running out, the phone always switches off.
   C There are two things wrong with the phone.

4 You will hear a boy and a woman in a shop.
   Why does the boy want to change the pullover?
   A It's the wrong size and the wrong colour.
   B It was too expensive.
   C He would rather have a T-shirt.

5 Listen to two friends talking.
   What has the girl done?
   A She has changed the colour of her hair.
   B She has had her hair cut and changed the colour.
   C She has had her hair cut shorter than it was before.

6 Listen to two friends talking about music at a party.
   What did the girl think about the music?
   A She didn't enjoy listening to the band.
   B She wanted to dance, but the music wasn't great.
   C The DJ didn't play good music for dancing.

TEST YOURSELF   UNITS 5 & 6

VOCABULARY

1 Complete the sentences with the words in the list. There are two extra words.

> charge | enter | extinct | flood | melt | record | release
> standby | stream | throw away | tour | waste

1 Is it OK if I _____ my mobile phone in your room?
2 It's getting warm now, so I think the snow will _____ soon.
3 Don't _____ water. You shouldn't stay in the shower for more than four minutes!
4 It's really easy to _____ songs – all you need is an internet connection!
5 They've made a new record, and they're going to _____ it next week.
6 You can't win the competition if you don't _____ it!
7 After the band released their new record, they went on _____ for six months.
8 If it carries on raining like this, there might be a _____ tonight.
9 There aren't many of these monkeys left in the world. They could be _____ in a few years.
10 Don't switch it off completely – leave it on _____ , OK?

/10

GRAMMAR

2 Complete the sentences with the words in the list.

> have been playing | have played | if | might not | unless | won't

1 I didn't study for the test. I _____ pass it, I'm sure!
2 Sorry, Mum. My shirt is really dirty. I _____ football in the park.
3 We won't have a picnic _____ it rains.
4 I don't feel very well, so I _____ go to the cinema tonight. I'm not sure.
5 I'll never finish this washing up _____ you help me. Please!
6 Everyone in the team is really tired. We _____ three games this week already!

3 Find and correct the mistake in each sentence.

1 He's being working here for over five months.
2 If it will rain, we'll stay at home.
3 I've been writing forty invitations for the party next week.
4 We might to go to the game later.
5 You won't do well in the test unless you don't study.
6 Ouch! I've been cutting my hand.

/12

FUNCTIONAL LANGUAGE

4 Complete the mini-dialogues with the words in the list.

> bit | feeling | how | matter | news | not | sounds | up

1 A Hi, Paul. What's the _____ ?
  B Nothing much. I'm just a _____ upset.
2 A What's _____ , Olivia? Why are you crying?
  B I'm crying because I'm happy. I won a competition.
  A _____ exciting! I'm really happy for you.
3 A How are you _____ ?
  B Well, _____ great. But I'll be OK, I think.
4 A I've got some _____ . We're going to get a new dog.
  B That _____ great! I'm sure you're really happy.

/8

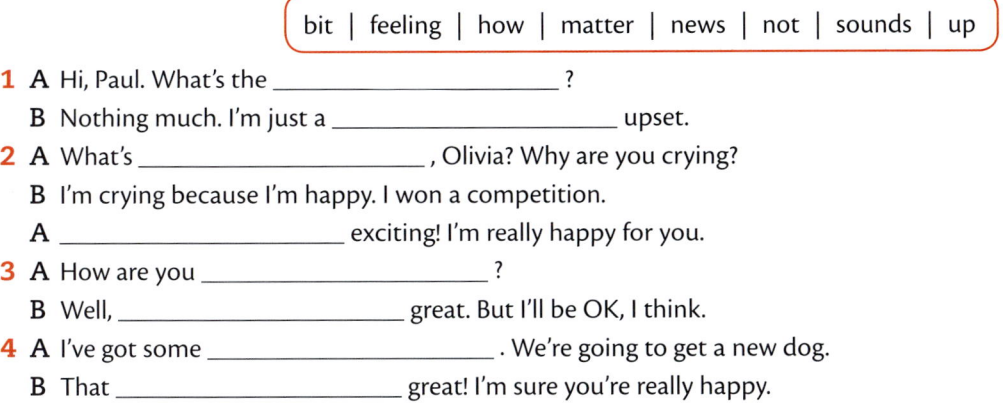

MY SCORE /30

22–30   10–21   0–9

This page is intentionally left blank.

PRONUNCIATION

UNIT 1
Intonation and sentence stress

1 🔊 1.06 Read and listen to the dialogue.

Henry I **know** … let's learn to **surf**!
Lucy   That's a **great** idea!
Henry Do you **think** so?
Lucy   Of **course**! We'll need **lessons**.
Henry I'll phone the **surf shop**!
Lucy   It'll be **fun** … we should **definitely** do it!

2 Which words show that Lucy likes Henry's idea?

3 🔊 1.07 Listen and repeat the dialogue.

UNIT 2
Word stress

1 🔊 2.05 Read and listen to the dialogue.

Sadie Jake, I can't **believe** it! Do you **recognise** that man over there?
Jake   I **suppose** it could be someone we **know** …
Sadie How could you **forget**? **Think**, Jake!
Jake   Oh, yeah! Now I **remember**! He's on that TV quiz show.
Sadie That's right. It's called '**Concentrate**'. I **wonder** what he's doing here?

2 How many syllables do the blue / red / green words have? Say these verbs and stress the correct syllable.

3 🔊 2.06 Listen and repeat the dialogue.

UNIT 3
Words ending in /ə/

1 🔊 3.02 Read and listen to the dialogue.

Joe   Why don't we go to the cinema? We can see *The Monster in the Computer*. Tammy Baker plays the monster.
Tess Well … there's also *River Adventure*. Tom Webster's a doctor in it.
Joe   I know he's a better actor than Tammy Baker but *River Adventure* is a lot longer. If we see the shorter film, we can have dinner after.
Tess OK – it looks much funnier, too. And let's go to the Super Burger for dinner!

2 Say the words ending in the short /ə/ sound.

3 🔊 3.03 Listen and repeat the dialogue.

UNIT 4
The short /ʌ/ vowel sound

1 🔊 4.05 Read and listen to the poem.

My little c**ou**sin from L**o**ndon's c**o**ming on M**o**nday.
She's y**ou**ng and l**o**vely – and very f**u**nny.
She l**o**ves the s**u**n and r**u**nning and j**u**mping.
She d**oe**sn't like st**u**dying or spending m**o**ney.

2 Say the words with the /ʌ/ vowel sound in blue.

3 🔊 4.06 Listen and repeat the poem.

UNIT 5
been: strong /biːn/ and weak /bɪn/

1 🔊 5.03 Read and listen to the dialogue.

Jill Where have you **been**? The party's already started.
Pete Shh! I've **been** hiding in the kitchen.
Jill We've **been** looking for you everywhere. We want to play a game.
Pete Well, I've **been** trying to find a **bin** to put this sandwich in. It's horrible!

2 Say the strong and weak forms of *been*, /biːn/ and /bɪn/. What other word sounds like /bɪn/?

3 🔊 5.04 Listen and repeat the dialogue.

UNIT 6
/f/, /v/ and /b/ consonant sounds

1 🔊 6.07 Read and listen to the advertisement.

Visit the **b**eautiful **v**illage of **V**ictoria!
The **v**illage is surrounded **b**y **f**orests and **f**arms.
There's a **f**antastic ri**v**er **f**or **f**ishing.
You can **b**uy souvenirs and see **v**ery old **b**uildings.
There are **b**uses to the **b**each **f**rom Monday to **F**riday.
You'll ne**v**er **f**orget your **v**isit to **V**ictoria!

2 Say the words with the /f/, /v/ and /b/ sounds.

3 🔊 6.08 Listen and repeat the sentences.

GET IT RIGHT!

UNIT 1
Present perfect vs. past simple

> Learners often use the present perfect when the past simple is required.
> We use the past simple to talk about events which have taken place at a specific time. We use the present perfect to talk about events where the time is not specified.
> ✓ I **went** on holiday with my family last year.
> ✗ I ~~have been~~ on holiday with my family last year.

Write positive answers to the following questions using the words given in the correct tense.

0 Have you started your new job? (last weekend)
   Yes, I have. I started my new job last weekend.

1 Have you seen the latest episode? (yesterday)
   _____

2 Have you been to France before? (two times)
   _____

3 Have you visited your grandparents recently? (a few days ago)
   _____

4 Have you seen John? (five minutes ago)
   _____

5 Have you changed your phone? (for a better one)
   _____

6 Have you earned any money recently? (over £100 last week)
   _____

UNIT 2
Present perfect with *for* or *since*

> Learners often use the present simple with *for* or *since* when the present perfect is required.
> We use the present perfect tense with both *for* and *since* referring to an earlier time which is still relevant now.
> ✓ I **have known** him for three months.
> ✗ I ~~know~~ him for three months.

Make new sentences in the perfect tense using the information given.

0 I started playing the guitar when I was six years old. I still play the guitar now.
   I've played the guitar since I was six years old.

1 We were friends when we were ten. We are still friends now.
   _____

2 I saw her when I was five. I did not see her after that.
   _____

3 I started working in the newsagent's two years ago. I work there now.
   _____

4 You moved to Madrid six months ago.
   _____

5 My family travelled abroad in 2014. They did not travel abroad after that.
   _____

6 I changed schools last school year.
   _____

UNIT 3
Comparatives and *than*

> Learners often use the wrong forms of adjectives, trying to use *more* where it is not possible, especially with *bigger* and *cheaper*.
> For adjectives with one syllable, we add *-er* for the comparative.
> ✓ In ten years' time my town will be **bigger** than now.
> ✗ In ten years' time my town will be ~~more big~~ than now.
> For adjectives with two syllables ending in *-y*, we make the comparative by adding *-ier*.
> ✓ I find English **easier** than French.
> ✗ I find English ~~more easy~~ than French.
> Learners sometimes use *that* instead of *than*.
> ✓ Sports clubs are much better **than** the gym.
> ✗ Sports clubs are much better ~~that~~ the gym.

Correct the following sentences.

1 I am much more happy than before.
   _____

2 If you go to Europe, the weather will be better in July that in February.
   _____

3 Which is more old, football or rugby?
   _____

4 The beaches are cleaner in the countryside that in the city.
   _____

5 It will make you fitter and more healthy.
   _____

UNIT 4
Any vs. – (no article)

> **Learners often miss out *any* where it is needed in questions and negative statements.**
> ✓ *Do you have **any** questions? If so, please visit me in my office.*
> ✗ *Do you have ___ questions? If so, please visit me in my office.*

Choose the correct answer, *any* or – (no article).

1. In the countryside there aren't *any* / – discos.
2. I didn't take *any* / – notice of it and deleted it again.
3. I have been doing *any* / – homework.
4. We need *any* / – time to work on this.
5. I have been here for four months and I can't live here *any* / – longer.
6. Do you have *any* / – money I can borrow?

will vs. *should*

> **Learners sometimes use *will* instead of *should*.**
> We use *should* to give advice to someone, or to mean that something is supposed to happen.
> ✓ *In my opinion, the subject you **should** talk about is the environment.*
> ✗ *In my opinion, the subject you ~~will~~ talk about is the environment.*

Choose the correct answer.

1. In my opinion, you *will* / *should* not move schools.
2. If you like the seaside, you *will* / *should* go to the south coast.
3. If we do it that way, it *will* / *should* be a disaster.
4. On this diet, you must eat healthy food, and you *won't* / *shouldn't* drink fizzy drinks.
5. *I'll* / *I should* meet you there if you like.
6. *Will* / *Should* we study everything for the test or just this unit?

UNIT 5
Present simple or present continuous vs. present perfect continuous

> **Learners sometimes use the present simple or the present continuous when the present perfect continuous is required.**
> We use the present perfect continuous to talk about how long we have been doing something. We often use it with *for* and *since* and a time period.
> ✓ *I **have been living** in this house for three years.*
> ✗ *I ~~live~~ in this house for three years.*
> ✗ *I ~~am living~~ in this house for three years.*

Correct the following sentences.

1. I try to do that for ages, but I can't manage it.
   _____
2. How long is Michael learning English?
   _____
3. I have always been going to work by train, because I live far away.
   _____
4. His friends laugh every time he is telling that joke – I don't know why.
   _____
5. I need to fill in your address – where have you been living?
   _____
6. Since last Wednesday I go to karate lessons.
   _____

UNIT 6
Future with *will*

> **Learners sometimes use the present simple tense when the future tense is required.**
> ✓ *We **will meet** at 9 pm tomorrow.*
> ✗ *We ~~meet~~ at 9 pm tomorrow.*

Correct the following sentences.

1. We normally will go there every Wednesday.
   _____
2. I think I will know what you mean.
   _____
3. So I see you on the 15th.
   _____
4. I'm sure you want to go there when you see these pictures.
   _____
5. When I will get home, I'll send you a text.
   _____
6. Who wins the next football match?
   _____

This page is intentionally left blank.

STUDENT A

UNIT 5, PAGE 54

Student A
1 You're a bit upset. There's a party at the weekend, but your mum says you can't go.
Talk to your friend about the problem.
2 Your friend looks a bit upset. Find out what the problem is and see if you can help.
Why don't you … ?
You could …
Can't you … ?

Does music rock your world? Find out your score!

5–8: Music doesn't rule your world. You like it and you probably listen to it, but it's not so important.

9–11: Music plays an important part in your life, but it isn't the only thing that matters.

12–15: Music is your world and you would find it difficult to live without it. You live, sleep and breathe music.

Key

Q1	A – 1	B – 2	C – 3
Q2	A – 3	B – 2	C – 1
Q3	A – 3	B – 1	C – 2
Q4	A – 1	B – 3	C – 2
Q5	A – 1	B – 2	C – 3

STUDENT B

UNIT 5, PAGE 54

Student B
1 Your friend looks a bit upset. Find out what the problem is and see if you can help.
   Why don't you … ?
   You could …
   Can't you … ?
2 You're a bit upset. It's your mum's birthday tomorrow and you haven't got any money to buy her a present. Talk to your friend about the problem.

Acknowledgements

The authors and publishers acknowledge the following sources of copyright material and are grateful for the permissions granted. While every effort has been made, it has not always been possible to identify the sources of all the material used, or to trace all copyright holders. If any omissions are brought to our notice, we will be happy to include the appropriate acknowledgements on reprinting and in the next update to the digital edition, as applicable.

Key: WL= Welcome; U = Unit.

Photography

All the photographs are sourced from Getty Images.

WL: Westend61; Eri Morita/The Image Bank/Getty Images Plus; ©fitopardo.com/Moment; johnandersonphoto/iStock/Getty Images Plus; Sven Hansche/EyeEm; VladOrlov/iStock/Getty Images Plus; maylat/iStock/Getty Images Plus; Jim Spellman/WireImage; Amanda Edwards/WireImage; imaginima/E+; mihalis_a/iStock/Getty Images Plus; MC_Noppadol/iStock/Getty Images Plus; GaryAlvis/E+; photllurg/iStock/Getty Images Plus; scibak/E+; Sinan Kocaslan/E+; Firmafotografen/iStock/Getty Images Plus; vovan13/iStock/Getty Images Plus; © by Martin Deja/Moment; bonetta/iStock/Getty Images Plus; Hemera Technologies/PhotoObjects.net/Getty Images Plus; SDI Productions/E+; epicurean/E+; Lucy Lambriex/DigitalVision; Burke/Triolo Productions/Photolibrary/Getty Images Plus; 8vFanI/iStock/Getty Images Plus; Judd Pilossof/Photolibrary/Getty Images Plus; Nazar Abbas Photography/Moment; alle12/E+; Barcin/iStock/Getty Images Plus; Adie Bush/Cultura; coastalrunner/iStock Editorial/Getty Images Plus; **U1:** Caroline Yeo/iStock/Getty Images Plus; kali9/E+; SDI Productions/E+; Minerva Studio/iStock/Getty Images Plus; Pollyana Ventura/E+; SolStock/iStock/Getty Images Plus; gustavofrazao/iStock/Getty Images Plus; edoardogobattoni.net/Moment; Rawpixel/iStock/Getty Images Plus; Westend61; robh/E+; mawielobob/iStock/Getty Images Plus; popovaphoto/iStock/Getty Images Plus; dendong/E+; JoeGough/iStock/Getty Images Plus; LauriPatterson/E+; Foodcollection; blackdovfx/iStock/Getty Images Plus; Jose Luis Pelaez Inc/DigitalVision; Bloom Productions/Taxi/Getty Images Plus; Anadolu Agency; Guy Edwardes/The Image Bank/Getty Images Plus; Martin Bernetti/AFP; Mint Images RF; Hero Images; **U2:** kali9/E+; SDI Productions/E+; Klaus Vedfelt/DigitalVision; Alistair Berg/DigitalVision; Jack S./500px; imagenavi; TPopova/iStock/Getty Images Plus; Andrea Donetti/EyeEm; Stockbyte; AlexLMX/iStock/Getty Images Plus; Jupiterimages/Stockbyte; studiocasper/E+; simon2579/DigitalVision Vectors; Viorika/iStock/Getty Images Plus; djgunner/DigitalVision Vectors; bluestocking/E+; hdagli/E+; LemonTreeImages/iStock/Getty Images Plus; buchsammy/Moment; DGLimages/iStock/Getty Images Plus; Tntk/iStock/Getty Images Plus; Echo/Juice Images; kajakiki/E+; Jamie Grill; AlexSava/E+; Jonas Gratzer/LightRocket; Michael Roberts/Moment; SteveStone/iStock/Getty Images Plus; PhotoMelon/iStock/Getty Images Plus; Turnervisual/E+; Roman Samokhin/iStock/Getty Images Plus; Westend61; mladn61/iStock/Getty Images Plus; ollo/iStock Unreleased; Bet_Noire/iStock/Getty Images Plus; kanvag/iStock/Getty Images Plus; tiler84/iStock/Getty Images Plus; **U3:** PeopleImages/E+; gilaxia/E+; DGLimages/iStock/Getty Images Plus; Marc Romanelli; Akihiro Sugimoto; Caiaimage/Paul Bradbury; Eddy Lemaistre/Corbis Entertainment; Phil Jones/500px/500Px Unreleased Plus; Ariel Skelley/DigitalVision; smutnypan/iStock/Getty Images Plus; Antonio_Diaz/iStock/Getty Images Plus; Petrified Collection/The Image Bank/Getty Images Plus; Tetra Images; jakkapan21/iStock/Getty Images Plus; xavierarnau/E+; monkeybusinessimages/iStock/Getty Images Plus; **U4:** Fabrice Lerouge/Onoky; Dmitry Ageev; Karrastock/Moment; Igor Emmerich/Corbis/VCG; Total Guitar Magazine/Future; Gonzalo Azumendi/The Image Bank/Getty Images Plus; Giakita/iStock/Getty Images Plus; Insights/Universal Images Group; Nic_Taylor/E+; DEA/A. Dagli Orti/De Agostini; kali9/iStock/Getty Images Plus; Morsa Images/DigitalVision; Hero Images; Westend61; Zave Smith/Image Source; **U5:** kzenon/iStock/Getty Images Plus; M_a_y_a/E+; Jon Feingersh Photography Inc/DigitalVision; Comstock/Stockbyte; Slavica/E+; millann/iStock/Getty Images Plus; Mike Marsland/WireImage; Kativ/E+; Pool/Samir Hussein/WireImage; stevegeer/iStock/Getty Images Plus; South_agency/E+; valentinrussanov/E+; Damir Khabirov/iStock/Getty Images Plus; Anna_Om/iStock/Getty Images Plus; wabeno/iStock/Getty Images Plus; pixhook/E+; studiocasper/iStock/Getty Images Plus; GeorgePeters/E+; C Squared Studios/Photodisc; tarasov_vl/iStock/Getty Images Plus; AlexLMX/iStock/Getty Images Plus; walterbilotta/iStock/Getty Images Plus; B2M Productions/Photodisc; Alphotographic/iStock Unreleased; **U6:** J & C Sohns/Picture Press/Getty Images Plus; courtneyk/iStock/Getty Images Plus; Ron and Patty Thomas/Taxi/Getty Images Plus; Philippe Turpin/Photononstop; Grafner/iStock/Getty Images Plus; FabioFilzi/iStock/Getty Images Plus; posteriori/E+; CircleEyes/iStock/Getty Images Plus; Buena Vista Images/The Image Bank/Getty Images Plus; Natthawut Nungsanther/EyeEm; Maik Mitschke/EyeEm; Fadel Senna/Stringer/AFP; serts/E+; rsiel/iStock/Getty Images Plus; tane-mahuta/iStock/Getty Images Plus; Annika Gültzow/EyeEm; Sylvain Cordier/Photographer's Choice RF.

Cover photography by David Sacks/The Image Bank/Getty Images; Alex Tihonov/Moment Open/Getty Images.

The following images are sourced from other sources/libraries.

U2: Michael Mcgurk/Shutterstock; **U4:** © 2019 Snap Inc.; © Pinterest 2019; Facebook © 2019; © 2019 Twitter, Inc.; © 2019 INSTAGRAM, INC.; © 2019 WhatsApp Inc.; **U6:** ©Incredible Edible Todmorden www.incredible-edible-todmorden.co.uk.

Illustrations

Dusan Lakicevic (Beehive Illustration) pp. 11; Ben Scruton (Meiklejohn) pp. 28, 35; Szilvia Szakall (Beehive Illustration) pp. 14, 32, 43.

Music

All the audios are sourced from Getty Images.

U5: Crispin Merrell; Frostie; Marcus Bressler; Vytenis Misevicius; JaerckG; nikosav; Emir Memedovski.

Documentary video stills

All the stills are sourced from Getty Images.

U1: Matthias Clamer; **U2:** Marc Romanelli/Image Bank Film: Signature; Kontent Real/Image Bank Film; **U3:** Sony Pictures Entertainment; **U4:** Laurence Dutton/Creatas Video; xijian/Creatas Video; **U5:** Sony Pictures Entertainment/Image Bank Film; **U6:** Scubazoo Images/Photolibrary Video; Milo Zanecchia/Ascent Xmedia/Image Bank Film.

Vlog & Grammar Rap video stills: Silversun Media Group.

Full video acknowledgements can be found in the online Teacher`s Resources.

Audio Production: Leon Chambers.

This page is intentionally left blank.

WORKBOOK
COMBO A 2
CEFR B1

TH!NK
SECOND EDITION

Herbert Puchta,
Jeff Stranks &
Peter Lewis-Jones
with Clare Kennedy

This page is intentionally left blank.

CONTENTS

Welcome   4

UNIT 1 Incredible people	10
Grammar	10
Vocabulary	12
Reading	14
Writing	15
Listening	16
Exam practice: B1 Preliminary for Schools	17

UNIT 2 A good education	18
Grammar	18
Vocabulary	20
Reading	22
Writing	23
Listening	24
Exam practice: B1 Preliminary for Schools	25
Consolidation 1 & 2	26

UNIT 3 On the screen	28
Grammar	28
Vocabulary	30
Reading	32
Writing	33
Listening	34
Exam practice: B1 Preliminary for Schools	35

UNIT 4 Online life	36
Grammar	36
Vocabulary	38
Reading	40
Writing	41
Listening	42
Exam practice: B1 Preliminary for Schools	43
Consolidation 3 & 4	44

UNIT 5 Music to my ears	46
Grammar	46
Vocabulary	48
Reading	50
Writing	51
Listening	52
Exam practice: B1 Preliminary for Schools	53

UNIT 6 No planet B	54
Grammar	54
Vocabulary	56
Reading	58
Writing	59
Listening	60
Exam practice: B1 Preliminary for Schools	61
Consolidation 5 & 6	62

Pronunciation   pages 118–119

Grammar reference   pages 122–124

Irregular verb list   page 128

WELCOME

A GETTING TO KNOW YOU
Asking questions

1 **Put the words in order to make questions.**

0 are / from / where / you
   <u>Where are you from</u> ?

1 you / 15 / are
   _____ ?

2 doing / you / are / what
   _____ ?

3 do / do / you / what
   _____ ?

4 do / like / doing / you / what
   _____ ?

5 like / you / TV / watching / do
   _____ ?

2 **Write the right question from Exercise 1 for each answer.**

0 A <u>Are you 15</u> ?
  B Yes, I am. Last Saturday was my 15th birthday.
1 A _____ ?
  B I'm just finishing my homework. I won't be long.
2 A _____ ?
  B Pakistan, but I live in the UK.
3 A _____ ?
  B Yes, I do, especially reality shows.
4 A _____ ?
  B Hanging out with my friends. That's my favourite thing.
5 A _____ ?
  B I'm a dentist.

3 **Answer the questions in Exercise 1 so that they are true for you.**

_____
_____
_____
_____
_____
_____

The weather

4 **Match the pictures with the sentences.**

0 It's dry and cloudy. [F]
1 It's warm and sunny. [ ]
2 It's cold and foggy. [ ]
3 It's hot and humid. [ ]
4 It's wet and windy. [ ]
5 It's rainy and freezing. [ ]

 A
 D
 B
 E
 C
 F

Families

5 **Complete the sentences with the words in the list.**

aunt | cousin | father | grandma | grandpa
husband | mother | sister | uncle | ~~wife~~

0 My mother is my father's <u>wife</u>.
1 My _____ is my mother's mother.
2 My _____ is my aunt's child.
3 My uncle is my aunt's _____ .
4 My aunt is my cousin's _____ .
5 My aunt is my father's _____ .
6 My _____ is my grandmother's husband.
7 My _____ is my cousin's father.
8 My _____ is my mother's husband.
9 My mother's sister is my _____ .

6 🔊 **W.01** Listen and complete the table.

	Relation to Zoe	Age	Nationality	Job
Jess				student
Tom				
Karen				

7 Choose three people from your family. Write one or two sentences about each one.

My aunt's name is Laura. She's from Brasilia.
She's 34 and she's a businesswoman.
_____
_____
_____
_____
_____

SUMMING UP

8 (Circle) the correct words.

A Hey, what ⁰*you are* / *are you* doing?
B I'm writing an email to my ¹*cousin / brother* Lucy in New Zealand.
A In New Zealand? What ²*does she do / is she doing* there? Is she there on holiday?
B Yes. Her mother – my ³*aunt / uncle* – is from New Zealand. They're there on holiday, visiting her family.
A That's nice. Is the weather good there right now?
B Yes, Lucy said it was ⁴*hot and sunny / freezing*.
A Hot? But it's January!
B In New Zealand, January is summer, remember?
A Oh, right. Listen. ⁵*Are you / Do you* going to the cinema tonight?
B No, why?
A There's a great film on at the moment. Come and see it with us!
B OK, thanks. But I'll finish my email first!

WELCOME

B EXPERIENCES
Meeting people (tense revision)

1 Match the pictures with the sentences.

1 She's met lots of famous people. ☐
2 She met a famous actor last night. ☐
3 She was having dinner with an actor when her phone rang. ☐

 A  B  C

2 Complete the sentences. Use *he* and the verb *eat* in the tenses in brackets.

0 ____*He ate*____ a really good curry last night. (past simple positive)
1 _____ any breakfast this morning. (past simple negative)
2 **A** _____ all his vegetables? (past simple question)
  B _____ (negative short answer)
3 _____ when I phoned him. (past continuous statement)
4 **A** _____ Japanese food? (present perfect question with *ever*)
  B _____ (positive short answer)

3 Complete the sentences with the correct forms of the verbs.

A Have you ever ⁰____*been*____ (be) late for a concert?
B Yes. I ¹_____ (be) late for a big concert last year. It was Ariana Grande.
A What ²_____ (happen)?
B Well, I ³_____ (miss) my train. So I ⁴_____ (get) to the concert hall at 9 o'clock, not 8 o'clock.
A ⁵_____ you _____ (see) the show?
B Yes. The concert ⁶_____ (start) at 8.30, so of course, when I ⁷_____ (go) in, the band ⁸_____ (play). But I ⁹_____ (see) about 75 per cent of the show. And it's the best concert I ¹⁰_____ ever _____ (see)!

Irregular past participles

4 Write the past participles of the verbs.

1 think _____   6 go _____
2 ride _____   7 see _____
3 have _____   8 win _____
4 drink _____   9 eat _____
5 read _____   10 wear _____

5

5 Complete the sentences with the correct verbs from Exercise 4.

0 Someone has ___drunk___ my orange juice!
1 This book's great. I've _____ it five times.
2 We haven't _____ the film yet. Is it good?
3 Zac loves motorbikes, but he's never _____ one.
4 I've got a suit, but I've never _____ it.
5 Sara isn't here. She's _____ to the park.
6 My team's never _____ a match!

6 Complete the sentences with the correct forms of the verbs.

0 No ice cream, thanks. I've ___eaten___ (eat) enough.
1 Oh, you're from Peru? I _____ (think) you were Spanish.
2 This is an interesting article. Have you _____ (read) it?
3 Louis has _____ (lose) his keys. Have you got them?
4 We _____ (run), but we still missed the train.
5 They _____ (go) to bed late last night, so they're tired today.
6 I know I've _____ (see) that man before, but I can't remember where.
7 Zoe _____ (wear) her new dress to the party last week.
8 We _____ (ride) 30 km on our bikes yesterday.

Losing things

7 🔊 W.02 Put the conversation in order. Then listen and check.

- ☐ Jack   What did you lose?
- ☐ Jack   So what did you do? Did you find it?
- ☐ Jack   What! That's not losing something – that's just a story about being untidy!
- ☐ 1 Jack   Have you ever lost anything really important?
- ☐ Jack   How did you find it? Where was it?
- ☐ Jack   That's terrible! How did you feel?
- ☐ Darcy My mobile phone. It wasn't expensive, but it had all my stuff on it.
- ☐ Darcy Well, I got my mum's phone and I rang my number. I heard it ringing. It was somewhere in my bedroom. I looked in the wardrobe. It wasn't there. Then I looked under the bed and there it was.
- ☐ Darcy It was the worst thing! It was like losing my whole life.
- ☐ Darcy Yes, I have.
- ☐ Darcy Yes, luckily I did.

8 Read the conversation again. Answer the questions.

0 What did Darcy lose?
   She lost her mobile phone.
1 How did she feel about losing it?
   _____
2 Why did she feel this way?
   _____
3 How did she find it?
   _____
4 Where did she find it?
   _____
5 What does Jack think about her story?
   _____

Furniture

9 Put the letters in order to make items in a house.

0 keds   ___desk___
1 elvsesh   _____
2 pretac   _____
3 reshwo   _____
4 otilte   _____
5 oreokc   _____
6 foas   _____
7 rirrmo   _____
8 archmira   _____
9 bedrarow   _____
10 nustaric   _____
11 palm   _____

10 Which of the items in Exercise 1 might you find in each room? Some items might be in more than one room.

1 bedroom
   wardrobe
2 living room
   _____
3 kitchen
   _____
4 dining room
   _____
5 bathroom
   _____

SUMMING UP

11 Circle the correct words.

A Why didn't you come to the match yesterday?
B Oh, I was busy. I ⁰*painted* / *was painting* my bedroom. I still ¹*haven't finished* / *didn't finish*.
A Are you just changing the colour of the walls?
B No, I've got some new things, too. Last weekend, I ²*bought* / *have bought* a new desk and some ³*shelves* / *curtains* for the window. I want to get a new lamp, too. But I ⁴*didn't see* / *haven't seen* anything I like yet.
A There's a new shop in town. I saw it when I ⁵*shopped* / *was shopping* last week. They've got some nice lamps.
B Thanks. I'll go and have a look.

C EATING AND DRINKING
Buying and talking about food

1 Complete the questions with the words in the list.

> got any | everything | How many | else
> How much | Would you like | help you

0 Have you _____got any_____ of those Spanish oranges?
1 Is that _____?
2 Can I _____?
3 _____ would you like?
4 _____ some of those?
5 Anything _____?
6 _____ is that?

2 🔊 **W.03** Complete the conversation with the phrases in Exercise 1. Then listen and check.

Assistant Good afternoon. ⁰_____Can I help you?_____
Customer Yes, I'd like some apples, please.
Assistant ¹_____
Customer Six big ones, please.
Assistant OK, ²_____
Customer Yes. ³_____
Assistant I'm afraid we haven't got any. We've got some really nice ones from South Africa. ⁴_____
Customer Sure. I'll have three.
Assistant ⁵_____
Customer Yes, it is. ⁶_____
Assistant That's £5.20 altogether.
Customer Here you are.
Assistant And 80p change. Thanks!

3 Circle the correct words.

0 I think there are *some* / *any* eggs in the fridge.
1 We don't want *some* / *any* cake, thanks.
2 I'd like 500 grams of cheese and *some* / *any* chicken.
3 Sorry. There isn't *some* / *any* rice left.
4 You haven't got *some* / *any* butter in your sandwich.
5 This soup is really good. Try *some* / *any*.

In a restaurant

4 Put the words in order to make sentences. Write W (waiter) or C (customer).

0 I / the / please / can / menu, / see
_____Can I see the menu, please?_____ [C]
1 ready / you / are / order / to
_____? [ ]
2 OK / everything / is
_____? [ ]
3 much / too / chicken / the / salt / on / there's
_____. [ ]
4 can / please / have / bill, / the / we
_____? [ ]
5 a / please / four, / for / table
_____. [ ]

5 Complete the sentences with *much* or *many*.

0 There are too _____many_____ people in this restaurant.
1 There's too _____ salt in this soup.
2 There are too _____ things on the menu.
3 There's too _____ noise in here.
4 There are too _____ vegetables on my plate.
5 This restaurant's a bit expensive. I can't spend too _____ money.

6 🔊 **W.04** Match the sentences in Exercise 5 with the replies. Then listen and check your answers to Exercises 5 and 6.

a You're right! It's disgusting. [ ]
b Eat them! They're good for you. [ ]
c Yes, I really don't know what to choose. [ ]
d Don't worry. It's your birthday, so I'll pay. [ ]
e Well, it's always busy at lunchtime. [0]
f Yes, let's go somewhere quieter. [ ]

Shops

7 Look at the pictures. Write the shops.

1 _____

3 _____

2 _____

4 _____

Things you have to do

8 Circle the correct words. Then match the sentences with the pictures in Exercise 1.

a You *have to / don't have to* tell the barista what size drink you want. ☐

b You *have to / don't have to* wait here. ☐

c You *have to / don't have to* try clothes on over there. ☐

d You *have to / don't have to* keep medicines away from children. ☐

9 What do these customer notices mean? Write sentences with *have to* or *don't have to*.

0 'Buy now, pay later.'
You can have the item now, but you don't have to pay for it yet.

1 'Please ask an assistant before trying on clothes.'
_____

2 'Cash only – no credit or debit cards accepted.'
_____

3 'We can deliver your shopping to your home.'
_____

SUMMING UP

10 Complete the conversations. Write one word in each space.

0 **A** Why are you going to the *department store* ?
   B To buy a birthday present for Mum.

1 **A** My pen's broken.
   B Well, you don't _____ to buy a new one. You can use mine.

2 **A** I'd like _____ olives, please. 250 grams.
   B OK, here you are. Anything _____ ?

3 **A** What's the matter?
   B I don't feel well. I've eaten too _____ sweets.

D LOOKING AHEAD
Plans and arrangements

1 Look at Abbi's diary. Write her plans for the day.

DIARY
TODAY
8 am – go for a swim with Lola
10 am – walk in park with Harry
1 pm – lunch with Mum and Dad
3 pm – dentist
6 pm – train to Liverpool
9 pm – film with Emily

0 At 8 am *she's going for a swim with Lola.*
1 After that _____
2 At 1 pm _____
3 Two hours later _____
4 At 6 pm _____
5 Finally, at 9 pm _____

2 Read the sentences and write I (intention) or A (arrangement).

0 We're having a coffee, too. [A]
1 They're going to travel there by bus. ☐
2 She's going to have yoghurt and cereal. ☐
3 We're meeting at the new shopping centre. ☐
4 I'm just having a check-up – I hope. ☐
5 We're seeing Lily James's latest film – I can't wait. ☐

3 Write about four arrangements you've got for this week.

_____
_____
_____
_____

Sports and sport verbs

4 Circle the correct words.

0 Do you want to *go / do / play* volleyball later?
1 We *went / did / played* skiing last weekend.
2 My friend Alex *goes / does / plays* rock climbing every weekend.
3 You have to *go / do / play* gymnastics on Fridays.
4 I hate tennis. I never want to *go / do / play* it again!
5 Mum *goes / does / plays* running every morning.
6 We go to the sports ground on Sundays to *go / do / play* some athletics.
7 Let's go to the gym. We can *go / do / play* karate.

Travel plans

5 Match the parts of the sentences.

0 We arrived late at the railway station and missed — *f*
1 It was late and we were tired, so we took — ☐
2 My mum's car is at the garage, so I rode — ☐
3 My friends left the cinema at 10 pm and caught — ☐
4 Last year we flew — ☐
5 Dad really wanted to get home, so he drove — ☐

a my bike to school today.
b the last bus home.
c to Colombia for our holiday.
d a taxi home from the airport.
e all night.
f the train by three minutes.

6 Write five sentences about the transport you use in your life.

0 *When we go on holiday, we usually fly.*
1 _____
2 _____
3 _____
4 _____
5 _____

7 🔊 W.05 Listen to the conversation and answer the questions.

0 Where is Martha going for her holiday?
   She's going to Italy.
1 How long is she going for?
   _____
2 How is she getting there?
   _____
3 When is she leaving?
   _____
4 What does she need to buy in town?
   _____
5 Why is Ben surprised?
   _____

8 🔊 W.05 Complete the conversation with the words in the list. Then listen again and check.

> flying | going | going to be | going to buy
> going to have | going to spend | leaving
> taking | taxi | train

Ben   Are you ⁰ *going to have* a holiday this year?
Martha Yes. We're ¹_____ two weeks in Italy.
Ben   Lucky you. Are you ²_____ ?
Martha No, we're not. We're ³_____ the train. It's ⁴_____ a real adventure.
Ben   That sounds really exciting.
Martha Yes, in fact, we're ⁵_____ next Monday. We're taking a ⁶_____ to the station and then it's the ⁷_____ all the way to Naples.
Ben   So, are you ready for the trip?
Martha Almost. I'm ⁸_____ to town tomorrow to buy a few last-minute things.
Ben   Like what?
Martha Well, I'm ⁹_____ some more summer clothes and then I need to go to the chemist's.
Ben   The chemist's? Why?
Martha I've got to get some sun cream.
Ben   Sun cream? But it's only May. It isn't hot enough to lie on the beach!
Martha Here it isn't, but it is in Italy!

SUMMING UP

9 Complete the email. Write one word in each space.

> 🏆 **Jack**
> Jackjones@thinkmail.com

Hi Jack,

You know our school volleyball team won the local championship last year, right? Well, this month we're playing teams from other cities in the UK.

Next Saturday, we're ⁰ *playing* against a team in Scotland. It's a long way, so we aren't ¹_____ the train – we're ²_____ there! I've never been on a plane before, so I'm really excited.

We're going to stay in Scotland until Monday. On Sunday, I hope to ³_____ some rock climbing. There are some great places for it up there. My friend Sebastian wants to ⁴_____ skiing, but I don't think there's enough snow.

I'll write when we come back and tell you all about it.

Bye for now,

Alessia

1 INCREDIBLE PEOPLE

GRAMMAR

Present perfect with just, already and yet → SB p.14

1 ★☆☆ Complete the sentences with *just*, *already* or *yet*.

My little sister is really smart.
1 She's _____ learned to walk. She took her first steps last week.
2 She hasn't learned to read _____, but she likes the pictures.
3 She's _____ learned to count from one to five and she's only one year old!

2 ★★☆ Look at Alex's to-do list for tidying his bedroom. Write sentences with *already* and *yet*.

- tidy desk ✓
- clean the floor ✗
- pick up towels and put them in bathroom ✗
- make bed ✓
- empty bin ✗
- hang up clothes ✓

Alex has *already tidied his desk*. _____
_____
_____
Alex hasn't _____
_____
_____

3 ★★★ Look at the pictures. What has just happened? Write sentences with the verbs in A and the words in B, and *already*, *just* or *yet*.

A	B
~~wake~~	~~up~~
fall	a goal
have	an accident
score	over
start	a trophy
win	to rain

0 *He has just woken up.*
1 They _____
2 They _____
3 She _____
4 She _____
5 It _____

Present perfect vs. past simple → SB p.17

4 ★☆☆ Match the questions with the answers.

0 Have you ever played volleyball? **b**
1 Where did you play? ☐
2 Did you enjoy it? ☐
3 Were you good at it? ☐
4 Has your team played teams from other countries? ☐
5 Has your team won any trophies? ☐

a No, I wasn't.
b Yes, I have.
c Yes, we've already won three competitions.
d At school.
e No, we haven't – not yet.
f No, not very much.

5 ★★☆ Complete the conversation. Use the present perfect or the past simple and the information in brackets.

It's Sunday afternoon.

Lucas Mum, I'm bored. What can I do?
Mum (finish your homework?)
0 *Have you finished your homework?*
Lucas (last night)
Yes, I finished it all last night.
Mum (tidy your room?)
1 _____
Lucas (yesterday)
2 _____
Mum (clean the fish tank?)
3 _____
Lucas (before lunch)
4 _____
Mum (wash your bike?)
5 _____
Lucas (on Friday)
6 _____
Mum (phone Jamie?)
7 _____
Lucas (this morning)
8 _____
Mum (watch that new film on Netflix?)
9 _____
Lucas (last night)
10 _____
Mum Well, I don't know. What about coming to the supermarket with me?
Lucas Erm … maybe not!

6 ★★★ Complete the text. Use the present perfect or past simple form of the verbs in the list. You can use some verbs more than once.

be | buy | ~~do~~ | get | have | live | look | not finish | not learn | stop | work

My grandmother is 65 and ⁰ *has done* a lot of things in her life. She ¹_____ born in the country and ²_____ on a small farm until she was 16. She ³_____ in many different places, but she always says the farm ⁴_____ the best place of all. She ⁵_____ school because she started working when she was 15. She ⁶_____ many different jobs in her life – she ⁷_____ a children's nurse, a dressmaker and a shop assistant, among other things. She ⁸_____ in a very expensive shop in London for several years. She ⁹_____ working after she ¹⁰_____ married. She ¹¹_____ five children and she ¹²_____ after the house. Grandma loves new things. She ¹³_____ just _____ a laptop, but she ¹⁴_____ how to use social media yet. I'm going to her house to help her now.

GET IT RIGHT!
Present perfect with just, already and yet

Learners often make word order errors with *just*, *already* and *yet*.

✓ I **have just** finished my homework.
✗ I ~~just have~~ finished my homework.
✓ He has not **passed his exam yet**.
✗ He has not ~~passed yet his exam~~.
✓ We **have already finished** our project.
✗ We ~~already have finished~~ our project.

Correct the sentences.

0 I already have sent a message about the party to my friends.
I have already sent a message about the party to my friends.

1 My brother has yet not had a summer job.
_____

2 My big sister already has learned to drive.
_____

3 My family and I have been just on holiday.
_____

4 Have you yet bought your mum a birthday present?
_____

5 The singer has released already five albums.
_____

6 I just have uploaded some photos.
_____

VOCABULARY
Personality adjectives

→ SB p.13

1 ★★☆ Circle the correct answers.

0 An active person   A loves theatre.   B is always doing something.   C sleeps a lot.
1 A brave person   A takes risks when it's necessary. B is often angry.   C doesn't like talking.
2 A creative person   A often makes mistakes.   B has original ideas.   C works very hard.
3 A charming person   A is very good-looking.   B has a lot of money.   C is kind and friendly.
4 A cheerful person   A often feels sad.   B enjoys life.   C often gets angry.
5 A laid-back person   A is very relaxed.   B can't wake up in the morning. C never goes out.
6 A confident person   A doesn't work hard.   B believes in him-/herself.   C will keep a secret.
7 A positive person   A sees the good in everything. B is frightened of the future. C is often bored.
8 A talented person   A has got a lot of money.   B isn't good at sports.   C is very good at something.

2 ★★☆ Read the text. Complete the adjectives. The first and last letters are given.

My ideal friend is very ⁰a<u>ctive</u> – that's important because I love sport and I want her to play basketball in my team. She's ¹c_____g and knows how to have fun, so she's a good person to hang out with. I need a friend who's really ²c_____e and is good at art, because I'm not and she could help me and give me some ideas.

Maybe it would be good if she was ³c_____l too – people sometimes say I'm too ⁴s_____s and don't laugh much. I'd like her to be ⁵p_____e as well – I don't like it when people only see the bad side of things.

3 ★★★ Write one or two sentences about people you know (friends or family). Use the adjectives in Exercises 1 and 2.

_____
_____
_____
_____

Collocations

→ SB p.17

4 ★★☆ Complete the sentences with the correct form of the verbs in the list. Use each verb twice.

do | form | get | have | lose | make | take

0 Jonah didn't ___have___ any homework last night.
1 The singer Leila Jenson _____ an appearance in this film.
2 How many presents did you _____ for your birthday?
3 Hundreds of people have _____ their lives in the hurricane.
4 I need more information before I can _____ an opinion.
5 The children _____ a really good time at the zoo yesterday.
6 Rebecca wasn't on time for school all week. She's _____ a bad reputation for being late!
7 Hurry up! You _____ a music lesson in ten minutes.
8 Wait a minute. I want to _____ a photograph.
9 We _____ a group to collect money for the hospital.
10 That isn't right! You've _____ a mistake.
11 I know it isn't very good, but I _____ my best.
12 Oh no! We've _____ the race. Our team is last.
13 Emily doesn't like _____ risks. She likes to be safe.
14 Have they _____ enough work for today?

WordWise: Phrases with just

→ SB p.15

5 ★★☆ Tick (✓) the five sentences that can be completed with *just*.

0 I've … cleaned the floor. ✓
1 That horror film, *The Blob*, is … terrifying. ☐
2 He can't tell you if you don't … ask. ☐
3 This dress is almost … perfect. ☐
4 The flower show was … amazing. ☐
5 He's … a child, but he's a talented artist. ☐
6 No problem, it was … a thought. ☐
7 Gemma has … phoned. She's on her way. ☐

6 ★★☆ Match the five sentences in Exercise 5 with the meanings of *just*.

1 a short time ago   0
2 only   ☐
3 really   ☐

REFERENCE

Personality adjectives
- serious
- cheerful
- brave
- positive
- talented
- creative
- active
- laid-back
- charming

COLLOCATIONS
- **make** a mistake / an appearance
- **do** your best / work
- **get** a present / a reputation
- **lose** a race / your life / something important / your home
- **take** a risk / a photograph
- **form** a group / an opinion

JUST
- It was **just** a joke.
- Tom's **just** arrived.
- The book was **just** fantastic!

VOCABULARY EXTRA

1 Complete the sentences with the words in the list.

amusing | bossy | curious | reasonable | reliable | smart

0 Amy's _____amusing_____ . She makes me laugh.
1 Coral's _____ . She's clever and knows a lot.
2 Aidan's _____ . He's fair and makes good decisions.
3 Zara's _____ . She always tells us what to do.
4 Seth's _____ . He always does what he has promised to do.
5 Jake's _____ . He's interested in how things work.

2 Think of a person you know for each adjective in Exercise 1.

0 bossy
   _____My big brother is bossy._____
1 amusing
   _____
2 curious
   _____
3 reasonable
   _____
4 reliable
   _____
5 smart
   _____

ALL IN A DAY'S WORK

Who are your heroes? We aren't talking about superheroes like Superman or Wonder Woman; we want to hear your opinions about *real* people who make big differences to other people's lives while they do their jobs. So, tell us about the people you think are heroes because of the amazing things they do every day as part of their work.

1 _____

Theo

Paramedics – the people who drive ambulances and help in medical emergencies – are my everyday heroes. The other day, my grandad had a bad fall. I tried to help him, but I couldn't do it by myself, so I called an ambulance. It arrived almost immediately and the paramedics helped Grandad straightaway. They were very professional and worked quickly, but they were also friendly and cheerful. By the time Grandad was in the ambulance, he was relaxed and smiling again.
Every time paramedics go out, it's an emergency and often a serious situation. Think how many people that team has helped already and how many lives it's saved!

2 _____

Caitlin

My neighbour, Anna, is a firefighter and she does an incredible – and dangerous – job. Firefighters don't just put out fires, they also help in all sorts of emergencies. Anna's rescued people from rivers, helped people stuck in the snow and she often has to go to traffic accidents. Firefighters have to be brave, smart and good at working in a team. As well as saving lives, they teach people how to prevent accidents. She says every day at work is different: even on quiet days, they have to be ready for action. Firefighters often take risks in order to rescue people. I really admire them for that.

Jodie

I live on the edge of a big city and until last year there was nothing for teenagers to do. Kids hung out on the streets and some of them got into trouble. Then Jonas, a youth worker, arrived and everything changed!
He's positive and easy-going, but he's also serious about his job. He wants to help us discover our talents – 'Be curious!' he says. He's organised lots of new activities for us, from songwriting to rock climbing! I can honestly say he's made an enormous difference to our lives. We've got interesting things to do now and a cool place to go in our free time. Jonas is our hero!

3 _____

READING

1 Read the article. Write the names of the jobs under the photos.

2 Read the article again. Write A, B or C next to the sentences.

This everyday hero …
0 has a lot of variety in his/her job. **B**
1 works with young people. ☐
2 helps teenagers during their free time. ☐
3 is interested in people's health. ☐
4 often works in frightening and dangerous situations. ☐
5 tries to introduce teenagers to new ideas. ☐
6 helps to make people get better. ☐

3 **CRITICAL THINKING** Read the questions and (circle) the best answers.

1 What do the everyday heroes in A, B and C have in common?
   A They all save lives.
   B They all help other people.
   C They all change people's lives.
   Because …

2 What are the personalities of the everyday heroes in A, B and C like?
   A They're caring and reliable.
   B They're friendly and popular.
   C They're brave and talented.
   Because …

DEVELOPING Writing

INCREDIBLE PEOPLE · UNIT 1

A description of a person I know well

1 **INPUT** Read the text that Poppy wrote about her friend Liam. Match the pictures with three of the paragraphs.

 1 ☐
 2 ☐
 3 ☐

○ I'm writing about my friend, Liam. I've known him for three years. We met when he moved to a house in my street.

○ He's a little older than me, but I always feel like he's much older! I think that's because he's very confident. He isn't afraid to disagree with adults. For example, I've never said 'No, I don't agree' to an adult, but Liam has! I admire him for that.

○ Another good point is that he's very honest. If he doesn't like something, he says so. He never says 'Oh yes, it's great' just to be the same as everyone else. In fact, this is why some people at school don't like him very much, I think.

○ Does he have any bad points? Yes! He's forgetful. Last week, he promised to come to my house and help me fix my bike. But he didn't come. I waited, then I phoned him. He's honest, so he said, 'Oh, no! I forgot. I'll come right now.' And he did. He arrived with a big smile, saying: 'I always forget. Sorry.' How could I be angry?

○ I hope we're going to be friends for a long time.

2 Read the text again. Match the paragraphs (A–E) with the topics.

0 Not-so-good things about Liam — D
1 The first good thing about Liam ☐
2 Final comment ☐
3 Introducing Liam and how they met ☐
4 Another good thing about Liam ☐

3 **ANALYSE** Which adjectives describe Liam? Tick (✓) three.

1 polite ☐   4 confident ☐
2 honest ☐   5 forgetful ☐
3 intelligent ☐   6 talented ☐

4 Look at the three boxes you ticked in Exercise 3. What examples does Poppy give to show that these adjectives describe Liam?

1 _____
2 _____
3 _____

WRITING TIP: describing a person

- Introduce the person. Give his/her name and say when and where you met.
- Explain why you like him/her. Use different adjectives to describe his/her personality (good and bad points!) and give examples.
- Finish with a comment about your friendship or your hopes for the future.

5 **PLAN** You are going to write about a person you know well. Choose a friend or a family member and write a plan. Use the Writing tip to help you.

Introducing the person
_____

Good and/or bad things about him/her
_____
_____

Final comment
_____

6 **PRODUCE** Write your description in 150–200 words. Use your notes from Exercise 5.

🎧 LISTENING

1 🔊 1.01 Listen to the conversation. Circle the correct words.

1 They're discussing *last weekend / going to a film / their parents*.
2 They both like *an actor / a film / London*.

2 🔊 1.01 Listen again. Mark the sentences T (true) or F (false).

0 Megan thinks last weekend was exciting. **T**
1 A film premiere is the first time a new film is shown. ☐
2 Megan wants to go to the premiere of Noah Centineo's new film. ☐
3 Megan thinks her parents will be happy for her to go. ☐
4 Joe has an aunt and uncle who live in London. ☐
5 Joe doesn't want to go to the film with Megan. ☐
6 Joe doesn't like Noah Centineo. ☐
7 Joe and Megan are going to talk to Megan's parents. ☐

3 🔊 1.01 Listen again. Complete the conversations. Use no more than three words.

1 **Megan** Well, you know that Noah Centineo is my favourite actor?
   Joe Yes, of course ⁰ *I know* that. So ¹_____?
2 **Megan** Well, I'm going to the premiere!
   Joe Oh, that's a ²_____!
   Megan Oh? Do you really think so?
   Joe Yes, you ³_____ do it. You've always wanted to meet him.
3 **Megan** Wow, that's great! Thank you. I'm just worried that my parents … ⁴_____, they won't like the idea.
4 **Joe** I know what you mean. But, hey, you know what? You've got to ⁵_____!

PRONUNCIATION
Sentence stress   Go to page 118. 🎧

DIALOGUE

4 🔊 1.03 Put the conversations in the correct order. Then listen and check.

Conversation 1
☐ **A** We can put a football match together between our street and Nelson Street.
[1] **A** I've got an idea for the weekend.
☐ **A** Let's speak to some people about it now.
☐ **B** I'll come with you. We can do it together.
☐ **B** A football match? That's a great idea!
☐ **B** Yeah? What is it?

Conversation 2
☐ **A** Thanks, but I'm not sure if we can do everything before Saturday.
[1] **A** Mark, why don't we have a party?
☐ **A** I don't know. Can people come on Sunday?
☐ **A** Well, the next day's Monday – that's why. You know, homework to do, that sort of thing.
☐ **B** A party? Yes! I'll help you if you want. Let's have it this weekend.
☐ **B** OK, so forget Saturday. But you should definitely do it. It could be Sunday.
☐ **B** Oh, don't worry about homework, Stella. Come on! You've got to make this happen!
☐ **B** Yes, I think they can. Why not?

PHRASES FOR FLUENCY   → SB p.18

5 Put the words in order to make phrases.

0 what / know / You ? *You know what?*
1 sure / you / are / ? _____
2 it / let's / face _____
3 that / and / that's _____
4 so / don't / think / I _____
5 of / sort / thing / that _____

6 🔊 1.04 Complete the conversations with the phrases in Exercise 5. Then listen and check.

0 **A** Hurry up. The film starts at 8.30.
   B *Are you sure?* I heard it starts at 9.00.
1 **A** How did the tennis match go?
   B I lost. _____, I'm awful at tennis!
2 **A** So what did you do over the weekend?
   B Not much – read, watched TV, _____.
3 **A** Oh, Dad! Can I please watch *The Voice*?
   B No, you can't. I said no TV _____.
4 **A** I know it's raining, but let's go for a walk.
   B _____? I'm staying right here!
5 **A** This song's just fantastic.
   B Well, _____. It's terrible.

B1 Preliminary for Schools

🎧 LISTENING
Part 1: 3-option multiple choice

1 🔊 1.05 For each question, choose the correct answer.

1 What's the weather like now?

5 Why is the girl excited?

2 What are they going to have for dinner this evening?

6 Where's the boy today?

3 What job does the boy's aunt do?

7 How did the girl travel to her friend's house?

4 Where is the boy going to go first?

  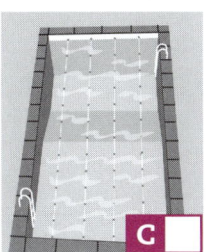

EXAM GUIDE: LISTENING PART 1

In B1 Preliminary for Schools Listening Part 1, you listen to seven short recordings. For each one, you have to answer a question by choosing one of three pictures.
- Read the questions carefully.
- Look at the three pictures and find similarities and differences between them.
- Identify the situation in each picture and think about the words you might hear.
- You will probably hear words from all the pictures, so don't choose a picture just because it contains the first word you recognise.
- Listen carefully to the dialogue and try to understand exactly what the speakers say about the things in the pictures.

2 A GOOD EDUCATION

GRAMMAR
Present perfect with *for* and *since*
→ SB p.22

1 ★☆☆ Complete the sentences with *for* or *since* and a number where necessary.

0 Matthew has worked as a computer games tester ___*for*___ three years.
1 I've lived in this house _____ 2018.
2 We've only had our pet rabbit _____ six weeks.
3 Lauren has played the guitar in the band _____ she was 16 years old.
4 This tree has been here _____ more than 200 years!
5 I've written poems _____ I was ten years old.
6 Charlotte has been in the football team _____ 2019, so she has been a footballer _____ _____ years.
7 Joshua has played tennis _____ he was four years old. He was born in 2012, so he has played tennis _____ _____ years.

2 ★★☆ Write sentences. Use the positive or negative form of the present perfect and *for* or *since*.

0 Thomas / not see / grandfather / two months
   Thomas hasn't seen his grandfather for two months.
1 Shiloh and Joss / be / singers / five years
   _____
2 Sophie / not play / football / she broke her leg
   _____
3 Jacob / not write / his blog / a long time
   _____
4 Dan / not go / to the dentist / a year
   _____
5 You and I / be / friends / we were kids
   _____
6 They / not see / a good film / ages
   _____
7 We / not go / on holiday / two years
   _____

3 ★★☆ Jessie wants to ask her friends some questions for a school project. Complete them with the present perfect of the verbs.

1 How long _____ (live) in your house?
2 What is your best friend's name? How long _____ (know) him/her?
3 How long _____ (be) at this school?
4 What's your favourite possession? How long _____ (have) it?

4 ★★★ Look at the table and write answers to Jessie's questions. Use the present perfect and *for* or *since*.

	Ella	Jack	Oliver
1	ten years	2010	three months
2	Sarah, 2018	Zayne, 2015	Dillon, a long time
3	five years	2019	September
4	bike, six months	dog, two years	laptop, May

1 Ella ___*has lived in her house for ten years.*___
2 _____
3 _____
4 _____

1 Jack _____
2 _____
3 _____
4 _____

1 Oliver _____
2 _____
3 _____
4 _____

5 ★★★ Answer the questions in Exercise 3 for you.

1 _____
2 _____
3 _____
4 _____

a, an, the or no article

→ SB p.25

6 ★☆☆ Circle the correct words.

Yesterday I went to ⁰(the)/ an park. I go there a lot, so I know it very well. I sat on ¹a / the grass and started to read my book. Then lots of ²the / – things started to happen.

You can play ³the / – ball games in the park, but ⁴the / – bikes aren't allowed. ⁵A / The boy on ⁶a / the bike was riding on the path. ⁷– / The park keeper started to run after ⁸a / the boy, but she couldn't catch him.

There were three small children playing ⁹– / the football, too. One of them kicked ¹⁰a / the ball, and it hit ¹¹a / the boy on his bike and he fell off. So the park keeper caught him! I think this was ¹²– / the really bad luck for the boy.

7 ★★☆ Complete the text with *a, an, the* or – (no article).

People have kept ⁰ _–_ cats as pets for thousands of years. In ancient times, ¹_____ most important reason for keeping animals was for food or ²_____ work. Cats are ³_____ example of how ⁴_____ animals can help ⁵_____ people, because they catch ⁶_____ rats and ⁷_____ mice.

These days, people keep cats as pets. Pet cats have ⁸_____ good life. They often sleep all day and people give them ⁹_____ tasty food – they don't have to catch it! Owners love their cats and think of them as members of ¹⁰_____ family.

A GOOD EDUCATION UNIT 2

8 ★★☆ Read the sentences. Tick (✓) the four that are grammatically correct.

1 I love the birds. ☐
2 I saw a beautiful bird in the park yesterday. ☐
3 The bird in the park was bigger than mine. ☐
4 It was flying in a sky. ☐
5 I think the bird was a parrot. ☐
6 I think the birds make really good friends. ☐
7 There are many different sizes of the birds. ☐
8 I saw a picture of the biggest bird in the world. ☐

PRONUNCIATION
Word stress   Go to page 118.

9 ★★★ Look at Exercise 8 again. Rewrite the four incorrect sentences so that they are correct.

_____
_____
_____
_____

GET IT RIGHT!

a(n) and no article

Learners often use *a(n)* where no article is needed, and no article where *a* is needed.

✓ I had **a** great time with my friends last Saturday.
✗ ~~I had great time with my friends last Saturday.~~

Complete the sentences with *a(n)* or – (no article).

0 I've got __a__ pet cat.
1 My brother works as _____ chef in a hotel.
2 Do you need to book _____ accommodation?
3 We haven't had _____ holiday for ages.
4 I'm _____ student at the University of London.
5 We need _____ information about this urgently.
6 I would like to buy _____ desk.

VOCABULARY
School subjects → SB p.22

1 ★☆☆ Put the letters in order to make school subjects.

0 You probably need a piano if you're a (sciuM) teacher. _Music_
1 We often use computers in Design and (Thecloongy). _____
2 (regGyhoap) teachers don't need maps now that there's Google Earth. _____
3 We have our (stiChryme) lessons in one of the science labs. _____
4 I love learning (shEling) because I want to visit London. _____
5 A calculator can be useful in a (thaMs) class. _____
6 I really enjoy (troyisH) lessons when they're about people, not just dates. _____
7 Our (amarD) teacher has been on TV and acted in a film! _____

2 ★★☆ Look at the photos. Write the subjects.

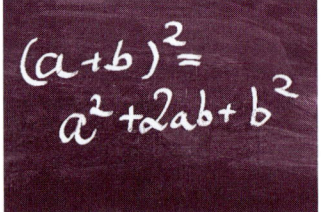
0 _Maths_

4 _____

1 _____

5 _____

2 _____

6 _____

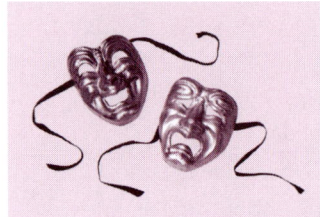
3 _____

7 _____

Verbs about thinking → SB p.25

3 ★☆☆ Find ten words about thinking.

W	R	U	O	R	T	G	K	O	B	R
C	O	N	C	E	N	T	R	A	T	E
S	G	F	G	M	I	K	E	E	Y	B
G	T	E	U	E	E	B	A	S	E	T
I	H	G	E	M	I	H	L	I	H	I
M	I	N	S	B	E	L	I	E	V	E
A	N	S	S	E	L	V	S	Y	K	E
G	K	G	L	R	T	E	E	N	Q	L
I	F	V	U	J	X	O	L	O	K	E
N	S	U	P	P	O	S	E	G	F	L
E	U	O	M	B	W	O	N	D	E	R
P	R	E	C	O	G	N	I	S	E	C

4 ★★☆ Complete the text with the words in Exercise 3.

Do you ⁰b_elieve_ in the idea of morning people and night people? I do. I've always found it difficult to ¹c_____ in the morning. I can never ²r_____ anything when we have a test in the morning.
I ³w_____ why schools don't start in the evening. I ⁴t_____ night people would love that. Can you ⁵i_____ starting school at 8 pm? Great! We could sleep all day! But I ⁶s_____ morning people would hate studying at night.
You can always ⁷r_____ morning people – they're so cheerful in the mornings and don't seem to ⁸r_____ that night people don't want to chat! So, am I a morning person or a night person? You can ⁹g_____ , can't you?

5 ★★★ Read and answer the questions so they are true for you.

1 Do you believe everything you read in magazines?
_____
2 What kind of thing(s) do you remember easily?
_____
3 What time of day do you concentrate best?
_____
4 What do you imagine you will be in the future?
_____

REFERENCE

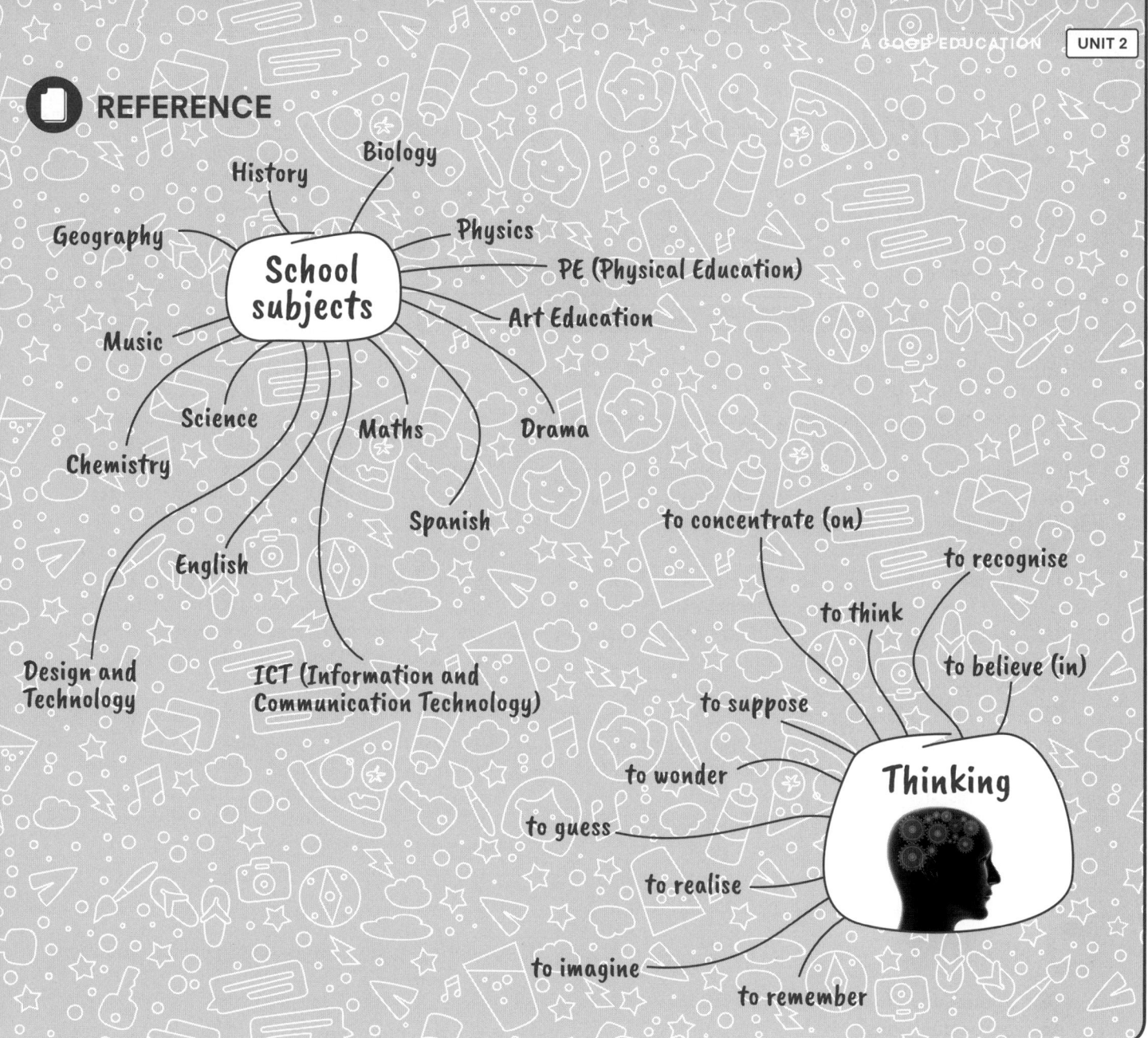

VOCABULARY EXTRA

1 Complete the definitions with the words in the list.

| ~~Citizenship~~ | Economics | French | Photography | Robotics |

0 In _____Citizenship_____ lessons, you study the laws, politics and economy of your country.
1 _____ is the study of how they make and use automated machines.
2 In _____ lessons, you learn to speak the language of France.
3 _____ is the study of money and business.
4 In _____ , you learn how to take good photos.

2 Write your school timetable in English. Write the days of the week, the times of the day and the subjects.

	Monday	Tuesday
9.00	Maths	Chemistry
10.00	PE	Drama

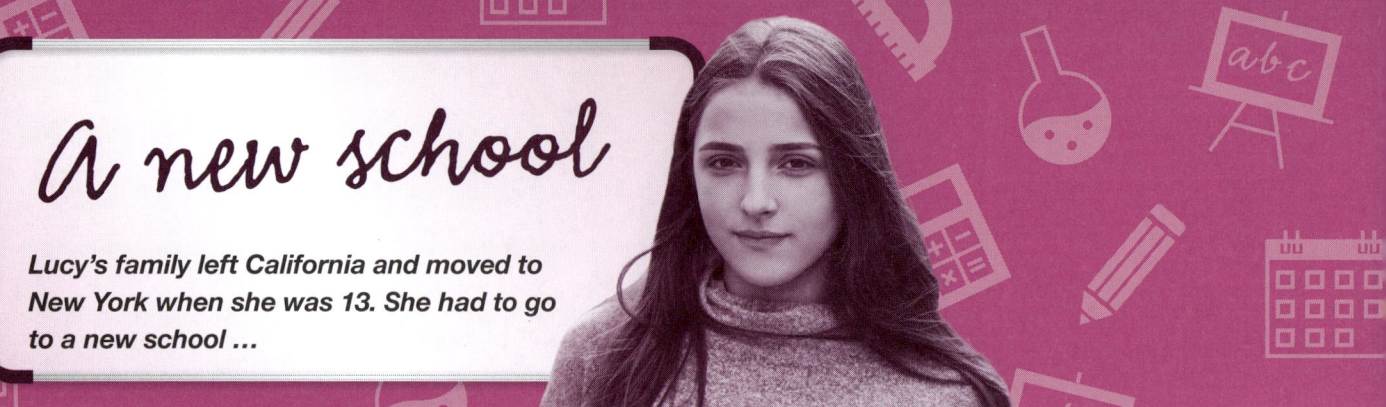

A new school

Lucy's family left California and moved to New York when she was 13. She had to go to a new school …

I remember it really well. My parents drove me to my new school and said goodbye to me. I **[A]** walked into the school. I didn't know what to feel. I was excited and scared and a bit nervous, all **[B]**. There were lots of other kids around. They were already in groups of friends, but none of them said hello or anything. It was a strange feeling for me, like I didn't really belong there. I wanted to be somewhere else, **[C]**.

The first thing I had to do was register, so I went to a room in the school that had a sign saying 'Administration'. They started asking me **[D]** questions. Suddenly, I felt like I was some kind of criminal. Then I went off to my first class. Wow, my first class was horrible. Perhaps it was because my accent or my clothes were different, but everyone just looked at me in such a strange way. And just like when I arrived, no one came to talk to me. Incredibly, that's still never happened: no one has ever taken the time to **[E]** or like me. I have friends because I made the first move to meet people.

Maybe the worst class that day, though, was Science. The teacher wasn't too bad. She introduced me **[F]** and showed me where to sit. But the other students? Well, they looked at me like I was a guinea pig or something they were going to use for an experiment. I hated every minute.

Then there was a break and I went to sit somewhere alone, **[G]**. But I thought they'd want me to keep trying, so I tried to be more positive in the next class. That didn't go so well, though. Everyone talked to other students, **[H]**. At the end of the day, I couldn't wait to get out of there.

But since I first started at the school, things have got better. Now I'm doing fine and I get OK grades. I've learned lots of things – but not what the teachers teach. I've learned that I'm strong and brave. I've learned that I will succeed even if some things aren't the way I want them to be.

READING

1 Read about Lucy's first day at a new school. Answer the questions.

 0 How did she feel about the school at the end of the first day?
 She couldn't wait to leave.

 1 What things made her feel bad?
 _____

 2 What surprised her most about the school?
 _____

 3 How does she feel about the school now?
 _____

 4 What has she learned from being at this school?
 _____

2 Read the text again. Match the phrases with the correct places (A–H).

0	at the same time	B
1	but I sat by myself	☐
2	missing my mum and dad	☐
3	but that wasn't possible	☐
4	took a deep breath and	☐
5	to the class	☐
6	all kinds of	☐
7	get to know me	☐

3 Underline two or three things Lucy says that you find interesting.

4 Write two questions that you'd like to ask Lucy. Then write what you think she'd say in reply.

 0 Q *What's your favourite subject at school?*
 A *Science. I like ICT, too.*

 1 Q _____
 A _____

 2 Q _____
 A _____

5 **CRITICAL THINKING** Read the questions and circle the best answers. Then explain why.

 1 Which sentence best describes Lucy's feelings now?
  A I always feel sorry for new students.
  B I'm enjoying the lessons and doing very well.
  C It was hard, but my experience was useful.
  Because …

 2 What do you think was the worst thing for Lucy?
  A the unfriendly students
  B being in a different country
  C the new school system
  Because …

DEVELOPING Writing

A GOOD EDUCATION — UNIT 2

An informal email

1 **INPUT** Read the email quickly. Tick (✓) the things Ed talks about.

1 how he feels about his routine ☐
2 the things he likes to watch on TV ☐
3 homework that he doesn't like to do ☐
4 a party for his birthday ☐

2 Read the email again and answer the questions.

1 How does Ed feel about weekdays?
  _____
2 What has changed in Tilly's life?
  _____
3 Why can't Ed write a longer email?
  _____

3 **ANALYSE** Find the short forms of the phrases below in the email. Complete them with the words in the list.

| I | Is | ~~It was~~ | I've |

0 ____It was____ good to get your last email.
1 _____ everything going well?
2 _____ hope you can come.
3 _____ got lots to do.

4 Read the email again. Find phrases that express these things.

0 What Ed says instead of *How are you*?:
  ____How's it going?____
1 Two ways that Ed starts to talk about a different topic: _____ and _____
2 Direct questions Ed asks Tilly: _____ and _____
3 Three ways he checks that Tilly understands what he's saying: _____ , _____ and _____
4 How he ends his email: _____

 Tilly
Tillysmith@thinkmail.com

Hi Tilly,

How's it going? Good to get your last email – it was fun to read. I liked hearing about your life, your routine and stuff, so I thought I could tell you about mine.

Most weeks are the same, but I guess that's true for everyone, right? Monday to Friday, well, they're school days, so that's a kind of routine. You know, get up at 7.30, go to school at 8.45, come home at 4.00 and do homework, then have dinner, and go to bed. Of course, lots of things make every day different, so I don't mind the routine. It's cool. We don't have the same lessons at school every day and I do different things in the evenings.

Anyway, I wonder how you're getting on at your new school. Everything going well? I'm sure it is!

By the way, it's my birthday next month – I'll be 15!! We're having a party on Saturday 12th.

Hope you can come. Let me know, OK?

So, what was I saying about routine and things? Yeah, right, homework – got lots to do, so I'm going to stop here. I really, really want to hear from you again soon, OK?

Take care,
Ed

WRITING TIP: an informal email

- Start your email by saying hello: *Hi, Hey, … .*
- First, ask how your friend is.
- Then say what you're writing about and why.
- Finish with a friendly expression.
- Use informal language. Imagine you are talking to your friend and use:
  - short sentences and contracted forms
  - direct questions
  - a friendly/informal style.

5 **PLAN** You are going to write an email to an English-speaking friend. Your friend wants to know about your weekend routine. Write a plan using the Writing tip to help you.

_____
_____
_____
_____

6 **PRODUCE** Write your email using informal language in 150–200 words. Use your plan from Exercise 5.

LISTENING

1 🔊 2.03 Listen to the three conversations. Match them with the correct photos. There is one photo you don't need.

A ☐

B ☐

C ☐

D ☐

2 🔊 2.03 Listen again. Circle the correct answers.

1 What is Kate asking to do?
   A go home because she feels ill
   B have extra time to finish some work
   C miss the biology lesson on Friday
2 Why won't Lily lend Max her skateboard?
   A She's going to use it later.
   B She's doesn't trust Max to look after it.
   C She doesn't know where it is.
3 What does the boy want to do?
   A stay out later than usual
   B have a party at home
   C invite Freddie to stay

DIALOGUE

3 🔊 2.04 Put the conversations in the correct order. Then listen and check.

1
1	Girl	Excuse me. Is it OK if I try this shirt on?
☐	Girl	Really? OK. Can I take a size 8, too?
☐	Girl	OK, thanks.
☐	Girl	I think so. This is a size 10.
☐	Woman	Well, I think it might be too big for you.
☐	Woman	Of course you can. Here's a size 8. OK. Tell me when you're finished.
☐	Woman	Of course. Have you got the right size?

2
1	Milo	Will, can I ask you something?
☐	Milo	Great, thanks. Oh – another thing.
☐	Milo	Well, I forgot to charge my mobile phone. Can I take yours?
☐	Milo	I understand. Thanks anyway.
☐	Milo	Can I borrow your jeans tonight – you know, the white ones?
☐	Will	Sure. What is it?
☐	Will	Sorry, no way! My phone goes with me everywhere.
☐	Will	Yeah, go ahead. I'm not wearing them.
☐	Will	Another thing? What is it?

Train to TH!NK

Thinking about texts

4 Read the text about Lucy on page 22 again. Circle the correct answers.

1 Where *wouldn't* you find this text?
   A in a magazine
   B on a website
   C in a newspaper
   D in a homework book
2 What is the main purpose of the text?
   A to complain about bad schools
   B to describe a personal experience
   C to entertain the reader
   D to persuade readers not to change schools
3 What is the best title for the text?
   A What I learned in a school that I didn't like
   B My first day at school
   C Good and bad teachers
   D How to do well at a new school

B1 Preliminary for Schools

READING
Part 4: Gapped text

1 Five sentences have been removed from the text below. For each question, choose the correct answer. There are three extra sentences which you do not need to use.

The Global Teacher Prize

There are plenty of prizes for good students but now there is an award for the best teacher in the world. **1**_____ It aims to celebrate the work of teachers and recognise how important their work is. The organisers believe that good teachers can change the lives of their students for the better.

The award started in 2015. It is open to all teachers in every country of the world. In its first year, over 5,000 teachers from 127 countries took part. So far, the winners have come from the US, Palestine, Canada, the UK and Kenya. **2**_____ Every year the winner receives one million dollars to spend on education in their community.

The 2019 winner was a teacher called Peter Tabichi. He teaches in a village school in a semi-desert area of Kenya. His class, like all the classes in his school, has over 50 students in it. Most of his students are from very poor families and the school has hardly got any classroom furniture and very little equipment. **3**_____ Despite these problems, this teacher started a 'talent club' to help his students. Some of them have even taken part in international science competitions. He also gives extra help to students with difficulties and regularly meets their families. **4**_____ In only three years, Tabichi's class has grown from 200 to 400 students.

5_____ In fact, the chosen teachers are always very proud of their success. However, they know they are only there because of their students. For a small school in a poor area, the prize money can make a huge difference to the school, its present and future students, as well as the whole local community.

A It only has one computer and a very slow internet connection.

B Tabichi was very excited to be chosen as the winner.

C The headteacher of the school was very proud.

D This new prize is called the Global Teacher Prize.

E Ten students from the school went to university last year.

F As a result, more teenagers have started going to the school.

G The students only enjoy some of the lessons at the school.

H The subjects they teach are varied too, and include Maths, English and Art.

EXAM GUIDE: READING: PART 4

In B1 Preliminary for Schools Reading Part 4, you read a text with five gaps. You have to choose the missing five sentences from eight options.

- Read the text quickly for general understanding.
- Look at the sentences. Remember there are three extra sentences.
- Read the sentences <u>before</u> and <u>after</u> each gap.
- Choose a sentence from A–H and try it in the gap.
- Re-read to check if the new sentence makes sense with the information surrounding the gap.
- Re-read the text with all the completed gaps to make sure the whole text makes sense.

CONSOLIDATION

🎧 LISTENING

1 🔊 **2.05** Listen and (circle) the correct option: A, B or C.

1 When did Freya start at the school?
   A Wednesday
   B Friday
   C Thursday
2 What is Freya's favourite subject?
   A Science
   B Art
   C Spanish
3 Where does Aron offer to take Freya?
   A the library
   B the school café
   C the school gym

2 🔊 **2.05** Listen again and answer the questions.

0 How many days has Freya been at the school?
   four days
1 How does it compare to her old school?
   _____
2 Who is her favourite teacher? What does he teach?
   _____
3 Why is Freya good at Spanish?
   _____
4 Where is the library?
   _____

Ⓖ GRAMMAR

3 Correct the sentences.

0 I've been at the County High School since five years.
   I've been at the County High School for five years.
1 It's a biggest school in our city.
   _____
2 I've yet taken some important exams.
   _____
3 But I haven't got the results already.
   _____
4 I've yet decided what I want to study at university.
   _____
5 I want to study the Spanish.
   _____
6 Bella is the my best friend at school.
   _____

🔤 VOCABULARY

4 Match the sentences.

0 He's so brave. **d**
1 Your sister's so laid-back. ☐
2 Have you heard Jim play the trumpet? ☐
3 My grandma's so active. ☐
4 Ethan's the most positive person I know. ☐
5 Ms Harrington's really cheerful. ☐

a Yes. He's so talented!
b She's always doing something.
c He can see the good in absolutely everything.
d He isn't scared of anything.
e She's always got a big smile on her face.
f Does she ever get angry?

5 Write the subjects these students are studying.

0 Oh, no! I've got paint all over my shirt.
Art

1 I love acting in front of the rest of my class. It's so much fun.
_____

2 The capital of Italy is … is … Oh, what is it?
_____

3 Twelve percent of 200 is 24, isn't it?
_____

4 I like learning about the past, but why do we have to learn all those dates?
_____

5 I can't believe it. I've forgotten my tennis racket.
_____

6 I love doing these experiments. It's so much fun.
_____

7 We're practising a song for the end-of-year concert.
_____

UNITS 1 & 2

DIALOGUE

6 🔊 2.06 **Complete the conversation with the phrases in the list. Then listen and check.**

> Are you sure? | I'll help you if you want.
> I've decided | just | Let's face it
> Of course you can. | That's a great idea.
> that sort of thing. | You know what?

Ben ⁰<u>I've decided</u> to start a homework club.
Chloe A what?
Ben A homework club. It's so we can get together, discuss lessons, help each other with our homework, ¹_____
Chloe ² _____ Can I be in it?
Ben ³ _____ I want you to be in it!
Chloe ⁴ _____ I could text some people.
Ben OK. Who are you thinking of?
Chloe What about David?
Ben David? ⁵ _____ He's way too smart. He doesn't need our help. ⁶ _____ , he won't want to join.
Chloe Yes, but he doesn't have many friends. Maybe he'd like to join to make friends.
Ben ⁷ _____ You might ⁸ _____ be right.
Chloe I might.
Ben In fact, it's perfect. We help him make friends and he helps us with our homework. Chloe, you're a genius!

📖 READING

7 Read the text. Mark the sentences T (true) or F (false).

0 Mrs Millington started teaching 15 years ago. **F**
1 Although she's a good teacher, she needs a bit more experience. ☐
2 Students are well behaved in her lessons. ☐
3 She really loves the subject she teaches. ☐
4 She worked for a travel company before she became a teacher. ☐
5 She has worked in different countries round the world. ☐
6 One reason she changed jobs is because she wanted to work near home. ☐
7 Although she's a brilliant teacher, she's sometimes a bit unfriendly. ☐

My Science teacher, Mrs Millington, is a really amazing person.

She's in her forties, but she's only been a teacher for five years. You'd never know she hasn't got very much experience because she's excellent in the classroom. She never has any trouble from students because her lessons are so interesting that everyone just listens to everything she says. She's really enthusiastic about Science and knows how to make her lessons interesting.

Before she was a teacher, she spent more than 20 years working as a research scientist. She worked at a lab in Australia for two years. She also took part in some international experiments, so she's travelled a lot. She brings all these experiences into the classroom and she explains why Science is so important in the real world. She loved her job, but she got tired of travelling so much and she wanted to work regular hours. That's when she made the decision to become a teacher. It seemed to be the perfect opportunity to finally follow her dream. I'm so happy she did. She's such a warm and positive person that when you're in her lessons, you don't even feel you're at school.

✏️ WRITING

8 Research a person who is famous for doing charity work. Write a paragraph (about 150–200 words) about him or her. Include the following information:

- who the person is
- what charity work he/she does
- what makes him/her so special

3 ON THE SCREEN

GRAMMAR
Comparative and superlative adjectives (review) → SB p.32

1  Complete the table.

Adjective	Comparative	Superlative
big	bigger	0 _the biggest_
1 _____	taller	2 _____
3 _____	4 _____	the prettiest
expensive	5 _____	6 _____
7 _____	more interesting	8 _____
9 _____	10 _____	the most difficult
good	11 _____	12 _____
13 _____	worse	14 _____

2 ★★★ Complete the text with the correct form of the adjectives.

I've just seen *First Man* and I can say that it's
⁰ ____the most amazing____ (amazing) film I've ever seen. It's brilliant. The special effects are incredible. They're ¹_____ (realistic) than any other special effects I've seen. You feel like you're in space with the actors. I really like space films. I thought *Gravity* was really exciting, but *First Man* is even ²_____ (exciting). Ryan Gosling and Claire Foy are two of ³_____ (professional) actors in Hollywood and they do some of the ⁴_____ (good) work of their careers in this film. Of course, the fact that Ryan Gosling is ⁵_____ (handsome) man in the world helps! The film is on at the Odeon until Friday. Tickets are ⁶_____ (cheap) in the afternoon than in the evening and the cinema is ⁷_____ (empty) then, too. But whatever you do, don't miss it!

PRONUNCIATION
Words ending with schwa /ə/
Go to page 118. 🎧

(not) as … as comparatives → SB p.32

3 ★☆☆ Look at the information about two cinemas. Mark the sentences T (true) or F (false).

Adjective	The Roxy	The Gate
price	£12	£10
number of seats	230	170
friendly staff	*	***
age of building	1920	2010
distance from your house	1.2 km	0.7 km
overall experience	***	***

0 The Roxy is more expensive than the Gate. **T**
1 The Roxy is smaller than the Gate. ☐
2 The Gate isn't as friendly as the Roxy. ☐
3 The Gate is older than the Roxy. ☐
4 The Roxy isn't as close as the Gate. ☐
5 The Roxy isn't as good as the Gate. ☐

4 ★★☆ Complete the sentences about the cinemas with the correct form of *be*, *(not) as … as* and the adjectives.

0 The Roxy ___isn't as cheap as___ (cheap) the Gate.
1 The Roxy _____ (friendly) the Gate.
2 The Gate _____ (big) the Roxy.
3 The Roxy _____ (modern) the Gate.
4 The Gate _____ (far) the Roxy.
5 The Gate _____ (good) the Roxy.

5 ★★★ Complete the second sentence so that it means the same as the first. Use no more than three words.

0 There has never been a film series as good as *Star Wars*.
  Star Wars is the ____the best____ film series ever.
1 The film is disappointing compared to the book.
  The film isn't _____ the book.
2 *Avengers: Endgame* is the most successful film of all time.
  No film has been _____ *Avengers: Endgame*.
3 *Toy Story 4* is funnier than *Toy Story 3*.
  Toy Story 3 _____ as *Toy Story 4*.
4 *Spider-Man* and *Superman* are equally bad.
  Spider-Man is _____ *Superman*.

Making a comparison stronger or weaker

→ SB p.33

6 ★★☆ Look at the pictures. Mark the sentences ✗ (not true), ✓ (true) or ✓✓ (the best description).

0

Owen   Callum

- A Callum is taller than his brother. ✓
- B Callum is a lot taller than his brother. ✓✓
- C Callum isn't as tall as his brother. ✗

1

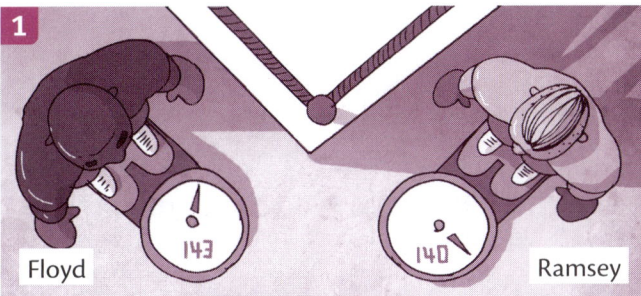
Floyd 143   140 Ramsey

- A Floyd is heavier than Ramsey. ☐
- B Floyd isn't as heavy as Ramsey. ☐
- C Floyd is a bit heavier than Ramsey. ☐

2

A £15   B £150

- A B isn't as expensive as A. ☐
- B B is much more expensive than A. ☐
- C A is cheaper than B. ☐

3

Ellie 99%   Ruby 25%

- A Ruby's test was far worse than Ellie's. ☐
- B Ellie's test was better than Ruby's. ☐
- C Ellie's test wasn't as good as Ruby's. ☐

7 ★★★ Complete the sentences so that they are true for you. Use *a lot*, *much*, *far*, *a little* and *a bit*.

0 I __am much shorter than__ my best friend.
1 Maths _____ English.
2 Playing sports _____ playing video games.
3 Chocolate _____ apples.
4 Winter _____ summer.
5 Rabbits _____ goldfish.

Adverbs and comparative adverbs

→ SB p.34

8 ★☆☆ Mark the underlined words ADJ (adjective) or ADV (adverb).

0 He plays football <u>worse</u> than I do. __ADV__
1 Her German is <u>better</u> than mine. _____
2 He speaks <u>more clearly</u> than you. _____
3 You walk <u>more quickly</u> than me. _____
4 It's raining a lot <u>harder</u> today. _____

9 ★★☆ Complete the sentences with the correct form of the words in brackets.

'Why can't you be more like your cousin Kyle?' my mum always says.

0 He talks to adults __more politely__ (polite) than you.
1 He studies _____ (hard) and always does _____ (good) than you at school.
2 His bedroom is _____ (tidy) than yours.
3 He runs _____ (quick) than you.
4 He writes _____ (careful) than you.
5 He treats me _____ (kind) than you.

GET IT RIGHT!
Comparatives and superlatives

Learners often incorrectly use *better* instead of *best* and *last* instead of *latest*.

✓ Friday is the **best** day of the week.
✗ Friday is the ~~better~~ day of the week.
✓ I use the internet to get the **latest** news.
✗ I use the internet to get the ~~last~~ news.

Circle the correct words.

0 This cinema always shows the *last* / (*latest*) films.
1 I don't think pizzas are *best* / *better* than hamburgers.
2 Was it the *last* / *latest* one left in the shop?
3 It was one of the *best* / *better* days of my life!
4 He likes to wear the *last* / *latest* fashion.
5 It's the *best* / *better* restaurant I know.

VOCABULARY
Types of films

→ SB p.32

1 ⭐⭐☆ Read the clues and complete the crossword. Who is the mystery film character?

This type of film …
0 is often set in the future or in space.
1 is always exciting, with lots of car chases, explosions and special effects.
2 makes you laugh.
3 is exciting and a bit scary at times, too.
4 is always scary.
5 tells you about the real world.
6 is popular with children.
7 involves a love story and some laughs.

0 S C I F I

2 ⭐⭐☆ Read the quotations. Write the type of film you think they come from.

0 'Quick! We've got 60 seconds to stop the bomb from exploding!' _action film_
1 'Deep in the caves of Colombia lives a bird that few people have ever seen.' _____
2 'The next Mars shuttle leaves at 15.00. Meet me at the space station.' _____
3 'Come on, Barney Bear. We've got a problem to solve.' _____
4 'I love you, Brad. I've always loved you. You're just too proud to know it!' _____
5 'Did you see its face? I tell you – that thing isn't human!' _____
6 'It was a rainy Thursday evening in New York – the perfect time for a murder.' _____
7 'Why would I want to be a member of a club that would have me as a member?' _____

Types of TV programmes → SB p.35

3 ⭐⭐☆ Put the letters in order to make types of TV programmes.

0 thac hows — _chat show_
1 swen — _____
2 elyairt ohws — _____
3 madra eiress — _____
4 nocrato — _____
5 mage wohs — _____
6 cimtos — _____
7 opsa proae — _____
8 roptss magroprem — _____
9 latent whos — _____

4 ⭐⭐⭐ Write the types of TV programmes.

WHAT'S ON?

0 'Tonight there's live action from Anfield, where Liverpool play Manchester City.'
sports programme
1 'Who will win the final of *The It Factor*: Jasmine and her amazing dog Scooby or the boy band Zap?' _____
2 'On the sofa tonight, answering Paula Nightingale's questions, is actor Lewis James.' _____
3 'Tonight on *Win It Or Lose It*, three couples compete for the top prize of £50,000.' _____
4 'Catch up on today's stories from the UK and around the world. Followed by the weather.' _____
5 'Minnie has a chance to make things right between Josie and James, but will she take it?' _____

WordWise: Expressions with *get* → SB p.33

5 ⭐☆☆ Complete the sentences.

0 The show doesn't finish until 11 pm, so I don't think we'll get h_ome_ before midnight.
1 I don't know how to get t_____ , so I need to look at the map.
2 Lee got very a_____ about the football match. They lost again.
3 You look really thirsty. I'll get you a d_____ .
4 After resting and taking his medicine for a week, he got b_____ .
5 It's an exciting film. You won't get b_____ .

UNIT 3 ON THE SCREEN

REFERENCE

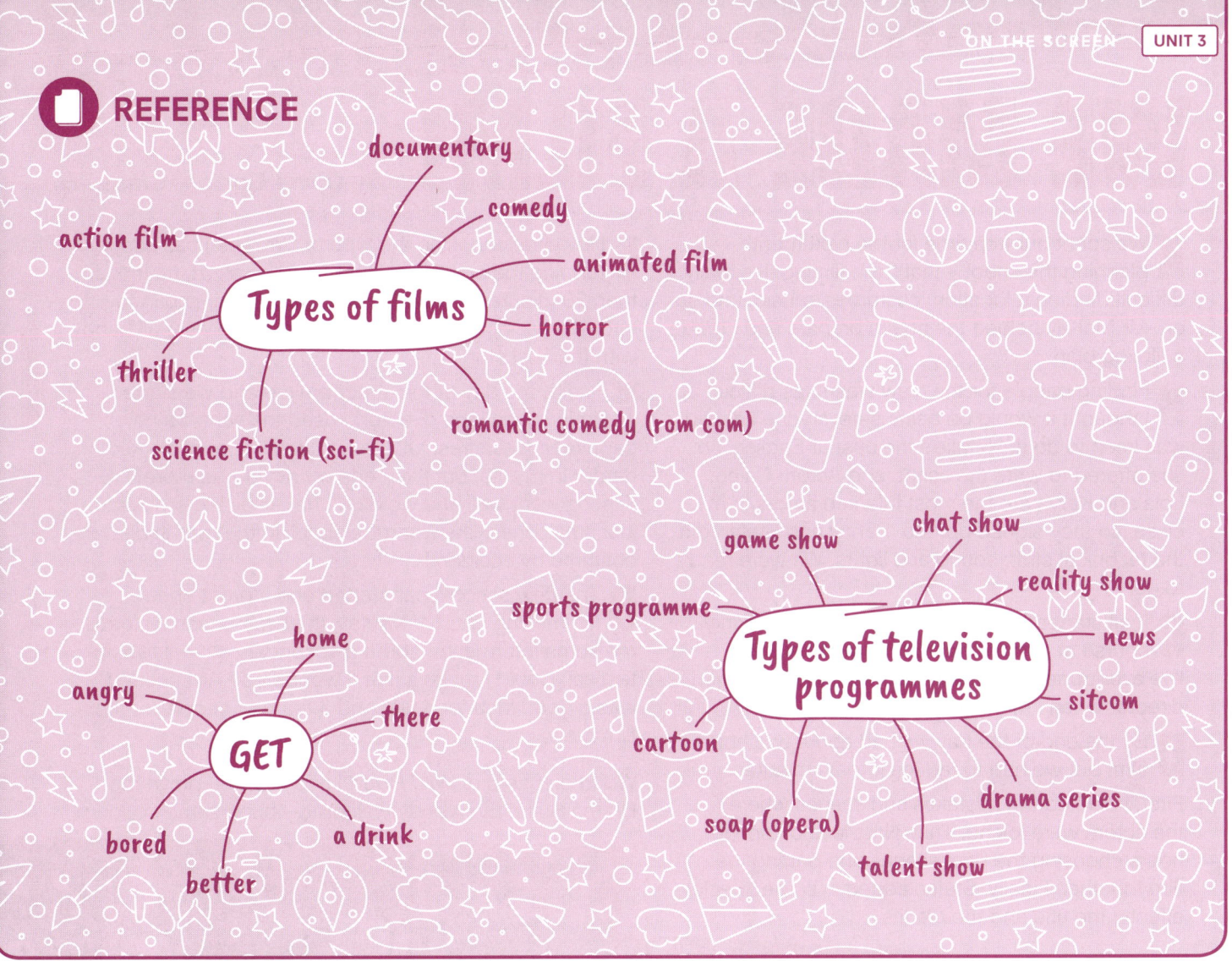

VOCABULARY EXTRA

1 Write the words in the correct column.

adventure | cooking | superhero | travel | ~~western~~

Film types	Types of TV programmes
western film	_____ show
_____ film	_____ show
_____ film	

2 Write the name of a film or TV programme as an example of each one.

0 western   _The Magnificent Seven_
1 travel   _____
2 superhero   _____
3 cooking   _____
4 adventure   _____

3 Which types of films and types of TV programmes do you like? Write your top three lists for each.

Favourite film types
1 _____
2 _____
3 _____

Favourite types of TV programmes
1 _____
2 _____
3 _____

WE MADE A FILM!

By Olivia Garton, Class 4B

A We spent our free time for the next month planning the shoot – that's the filming. It's really difficult: finding a location, costumes, music, and so on. Mr McKay helped the actors prepare and I made a filming plan.

B Finding people for the crew wasn't as difficult as I thought it would be because everyone I asked was keen to do it. Natalie's the best at English, so she offered to write the script, and Aaron, Caleb, Lola and Katya are the most talented actors in my class, so they signed up, too. Penny and Stefan did the technical stuff: sound and lights. We were ready to go!

C It all started last year when I did a filmmaking course at summer camp. It's the best thing I've ever done and I decided I'm going to be a film director when I'm older!

D By the end of the day we had about two hours of film, but we had to reduce it to 20 minutes. First, I deleted the mistakes and scenes where the actors were joking. Then Natalie and I spent hours choosing the best scenes and putting the film together. Finally, Stefan added in some special effects, the title and the credits.

E However, choosing the type of film wasn't as easy as forming the crew! The film had to be short, no longer than 20 minutes. We had lots of great ideas and in the end, we decided on an original drama. We were all happy with the final story.

F Finally, the day of the shoot arrived and we started filming. I was the director! I used the school's new camera. It was stressful! I don't think I've ever worked harder in my life, but I've certainly never had more fun. Filming went well and we didn't have any big problems – just small ones, like when Caleb fell in the river in his costume by accident!

G The new school year started and I forgot about filmmaking until Mr McKay, the Drama teacher, gave me some information about a secondary school film festival. Could I make a film, I wondered? All I needed was a good idea for a film and a team of people for the film crew.

World premiere of *Wild River*! Friday at 4.30 pm in the Drama Suite. Everybody welcome – bring some popcorn!

READING

1 Read the article. Put the paragraphs in order.

1 _C_   3 ___   5 ___   7 ___
2 ___   4 ___   6 ___

2 Read the article again. Mark the sentences T (true) or F (false). Correct the false information.

0 Olivia wants to be a script writer when she is older. [F]
  She wants to be a film director.

1 One of Olivia's teachers asked her to make a film. [ ]
  _____

2 Olivia couldn't find the right people for the film. [ ]
  _____

3 It was more difficult to choose the type of film than to form the film crew. [ ]
  _____

4 There was a lot of preparation to do before filming. [ ]
  _____

5 The day of filming was the busiest day in Olivia's life. [ ]
  _____

6 They deleted the most exciting scenes from the film. [ ]
  _____

3 **CRITICAL THINKING** Read the questions and (circle) the best answers. Then explain why.

1 Did Olivia and her classmates work together well?
  A no
  B yes
  C We can't know the answer to this.
  Because …

2 Olivia wrote this article to
  A describe a new experience.
  B encourage students to make films.
  C explain how to make a film.
  Because …

DEVELOPING Writing

ON THE SCREEN UNIT 3

A for and against essay

1 **INPUT** Read the essay quickly. Does the writer agree with the title?

_____

2 Read the essay again. Do you agree with the writer? Think of one additional argument to support *your* opinion.

_____
_____

3 **ANALYSE** Complete the sentences with the letters A–D.

1 Paragraph _____ agrees with the essay title.
2 Paragraph _____ disagrees with the essay title.
3 Paragraph _____ gives the writer's opinion.
4 Paragraph _____ is a general introduction to the topic.

4 The underlined words in the essay are linking words. Put these linking words in groups of the same meaning.

however | in addition | in conclusion
in my opinion | moreover | on the other hand
personally | to sum up | what's more

Finally	Also
1	1
2	2
	3
But	**I think**
1	1
2	2

'Going to the cinema is a waste of time.' Discuss.

A Everyone loves going to the cinema. <u>However</u>, we can watch films at home on television, online or on DVD. So, is going to the cinema a waste of time?

B A visit to the cinema can be expensive. Tickets aren't cheap and snacks cost a lot. Streaming a film or buying a DVD is cheaper and you can watch it as many times as you like. Watching a film on a widescreen television with digital audio, is nearly as good as being in a cinema. <u>Moreover</u>, what's more fun than inviting your friends, making popcorn and having a film night at home?

C <u>On the other hand</u>, a trip to the cinema is an enjoyable way to spend time with friends. <u>What's more</u>, modern cinemas offer you an amazing experience: comfortable seats, huge screens and excellent sound systems. You get so involved in the film that you feel like you're part of it!

D <u>To sum up</u>, I think going to the cinema is a good way to spend time. For me, it's definitely the best way to enjoy a film. <u>Personally</u>, I don't go to the cinema very often, so when I do, it's really special.

WRITING TIP: a for and against essay

- Organise your essay into paragraphs:
  1 Introduce the topic in general
  2 Agree with the title
  3 Disagree with the title
  4 Conclusion with your opinion
- Use linking words to connect your ideas.
- Use formal language.

5 **PLAN** You are going to write a for and against essay with the title: 'Watching television is a waste of time.' Think of some ideas for and against the title, then write a plan. Use the Writing tip to help you.

6 **PRODUCE** Write your essay in about 200 words. Use your plan from Exercise 5.

🎧 LISTENING

1 🔊 3.03 **Listen to the four conversations. Match them with the correct photos.**

A

C

B

D

2 🔊 3.03 **Listen again and answer the questions.**

0 Why does the man change his mind about getting some help?
Because he drops the TV and wants help to clear it up.

1 Why can't the man open the web page?
_____

2 What DVD does the shop assistant recommend?
_____

3 Why won't the TV work?
_____

DIALOGUE

3 🔊 3.04 **Put the words in order to make requests and offers. Then listen and check.**

Offers

0 any / help / you / do / need
Do you need any help? ?

1 help / I / you / can
_____ ?

2 OK / everything / is
_____ ?

Requests

3 something / you / help / could / with / me
_____ ?

4 hand / lend / you / me / can / a
_____ ?

5 few / you / minutes / got / have / a
_____ ?

4 Match the offers and requests in Exercise 3 with the replies. Sometimes there is more than one correct answer.

a No, I'm all right. ☐
b Sure – what is it? ☐
c I do, actually. 0
d Not really. I can't get the TV to work. ☐
e Of course I can. ☐
f Sure. Now, let me see. ☐

5 Write a short conversation about the picture.

PHRASES FOR FLUENCY → SB p.36

6 🔊 3.05 **Put the conversation in the correct order. Then listen and check.**

☐ Phoebe   I always knew I would be. In fact, I had a dream about it when I was a little girl.
☐ Phoebe   Well, this one did!
1 Phoebe   Guess what? I've got a part in a soap opera!
☐ Phoebe   I am. Have a look. It's a letter from the TV company.
☐ Oscar   What? You aren't serious!
☐ Oscar   Oh, come on! Dreams don't mean anything.
☐ Oscar   Wow! It's true! Looks like you're going to be famous after all.

7 🔊 3.06 **Complete the conversations with the phrases in the list. Then listen and check.**

after all | come on | ~~Guess what~~ | have a look
In fact | Looks like

Conversation 1

A ⁰ *Guess what* ? I won the singing competition.
B Oh, ¹_____ ! You aren't a good singer.
²_____ , you're terrible!
A You're just jealous.

Conversation 2

A So did you fail the test?
B No, I got 95 percent!
A What?!
B Here – ³_____ if you don't believe me.
A It's true!
B ⁴_____ I'm pretty clever
⁵_____ !

B1 Preliminary for Schools

LISTENING
Part 2: 3-option multiple choice

1 🔊 3.07 **For each question, choose the correct answer.**

  1 You will hear two friends talking about a film. What did the girl think of the film?
    A It was really good.
    B She enjoyed parts of it.
    C She disliked the music.

  2 You will hear a girl talking about an experience. What was it?
    A a concert
    B a song contest
    C a talent show

  3 You will hear two friends talking about a TV programme. What type of programme was it?
    A a soap opera
    B a reality show
    C a sports programme

  4 You will hear a boy talking about a book. How did he feel about it?
    A amazed
    B bored
    C scared

  5 You will hear part of a radio programme. What type of programme is it?
    A a chat show
    B the news
    C a sports report

  6 You will hear two friends making plans. What do they decide to do?
    A go to the cinema
    B go to a restaurant
    C watch films at home

EXAM GUIDE: LISTENING PART 2

In B1 Preliminary for Schools Listening Part 2, you listen to six dialogues and answer questions by choosing one answer from three options. The questions are generally about opinions and attitudes, or a general question about the situation, not details or facts.
- Before you listen, read the questions and look at the options. This will give you a general idea about what you're going to hear.
- The first time you listen, choose an answer or eliminate an option you are sure is wrong.
- The second time you listen, make a final choice.

4 ONLINE LIFE

GRAMMAR
Indefinite pronouns (everyone, no one, someone, etc.) → SB p.40

1 ★☆☆ Circle the correct words.

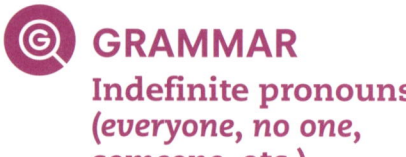

The new XR4 has landed!

It's ⁰(everything)/ something you could want in a tablet and more.

It's so simple that ¹no one / anyone can use it, but if there's ²everything / anything you don't understand, our technical team is ready to help you.

Its amazing network coverage means you have internet access ³everywhere / somewhere you go.

If there's ⁴something / nothing you need to remember or somewhere you need to be, the alarm system will make sure you don't forget.

If you order before Christmas, there's ⁵nothing / everything to pay until March.

The new XR4 – ⁶someone / no one should leave home without it!

2 ★★☆ Complete the sentences with the words in the list.

> ~~anyone~~ | anything | anywhere | everyone
> no one | nowhere | something | somewhere

0 This party's boring. I don't know ____anyone____ .
1 I'm sure I've seen that man _____ before, but I can't remember when.
2 Ava's really enjoying her new school. _____ has been so friendly to her.
3 There are no seat numbers in this cinema – you can sit _____ you like.
4 It wasn't me. I didn't do _____ , I promise!
5 Have you spoken to Connor? There's _____ he wants to tell you.
6 There are no trees here, so there's _____ to hide from the sun.
7 It's a secret. Tell _____ !

3 ★★★ Complete the second sentence so that it means the same as the first. Use no more than three words.

0 Leah is really popular. ____Everyone____ likes Leah.
1 I'm really bored. There's _____ do.
2 Are you hungry? Do you want _____ eat?
3 There's danger everywhere. _____ safe.
4 The cat has disappeared. I can't find _____ .
5 He's following me. He's _____ I go.

all / some / none / any of them → SB p.41

4 ★☆☆ Match the parts of the sentences.

0 We've got hundreds of DVDs, but — c
1 I've got a lot of pens, but
2 There were ten teams in the competition, but
3 Twenty students took the final test and
4 The cats have already eaten, so

a all of them passed.
b don't give any of them more food.
c we don't watch any of them now.
d none of them played very well.
e I don't think any of them work.

5 ★★☆ Complete the sentences with *all*, *some*, *any* or *none*.

0 I've got lots of friends, but ____none____ of them remembered my birthday.
1 We like most of his films, but _____ of them are awful.
2 They can't say which game they like best. They love _____ of them.
3 I don't like _____ of these songs. They're all terrible!
4 He's got 2,000 stamps. _____ of them are very rare.
5 Three buses came, but _____ of them were full.

PRONUNCIATION
The short /ʌ/ vowel sound
Go to page 119. 🎧

should(n't), had better, ought to → SB p.43

6 ★☆☆ Match the sentences with the pictures.

0 You should buy it. It looks good on you. **C**
1 We ought to leave now. It's going to rain. ☐
2 You'd better see a doctor about that. ☐
3 There's a lot to do. We ought to start now. ☐
4 You shouldn't touch those. They might be hot. ☐
5 We'd better hide – quick! ☐

UNIT 4 — ONLINE LIFE

7 ★★☆ Write advice with the phrases in the list.

activate flight mode on your tablet | attach it as a file | ~~change to a different provider~~ | choose a different password | delete it | go online and find it cheaper | open it | upload it onto your blog

0 My phone never has a signal.
   You'd better change to a different provider.
1 I don't know who this email is from and it's got a strange-looking attachment.
   _____
2 This email's got lots of important information in it.
   _____
3 I like this backpack, but it's £50. That's expensive!
   _____
4 The plane's about to take off.
   _____
5 This photo's really embarrassing. I don't want anyone to see it.
   _____
6 I need to send this photo to Nico.
   _____
7 This web page contains loads of my personal details.
   _____

GET IT RIGHT!

all vs. everyone

Learners sometimes confuse *all* and *everyone*.

***Everyone* is a pronoun that refers to a group of people.**

✓ In the cinema we bought popcorn for **everyone**.
✗ In the cinema we bought popcorn for ~~all~~.

***All* is used to modify a noun or pronoun.**

✓ My family have **all** got mobile phones.
✗ My family have ~~everyone~~ got mobile phones.

Complete the sentences with *everyone* or *all*.

0 I hope ___everyone___ likes the cake I've made.
1 My friends have _____ got jobs.
2 There should be enough lemonade for us _____ to have some.
3 Has _____ finished their work?
4 Does _____ that you know have a laptop?
5 I would like to introduce myself to _____ members personally.
6 After that, _____ of us got a ball and tried to throw it as far as possible.

VOCABULARY
IT terms
→ SB p.40

1 ★★☆ Match the parts of the sentences.

0 Before take-off, please activate — **d**
1 Don't open that
2 I haven't got any network
3 Our holiday is almost over and I haven't uploaded
4 If you can't buy it in the shops, go
5 To open that file, you need to install

a any photos to Instagram yet.
b coverage, so I can't make a call.
c this program first.
d flight mode on your mobile devices.
e attachment. It could have a virus.
f online and buy it.

2 ★★☆ Complete the sentences with an appropriate verb.

8 STEPS TO ONLINE SECURITY

0 Never ___open___ an attachment if you don't know where it's come from.
1 Think twice before you _____ a message on social media.
2 Don't _____ photos of people onto social media sites without asking them.
3 Be careful if you _____ in passwords in a public place.
4 Always _____ emails that you don't want other people to read.
5 Don't _____ apps from online stores you've never heard of.
6 Don't _____ any files from websites you don't know.
7 Check what a program is before you _____ it onto your laptop.

3 ★★★ Complete the sentences.

1 That's a great photo. You should u_pload_ it to your s_____ m_____ pages.
2 If you like making music, you should b_____ this a_____. It helps you mix different songs.
3 I forgot to a_____ the f_____ before I sent the email.
4 I deleted the m_____ without reading it.
5 You need to enter your email address and then k_____ in your p_____.
6 It takes ages to d_____ big files.

Language for giving advice
→ SB p.43

4 ★☆☆ Complete the sentences with *advise* or *advice*.

0 Don't take his ___advice___. He doesn't know what he's talking about.
1 Our teachers always _____ us not to leave our homework until the last minute.
2 I must _____ you not to call her after 8 pm.
3 My mum always gives me good _____ .

5 ★☆☆ Circle the correct answers.

The most useful advice I ever got was from my grandfather. He said: 'Never take ⁰ ___advice___ from anyone.' But I was only 18 and didn't know how useful it was, so I ¹_____ his advice and let people give me advice ²_____ everything. I ³_____ advice on what to wear and what to eat. My bank manager advised ⁴_____ save my money; friends advised me to spend it. My mother advised me to marry young; my father advised me ⁵_____ it. I got so much advice ⁶_____ so many people that I didn't know which advice to ⁷_____ and which advice to ignore. My grandfather was right. Now I've stopped ⁸_____ advice and life is much simpler!

0 **A** advice   B advise   C advisable
1 A took   B followed C ignored
2 A about   B in   C over
3 A had got   B got   C had
4 A to me   B me to   C me for
5 A for   B against   C on
6 A from   B for   C with
7 A get   B offer   C follow
8 A taking   B giving   C ignoring

6 ★★☆ Answer the questions for you.

1 What are you good at giving advice about?
_____
_____
2 What's the worst advice you've ever had?
_____
_____
3 Whose advice do you always follow and why?
_____
_____
4 Are you good at taking advice? Why / Why not?
_____
_____
5 Do you like giving advice? Why / Why not?
_____
_____

7 ★★★ Write about the best advice you've ever had (about 50 words). Who gave it to you and why was it good advice?

UNIT 4 — ONLINE LIFE

REFERENCE

IT terms
- to install a program
- to upload a photo
- to delete a message
- to buy an app
- to attach a file
- to have network coverage
- to activate flight mode
- to download a file
- to open an attachment
- to key in your password

LANGUAGE FOR GIVING ADVICE

bad / good / practical / useful advice	to ignore (someone's) advice
advice about (something)	advisable
to ask for / get advice from (someone)	to advise (someone) (to do something)
to give / offer (somebody) advice	to advise against (something)
to take / follow (someone's) advice	

VOCABULARY EXTRA

1 Match the words.

0 click on — c
1 hash
2 like
3 web
4 video
5 save

a tag
b browser
c a link
d a file
e a photo
f call

2 Complete the sentences with the words in the list.

file | hashtag | liked | link | video call | web browser

0 Lois saved the _____file_____ and shut down the laptop.
1 My grandma lives really far away, but we _____ her every week so she can see our faces!
2 Which _____ do you use for research?
3 So, you open the page … right, then click on the _____ and a new window opens.
4 That was a brilliant photo! I _____ it and shared it with all my friends.
5 Send your comments to # (_____) special days.

39

DIGITAL EXPERTS NEEDED!

Parents and grandparents always know who to ask when they have problems with their phones or digital gadgets – the nearest teenager, of course! So various organisations around the country have had the brilliant idea of connecting teenage digital experts to people in need of help with technology. What's happening in your area?

Comments   (3) replies

A Phoebe and Logan

We're members of our school's Good Citizens project. So we spend every Wednesday afternoon at a club for senior citizens – that means older people who don't work anymore. They bring along their laptops, tablets and phones to ask us for advice on how to use them. It's a simple idea and works really well! Most of their questions are about Skype and downloading photos and videos. These are great ways for people to keep in touch with family and friends living far away. I think what we do is a sort of exchange: they learn some digital skills from us and we learn more about life from talking to them!

B Noemi

I'm in the SOS Tech group at my youth club. There are about ten of us and we go to the community centre every Saturday morning to teach people how to use their digital gadgets. All sorts of people come for help – it's not only older people that don't feel confident about using computers. The other day, I showed a woman how to do her shopping online because she couldn't drive after an operation on her leg. Another man came in with a new tablet. He decided he'd better learn to use it because he didn't want to be left behind! What do I get out of it? Well, I've discovered that I enjoy explaining things to people, so I'm thinking about becoming a teacher!

C Louis

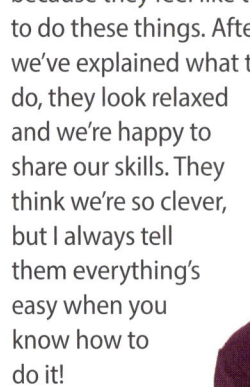

You should see the computer room in our public library on a Tuesday evening! It's one of the busiest places in town. People can come in and ask for advice about technology. I'm on the team of experts and we try to help everyone. If you haven't got access to a computer these days, life can be difficult. We help people find information online, show them how to fill in online forms, how to use job sites, things like that. At first, people are often embarrassed because they feel like they should know how to do these things. After we've explained what to do, they look relaxed and we're happy to share our skills. They think we're so clever, but I always tell them everything's easy when you know how to do it!

READING

1 Read the posts. Tick (✓) the best title.

A Sharing your digital skills ☐
B The trouble with technology ☐
C Teens teach IT at school ☐

2 Read the texts again. Write A, B or C to answer the questions.

Which student or students …

0 has discovered something they enjoy? **B**
1 helps people who sometimes feel embarrassed? ☐
2 gives advice to elderly people? ☐
3 helps people keep in contact online? ☐
4 works at the weekend? ☐
5 thinks technology is easy to deal with once you know how? ☐

3 CRITICAL THINKING Who would say these things about the projects in the text? Mark each sentence A (the students) or B (the people they help).

B 0 I want to be able to use new technology.
☐ 1 It's so interesting talking to them.
☐ 2 It was a complete mystery, but now I understand.
☐ 3 They're very patient and explain things very clearly.
☐ 4 It's so easy for me and I feel I'm helping others.
☐ 5 You hear a lot of negative things about us, so it's good to show we aren't all bad!

DEVELOPING Writing

ONLINE LIFE — UNIT 4

A blog: giving advice

1 **INPUT** Read the blog entry quickly. Why is Johnny's father angry?

_____

Blog | About | News | **Advice** | Community

Hi – I'm Johnny Tipp.
Welcome to my top 'tipps' blog!

TIPP 1 What to do when your laptop stops working

I'm writing on my ⁰___tablet___ because my laptop isn't working. A few days ago, I was writing my ¹_____ when a message appeared on the screen. It said there was a problem with my ²_____ and I should restart it. So I did exactly that, but the same message reappeared. After repeating this five times, I realised the problem was serious, so I looked ³_____ for a solution, using my phone. I found a site that promised to fix everything. But was it too good to be true? Here's what I learned …

TIPP 1.1 *You should never trust sites that promise to 'fix everything'.*
I only had to ⁴_____ a file onto my laptop and then ⁵_____ it.

TIPP 1.2 *You should never download files from sites you don't know.*
Next, a message appeared: 'Please enter your credit card details.' So, I used my dad's credit card.

TIPP 1.3 *Never pay before you see results.*
Then the laptop ⁶_____ everything on it, shut down and hasn't worked since. When Dad got home, he was really tired from work, but I had to tell him the whole story.

TIPP 1.4 *You'd better not tell bad news to a tired person.*
He got very upset with me, and it didn't get any better when he found out that £1,000 was missing from his bank account!

2 Complete the blog entry with the words in the list.

blog | deleted | download | install
machine | online | ~~tablet~~

3 **ANALYSE** Read the blog entry again. Put the events in the correct order.

- [1] Johnny writes his blog.
- [ ] He tells his dad about the problem.
- [ ] He installs a program.
- [ ] His laptop tells him it has a problem.
- [ ] His laptop crashes.
- [ ] He goes online to find a solution.
- [ ] He uses his dad's credit card.
- [ ] He downloads a program.

WRITING TIP: giving advice

- Organise the advice into short steps. Use bullet points or numbers.
- The advice or instructions should be clear and easy to understand.
- Give examples from your own experiences.
- Use the imperative and *should / ought to / 'd better*.
- Write in a friendly style and use informal language.

4 **PLAN** You are going to write a blog entry giving advice.

1 Choose a topic you know something about or explain how to do something. For example: keeping a pet / making a cake / fixing a bike.
2 Make a list of the advice you want to include.
3 Organise the advice in order and write a plan. Use the Writing tip to help you.

5 **PRODUCE** Write a blog entry giving advice to your readers in 170–200 words. Use your plan from Exercise 4.

LISTENING

1 🔊 4.02 Listen to William and Selena talking about passwords. According to Selena, which of these is a strong password?

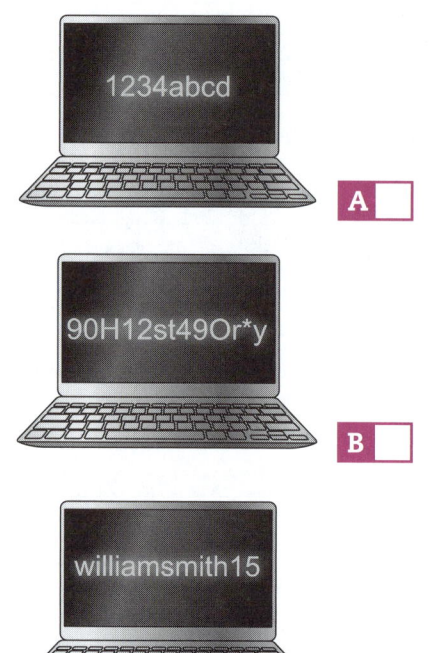

A ☐

B ☐

C ☐

2 🔊 4.02 Listen again. Complete the gaps in William's notes with one or two words.

0 You should use a ___different___ password for every website.

1 You shouldn't _____ your passwords to other people.

2 A good password has got numbers, _____ letters, lowercase letters and punctuation marks.

3 If you use words that have a _____ _____ for you, they will be easier to remember.

4 It's best to never _____ _____ your password anywhere, so people can't find it.

5 Use numbers such as your lucky number, your house number or your _____ _____ .

DIALOGUE

3 Put the words in order to make sentences.

0 shouldn't / password / use / always / You / same / everything / the / for
   You shouldn't always use the same password for everything.

1 other / You / password / tell / people / shouldn't / your
   _____
   _____

2 ought / password / good / A / letters and / have / in / numbers / it / to
   _____
   _____

3 difficult / guess / A / for / password / somebody / to / be / must / else
   _____
   _____

Train to TH!NK

Logical sequencing

4 Put the actions in a logical order.

1 ☐ Ask for some advice.
   ☐ Get some bad advice.
   ☐ Take the advice.
   [1] Have a problem.
   ☐ Get some good advice.
   ☐ Ignore the advice.
   ☐ Ask someone else.

2 ☐ Send your message.
   ☐ Write a reply.
   ☐ Add an attachment.
   ☐ Delete the first message.
   ☐ Log onto your email.
   ☐ Key in your password.
   [1] Go online.
   ☐ Read a message.

5 Connect the first and last events in the lists with your own ideas.

1 1 Find an old friend on a social networking site.
   2 _Send the friend a message asking about their life._
   3 _____
   4 _____
   5 Delete the friend!

2 1 See a great new band on TV.
   2 _____
   3 _____
   4 _____
   5 Go and see their show.

B1 Preliminary for Schools

 READING
Part 2: Matching

EXAM GUIDE: READING PART 2

In B1 Preliminary for Schools Reading Part 2, you have to match the texts to the people.
- Read profiles 1–5 and underline the important information.
- When you've read all the texts, go back and check that the text you've chosen matches the information in the profile <u>exactly</u>. If it doesn't, re-read the other options.

1 For each question, choose the correct answer.

The young people on the right all need to find some information online for a geography project.
Underneath, there are eight websites. Decide which website would be most suitable for each person.

1 Simon's geography project is about comparing cities around the world. He wants to see interviews with people talking about where they live and ways cities are protecting the environment.

2 Tara wants to research places that have difficult weather conditions. She'd also like to see how the population and industry of these locations is changing.

3 Marek needs to see the geography of each continent. He's keen to see the types of products regions are famous for and who they sell them to.

4 Aysha would like to research famous tourist attractions and see how many people visit them each year. She'd like to find historical photos of these attractions.

5 Pedro needs information about how countries move goods around to different locations. He also wants to know about festivals around the world and their history.

 WEBSITES ABOUT WORLD GEOGRAPHY

A StudyCentre.cxm | StudyCentre.com lets you explore celebrations that cultures around the world have each year. Look at ways they've changed over time and see how ancient celebrations sometimes share similar traditions. Find details about the things different regions produce and the transport used to send them abroad or within their own homelands.

B history101.cxm | This website has some videos from the 1880s showing typical city street scenes. You can compare them with modern videos to see how cities around the world have grown and developed. Find details about the kinds of goods each region is well known for, and how this has changed over the past hundred years.

C info-point.cxm | Find out the kinds of things countries are most well known for making and which countries buy them from abroad. This data is updated annually, so you can see new trends with these goods. You are also able to access detailed maps that show a country's mountain ranges, rivers and lakes, and historic routes that were used for trade purposes.

D land-mark.cxm | Every country has landmarks that tourists from around the world come and visit. At land-mark.com, you can see pictures of these attractions and read the history behind them. There are also details of each country's most well-known celebrations and when they take place in cities all over the world.

E GreenData.cxm | Go to GreenData.com to compare which countries are world leaders at protecting their wildlife and forests. See pictures of national parks in each continent and the annual number of visitors. This website also shows the amount of rainfall each country has annually and the weather conditions in each region.

F Xplain.cxm | Xplain.com follows regional trends on every continent, so you can find how many people move to various locations because of work and business opportunities. It also shows how villages, towns and cities deal with anything from floods to incredible amounts of snowfall and what it's like to live in some of the hottest and coldest places on Earth.

G A2Z.cxm | This website is a great place not only to find facts about a country but also to see some of the oldest pictures available of important landmarks from all over the world. See how they have changed over time by looking at recent videos of them. A2Z.com also shows you the number of people who travel to them each year.

H Edu-Hub.cxm | This educational website provides the most recent data on each country's capital, so you can see their similarities and differences. Find out how each of these locations are reducing pollution and increasing green spaces in their downtown areas. Edu-Hub.com also has videos of teens sharing their stories about what it's like to grow up in these places.

CONSOLIDATION

LISTENING

1 🔊 4.03 Listen to the conversation. Tick (✓) A, B or C.

1. What kind of show is *Priceless*?
   - A a chat show ☐
   - B a sports show ☐
   - C a game show ☐
2. What time does *Let Him Go* start?
   - A 8 pm ☐
   - B 9 pm ☐
   - C 11 pm ☐
3. What kind of film is *Let Him Go*?
   - A a sci-fi film ☐
   - B a horror film ☐
   - C a comedy film ☐

2 🔊 4.03 Listen again and answer the questions.

0. Why does Mike want to stay in?
   Because he's a bit tired.
1. What day of the week is it?
   _____
2. What kind of film is *By Tomorrow*?
   _____
3. What happens in *Let Him Go*?
   _____
4. What does Milly want Mike to make?
   _____

VOCABULARY

3 Look at the word snake. Find 12 types of films and TV programmes and write them in the correct column. Some can go in both.

TV shows	Types of films
	sci-fi

4 Complete the text with the words in the list. There are three words you don't need.

> against | attach | ~~buy~~ | download
> followed | for | ignored | key
> on | open | post | useful

One of the problems with modern technology is the number of passwords you need to remember. Every time I want to ⁰_____*buy*_____ an app, check my email or ¹_____ a photo on social media, I have to ²_____ in a password. My laptop even sometimes asks for one if I want to ³_____ a file or ⁴_____ an attachment. What makes it worse is that all these passwords have to be different. So I asked a friend of mine ⁵_____ some advice. He advised me ⁶_____ keeping them on my laptop. He told me to write them all down in a file and send it to myself and keep it in my email inbox. It sounded like ⁷_____ advice, so I ⁸_____ it and did exactly what he said. So my passwords are all safely stored in my email inbox. The only problem is that I can't remember the password to access it!

GRAMMAR

5 Rewrite the sentences with the words in brackets.

0. I don't know anyone kinder than her. (kindest)
   She's the kindest person I know.
1. The film was hated by everyone. (no one)
   _____
2. You should study more if you've got a test tomorrow. (better)
   _____
3. The weather was a lot nicer yesterday. (worse)
   _____
4. Polly is nearly as tall as Angus. (a bit)
   _____
5. The best thing for you to do is to tell the truth. (ought)
   _____
6. Is this house empty? (anyone)
   _____
7. I'm a bad singer, but I'm better than Perry. (badly)
   _____
8. It's really important for me to finish this today. (must)
   _____

UNITS 3 & 4

DIALOGUE

6 🔊 4.04 Complete the conversation with the phrases in the list. Then listen and check.

> after all | Can you lend me a hand?
> have a look | ~~have you got a few minutes?~~
> I can do it for you | In fact
> Is everything OK? | looks like | ought to

Vicky Ted, 0 _have you got a few minutes?_

Ted Sure. Yes, I have.
1 _____

Vicky Not really. I'm trying to download this file, but it isn't working.
2 _____

Ted Of course. Let me take a look.
[after a few minutes]

Ted That's very strange.
It 3 _____
you've got a virus on your laptop.

Vicky A virus!

Ted Yes, 4 _____ .
Each time I try and open this window, it just shuts down.

Vicky Oh, no. Is it serious?

Ted Not really.
5 _____ ,
I had the same one on my laptop, so I know exactly what to do.

Vicky Great. So, can you fix it?

Ted Yes, I can. I'm just running a program now. But you really
6 _____
update your virus protection.
7 _____ ,
if you want.

Vicky Thanks. That would be great.

Ted Oh. Oh dear.

Vicky What?

Ted Well, it didn't do that before. It seems your laptop's gone completely dead. Very strange. Maybe I didn't know that virus 8 _____ .

READING

7 Read the text and match the phrases with the correct places (A–F). There is one phrase you don't need.

0 you didn't have a chance of seeing it again [A]
1 in the house ☐
2 apart from things like live sports events, ☐
3 like they did when my parents were children ☐
4 whenever and wherever they like ☐
5 better sound and ☐
6 they watched the night before ☐

BYE-BYE TV?

Hey everyone! While I was watching my favourite Netflix series on my tablet, I thought, does anybody still sit down and watch TV these days?

When my parents were growing up, people only had a few channels to choose from. If you missed your favourite programme, it was just bad luck – **[A]** (unless you had a video recorder), but the TV was the centre point of the house. Families planned the programmes they wanted to watch and made sure they finished their dinner before the programme started. At school, children talked about the shows **[B]** and because there weren't many programmes for kids, they all watched the same thing. Can you imagine that? Now there are tons of options!

When I was growing up, TV screens were bigger and a lot thinner than the TVs of my parents' time. We had **[C]** a remote control to change channels. But the TV was still an important piece of furniture **[D]** and we all sat around it on a Saturday night to watch something as a family.

Nowadays the TV just doesn't seem to be so important, and **[E]** people can choose what they want to watch and when they want to watch it. They don't even need to watch it on a TV. They can download or stream programmes and watch them on their tablets and phones **[F]**, thanks to mobile devices. Watching TV has become a much more individual activity and in many houses the TV set sits forgotten in the corner of the room. Is it time to say goodbye to the TV?

WRITING

8 Write a short text (about 120–150 words) about your favourite TV programme. Include the following information:

- what it is
- what it's about
- when you watch it
- why you like it

5 MUSIC TO MY EARS

GRAMMAR
Present perfect continuous → SB p.50

1 ★☆☆ Match the sentences with the pictures. <u>Underline</u> examples of the present perfect continuous.

0 They<u>'ve been watching</u> TV all evening. [A]
1 He's been waiting for a long time. ☐
2 It's been snowing for days. ☐
3 She's been running for 62 hours. She's trying to break the world record. ☐
4 He's been talking to them for hours. ☐
5 She's been playing her favourite instrument all morning. ☐

2 ★★☆ Complete the sentences. Use the present perfect continuous (positive or negative) of the verbs.

0 She<u>'s been reading</u> (read) that book for more than a week now.
1 Dylan's in bed. He _____ (feel) well for about three hours.
2 Dinner's going to be good. Dad _____ (cook) all afternoon.
3 What awful weather. It _____ (rain) all day.
4 Lara looks really tired. She _____ (sleep) very well.
5 I _____ (study), so I don't think I'm going to pass this test.

3 ★★☆ Complete the text. Use the present perfect continuous of the verbs in the list.

dream | talk | think | ~~try~~ | write

I ⁰<u>'ve been trying</u> to contact you. Is your phone broken? I want to ask you a question: will you join 'The Cool Four'? Jared, Nina, Zoë and I have started a band! As you know, I ¹_____ songs for years, and I ²_____ of having my own band. I'm sure people ³_____ that I'd never do it. Well, they're wrong! Jared, Nina and Zoë are here now, and we ⁴_____ about the name of the band if you join us! How does 'The Cool Five' sound?

4 ★★☆ Write present perfect continuous questions.

0 [e] why / she / cry
<u>Why has she been crying</u>?
1 ☐ how long / she / speak / to the teacher
_____?
2 ☐ how long / you / try to phone me
_____?
3 ☐ what / you / do
_____?
4 ☐ how long / Bethany / practise / the piano
_____?

5 ★★☆ Complete the sentences. Use the present perfect continuous of the verbs.

a She<u>'s been playing</u> (play) since 10.30.
b I _____ (try) to reach you for two days.
c They _____ (discuss) the exam for an hour.
d We _____ (tidy) our room.
e She _____ (feel) sad about her cat.

6 ★★★ Match the questions in Exercise 4 with the answers in Exercise 5. Write a–d in the boxes.

PRONUNCIATION
Strong and weak forms of *been* /biːn/ and /bɪn/
Go to page 119. 🎧

Present perfect simple vs. present perfect continuous → SB p.53

7 ★☆☆ **Match the sentences.**

0 He's been wearing these jeans for years. *f*
1 He's bought a new pair of jeans. ☐
2 She's been recording since 7 am. ☐
3 She's recorded all the songs for her new album. ☐
4 They've been playing all evening. ☐
5 They've played concerts in many countries. ☐

a She's tired and hungry.
b They've got fans all over the world.
c But they're too big for him.
d But they haven't played their best song yet.
e She can go home now.
f He needs to buy a new pair.

8 ★★☆ **Complete the sentences. Use the present perfect simple or present perfect continuous.**

0 We *'ve been practising* all afternoon.
   We *'ve practised* 20 songs. (practise)
1 We _____ at photos for hours.
   We _____ at all my albums! (look)
2 She _____ 50 messages today!
   She _____ emails since eight o'clock. (write)
3 We _____ to songs all evening.
   We _____ to five albums. (listen)
4 They _____ the guitar since 2015.
   They _____ a lot of concerts. (play)
5 She _____ 300 pictures.
   She _____ for many years. (paint)

9 ★★★ **Write questions with *How long* and the present perfect simple or continuous.**

0 you / play / the piano
   How long have you been playing the piano ?
1 he / know / Greg
   _____ ?
2 they / play / in a band
   _____ ?
3 you / have / your guitar
   _____ ?
4 she / listen / to music
   _____ ?
5 they / be / teachers
   _____ ?
6 we / live / in this house
   _____ ?

10 ★★★ **Complete the questions. Use the correct form of the verbs in the list.**

be | hear | ~~know~~ | play | study

0 How long *have you known* your best friend?
1 What's your favourite sport and how long _____ it?
2 What class are you in now and how long _____ in it?
3 How long _____ English?
4 What's the most interesting information you _____ today?

11 ★★★ **Write your answers to the questions in Exercise 10.**

0 _____
1 _____
2 _____
3 _____
4 _____

GET IT RIGHT!

Present perfect continuous vs. past continuous

Learners sometimes use the past continuous when the present perfect continuous is required.

✓ I've **been looking** for a new phone since last week.
✗ I ~~was looking~~ for a new phone since last week.

Complete the sentences with the correct form of the verbs.

0 Over the last few weeks I *'ve been training* (train) for the race.
1 We _____ (eat) breakfast when we heard the news.
2 Nathan _____ (wait) to see the latest *Star Wars* film for months.
3 Heidi _____ (work) there last year, but she left in December.
4 My brothers _____ (play) the violin for two years.
5 They _____ (get) this discount for the last three years.
6 You left the meeting because your phone _____ (ring).

VOCABULARY
Making music → SB p.50

1 ★☆☆ Complete the text with the words in the list.

> ~~started a band~~ | wrote / songs and lyrics
> recorded / single | download | played gigs
> entered the charts | released | went on / tour

When Mick Jagger ⁰ _started a band_ called The Rolling Stones in 1962 with a few friends, he had no idea how successful they would become. The Stones ¹_____ their first _____, *Come On*, a song by the singer Chuck Berry, and ²_____ it on 7 June, 1963. They never performed it when they ³_____ because it wasn't 'their' song. But their fans found out about the record, and so many people bought it that it ⁴_____ in the UK and went to number 21. Of course, in those days, fans had to go to record shops; they couldn't just ⁵_____ music from the internet! Mick Jagger and Keith Richards ⁶_____ a lot of _____ _____ that became very famous. In 1964, The Rolling Stones ⁷_____ their first _____ of the US. When they came back, they had their first number one hit in the UK, *It's All Over Now*.

Musical instruments → SB p.53

2 ★☆☆ Put the letters in order to make musical instruments.

1. The _drums_ (sdmur) and the _____ (sabs aitugr) are responsible for the rhythm in a band.
2. The _____ (rmutpte) and the _____ (nxohpasoe) are wind instruments.
3. _____ (ysedbaokr) are electronic instruments similar to a _____ (iaopn).
4. The _____ (linvoi) and the _____ (griuat) are both examples of string instruments.

3 ★★☆ Tick (✓) the sentences that are true for you. Correct the ones that aren't.

1. I never listen to jazz. ☐
   _____
2. I prefer pop to rock. ☐
   _____
3. I like songs with good melodies. ☐
   _____
4. I don't really like rap. ☐
   _____
5. I never listen to the lyrics of a song. ☐
   _____

WordWise: Phrasal verbs with *out* → SB p.51

4 ★☆☆ Circle the correct answers.

0. We need help. Who could ___ this out for us?
   A come   **C sort**
   B start   D go
1. I'm afraid I'm ___ out of ideas. I'm not sure what to do.
   A coming   C sorting
   B running   D finding
2. I love ___ out with my friends.
   A finding   C sorting
   B starting   D going
3. My cousin ___ out writing for the local newspaper. Now he's a journalist on TV.
   A started   C sorted
   B found   D went
4. Nobody saw what happened, so it's difficult for the police to ___ out the truth.
   A come   C go
   B run   D find
5. They haven't had a new song for two years, but their new album should ___ out soon.
   A sort   C go
   B find   D come

5 ★★☆ Match the questions with the answers.

0. Why won't you join us at the cinema tonight? [c]
1. We have a real problem with this. ☐
2. When did this book come out? ☐
3. What was your brother's first job? ☐
4. Can I talk to Jenny? ☐
5. What if your dad finds out about it? ☐

a. I can't remember. I bought it a long time ago.
b. Well, he won't be happy, that's for sure.
c. I've run out of money. I just can't afford to go.
d. Sorry. She's gone out with her sisters.
e. Oh, don't worry. I'm sure we'll sort it out.
f. He started out as a drummer.

6 ★★★ Answer the questions so they are true for you.

1. How many times a week do you go out?
   _____
2. Are any of your friends good at sorting out problems? How do they do it?
   _____
3. Do you watch new films as soon as they come out?
   _____
4. Does your phone often run out of credit?
   _____

REFERENCE

Making music
- download a song
- write songs and lyrics
- enter a talent show
- go on tour
- start a band
- record (a single)
- release (a single)
- enter the charts
- win a competition
- play a gig

Musical instruments
- trumpet
- violin
- guitar
- piano
- drums
- saxophone
- keyboard
- bass guitar

OUT

My dad **started out** making tea for the bosses. Now he's the boss of the company.

I only **found out** about his accident when I read about it in the paper.

The printer's **run out** of ink. We need to buy some more.

The new Minecraft game **comes out** next Friday. I can't wait.

Do you want to **go out** tonight? The cinema or a restaurant, maybe?

If you tell me what the problem is, we can **sort** it **out** together.

VOCABULARY *EXTRA*

1 Circle the correct words.

1. The band is in the studio *performing / recording* their album.
2. Lewis Capaldi has many hit *songs / dances*.
3. My favourite singer is performing *direct / live* on TV tonight.
4. It isn't easy to make a great *album / concert*.
5. I really like this group, but I wish they would record some original songs, not just *covers / lyrics*.
6. You need a good internet connection to *sing / stream* music on your phone.

2 Complete the sentences with the words in the list.

album | covers | live | singles | song | streaming | ~~studio~~

1. Fine Feathers are in the ___studio___ and they're recording an _____ , Wind Songs.
2. They're playing a concert in their hometown so their fans can see them perform _____ . They're going to play some new songs and some well-known _____ .
3. They've got a hit _____ , Bad News, and it's top of the _____ chart. I keep _____ it on my phone – it's such a good song!

A HIDDEN STAR

A young man dreams of a career in music. He gets a chance to record two albums, but they don't sell. For many years, he lives on very little money. He has no idea that in the meantime his songs have become extremely popular in other countries, and that his fans believe he's dead.

It sounds like a fairy tale, but it isn't. It's an incredible but true story and this is only the half of it.

Sixto Rodriguez was the son of Mexican immigrants to the US. He released his first album, *Cold Fact*, in 1970, and his second, *Coming from Reality*, a year later. But nobody bought his music, so he had to do all kinds of jobs to earn enough to support him and his family. Life was hard.

In the meantime, his music was becoming a huge success in three countries on the other side of the world: Australia, New Zealand and, in particular, South Africa. There, Rodriguez was a huge star, more popular than The Rolling Stones. But people were saying he was dead, and he himself had no idea about the success of his music.

Then, finally, in December 1994, 24 years after he released *Cold Fact*, a young South African fan named Stephen 'Sugar' Segerman and Craig Bartholomew, a journalist, decided to find out more about Rodriguez. They started a website called The Great Rodriguez Hunt, and they organised for a photo of his face to be put on milk cartons in the US, with the question 'Have you seen this man?' Rodriguez's daughter saw one and the rest is rock history.

In March 1998, he was invited on a big tour across South Africa. Rodriguez played six concerts all over the country, in stadiums filled with thousands of young people who knew every word to every one of his songs.

Malik Bendjelloul, a Swedish filmmaker, made a documentary film called *Searching for Sugar Man*. The film told the story of how Segerman and Bartholomew tried to find out if Rodriguez was still alive and how they found him. When the film got a nomination for an Oscar, the director asked Rodriguez to come to the ceremony, but he refused because he was afraid all the attention would be on him and not the filmmakers. Although the film has helped to make his music successful around the world, Rodriguez doesn't have a rock star lifestyle. He's been living in the same simple house in Detroit for 40 years, and he doesn't have a car, a mobile phone or a TV.

READING

1 Read the article quickly. Complete the fact file.

FACTFILE

Name: ⁰ *Sixto Rodriguez*

Album titles: ¹ _____
² _____

First concert tour (date): ³ _____

Country (of the concert tour): ⁴ _____

2 Read the article again. Mark the sentences T (true) or F (false). Correct the false information.

0 Sixto Rodriguez was born in the US, but his parents were Brazilian. **F**
His parents were Mexican.

1 Lots of people knew his music in South Africa. ☐
_____

2 His daughter put a picture of him on milk cartons. ☐
_____

3 Twenty-four years after *Cold Fact*, he played in front of thousands of fans in South Africa. ☐
_____

4 The fans in South Africa knew all of the lyrics of his songs. ☐
_____

5 He has recently made a film about his life. ☐
_____

3 When she saw the advert, Rodriguez's daughter phoned Stephen 'Sugar' Segerman. Use your imagination to write the first six lines of that phone call.

Daughter *Hello, is that Stephen Segerman?*
Segerman _____
Daughter _____
Segerman _____
Daughter _____
Segerman _____

4 **CRITICAL THINKING** Put the events in Rodriguez's life in the correct order.

☐ **A** Two music fans found Rodriguez in the US.
☐ **B** His music became famous all over the world.
1 **C** Rodriguez made two albums.
☐ **D** He did a concert tour in South Africa.
☐ **E** He was a famous musician in New Zealand, Australia and South Africa.
☐ **F** There was a film about him.
☐ **G** He did ordinary jobs and didn't earn much.
☐ **H** People thought Rodriguez was dead.

DEVELOPING Writing

MUSIC TO MY EARS — UNIT 5

A magazine article

1 INPUT Read the article quickly and answer the questions.

0 What's the singer's real name?
  Her real name is Ella Marija Lani Yelich-O'Connor.
1 Where did she grow up?
  _____
2 What do experts think of her?
  _____
3 What does the writer think of her?
  _____

Ruling the world

A In 2013 a song called 'Royals' made a young singer called Lorde famous all over the world. Lorde's real name is Ella Marija Lani Yelich-O'Connor and she grew up in New Zealand. <u>She has been working in the music business since she won a talent show at the age of 12.</u>

B <u>Ever since Lorde appeared on TV screens for the first time, critics have been praising her fantastic voice.</u> She has an incredible feel for music and a unique talent for writing lyrics. She says her love for words has been as important as her love for music, and both have helped her to become a star.

C Lorde is still very young. <u>She became a star when she was 17</u>, and has had a number of successful songs since then. *Tennis Court* came out in the UK just after the Wimbledon Tennis Championship in 2013. She released her second album, *Melodrama*, in 2017 and started a world concert tour.

D I have been fascinated by Lorde's music and her personality since I first saw her in a video. Her songs make me happy and I love singing along to them. If you don't know Lorde, listen to some of her music – you'll love it!

2 Match the content (1–4) with the paragraphs (A–D).
 ☐ 1 the writer's personal opinion
 ☐ 2 the singer's early life
 ☐ 3 examples of her music
 ☐ 4 experts' opinions

3 ANALYSE Look at the <u>underlined</u> sentences in the text. Find examples of verb forms which refer to …

A something that happened at a specific time in the past.
 She became a star when she was 17.
 _____

B something that started in the past, and is still continuing.
 _____
 _____

C how long something has been happening.
 _____
 _____

WRITING TIP: a magazine article

- Think of an interesting title to attract the readers' attention.
- Start with an interesting opening line or a direct question to the reader.
- Organise your text in paragraphs.
- In the last paragraph, give your opinion and/or make a suggestion of something the reader should do.

4 PLAN You are going to write an article about a singer or a musician alive today.
 1 Choose a singer or musician.
 2 Research the information in Exercise 2 points 2–4 about the singer or musician.
 3 Use your notes to write a plan. Use the Writing tip to help you.

5 PRODUCE Write an article about the singer or musician in about 200 words. Use your plan from Exercise 4.

51

LISTENING

1 🔊 5.02 **Listen to the conversations and answer the questions.**

Conversation 1

0 What do Tony's friends like that he doesn't?
Listening to music while doing other things.

1 Why can't he listen to music while he's doing something else?
_____

2 When does he like to listen to music?
_____

Conversation 2

3 How does Rachel feel about music?
_____

4 Do her teachers allow her to listen to music during the lessons?
_____

5 How does music make her feel?
_____

Conversation 3

6 Where does Ryan find new music?
_____

7 What are his favourite types of music?
_____

8 Does he listen to music when he works?
_____

DIALOGUE

2 🔊 5.02 **Match the questions with the answers. Then listen again and check.**

0 Why's that? — **d**
1 So, don't you ever listen to music? ☐
2 Does it relax you? ☐
3 Could you live without music? ☐
4 Do you dance a lot? ☐
5 When do you listen to that? ☐

a Yeah, it helps me see pictures.
b Not as often as I'd like to.
c Well, when I need to concentrate.
d Because I can't concentrate on both things.
e No, I don't think I could.
f Of course I do! I like music.

PHRASES FOR FLUENCY → SB p.54

3 🔊 5.03 **Put the conversation in the correct order. Then listen and check.**

☐	Emily	It's The Fallen – they're playing in the town hall on Saturday.
☐	Emily	Why don't we invite Yuri to come along?
1	Emily	Charlie, Charlie!
☐	Emily	Why not? He loves them.
☐	Emily	Well, if you say so. It's just me and you, then.
☐	Emily	Yes, really. I've already got my ticket. I can't wait! It's going to be the show of the year.
☐	Charlie	Tell me about it. They're my favourite band. I'm definitely going, too.
☐	Charlie	Yuri? No way.
☐	Charlie	What's up, Emily?
☐	Charlie	What?! Really?
☐	Charlie	Listen, there's no point in trying to change my mind. Yuri and I … well, we just don't like each other. I'd rather not invite him.

4 **Complete the conversations with the phrases in the list.**

> if you say so | there's no point in | I can't wait
> no way | tell me about it | what's up

0 A Stephen King is the best writer in the world.
  B _If you say so_. I prefer Suzanne Collins.
1 A I've told her again and again that she's wrong.
  B _____ talking to her. She just won't listen.
2 A Wow, that lesson was boring.
  B _____. I almost fell asleep twice!
3 A Let's climb that tree.
  B _____. That's far too dangerous.
4 A Hey, Tom. I need to talk to you.
  B OK, Jules. _____?
5 A I'm so happy it'll be summer soon.
  B Me, too. _____ to go swimming.

B1 Preliminary for Schools

🎧 LISTENING
Part 3: Gap-fill

1 🔊 **5.04** For each question, write the correct answer in the gap.

Write **one** or **two words**, or a **number**, or a **date** or a **time**.
You will hear a teacher talking about a school trip to a museum.

Museum of Popular Music

The building was once a ¹_____ .

The main exhibition is about music from ²_____ to the present.

A special exhibition has a display of musicians' ³_____ .

There is a 30-minute film about the history of ⁴_____ .

You can see what it's like in a professional ⁵_____ .

The museum gives students a gift if they do a ⁶_____ about the exhibition.

EXAM GUIDE: LISTENING PART 3

In B1 Preliminary for Schools Listening Part 3, you listen to one person speaking about something. While you listen, you have to complete some notes. There are six gaps and you have to write one or two words, or a date or a time in each gap.

Before you listen:
- Read through the notes.
- For each gap, think about the type of word/s you expect to hear, for example: name, number, date, time.

While you listen:
- Remember you will hear the information in the same order as the notes.
- Focus on the information you need to complete the notes.
- Start completing the gaps when you listen for the first time.
- The second time you listen, check your answers and any gaps you were unable to complete the first time you listened.

6 NO PLANET B

GRAMMAR
will (not), may (not), might (not) for prediction → SB p.58

1 ★☆☆ Match the sentences with the pictures.

0 Mum won't be happy when she sees her car. **F**
1 Mum will be happy when she sees her car. ☐
2 Don't eat it all. You'll be ill. ☐
3 Don't eat it. It might be poisonous. ☐
4 She may not finish her book tonight. ☐
5 She won't finish her book tonight. ☐

2 ★★☆ Complete the sentences. Use *will* or *won't* and the verbs in the list.

be | believe | cost | get | like | remember

0 He's grown a lot. He __will be__ taller than me soon.
1 I don't know how much the tickets _____ .
2 Wow! They _____ me when I tell them!
3 Listen carefully. Otherwise you _____ what I tell you.
4 Don't worry. I _____ there as soon as I can.
5 The cake is for Amanda. I'm sure she _____ it.

3 ★★☆ Circle the correct words.

0 I'm nervous. Mum *might* / *won't* get angry.
1 Wait there. I *'ll* / *might* be two minutes.
2 I don't know the answer. Who *won't* / *might* know?
3 Both teams are good. I've got no idea who *will* / *won't* win.
4 It's getting late. We *may* / *may not* miss the train.
5 I'll tell you, but you *might* / *won't* believe me.
6 They probably *won't* / *might not* come at all.

4 ★★★ Write predictions with suitable modal verbs.

0 there / only be / electric cars / 20 years from now (certainty)
   There will only be electric cars 20 years from now.
1 we / visit / the US / next summer (possibility)
   _____
2 I / watch / a film / in English / next week (possibility)
   _____
3 My friends / not see / a match / on Sunday (certainty)
   _____
4 next month / there / be / a lot of rain (possibility)
   _____
5 Samuel / go / to university / one day (certainty)
   _____
6 Maria / watch TV / tonight (possibility)
   _____

5 ★★★ Tick (✓) the predictions in Exercise 4 that are true for you. Change the others so that they are true for you.

1 ☐ _____
2 ☐ _____
3 ☐ _____
4 ☐ _____
5 ☐ _____
6 ☐ _____

6 ★★★ Write six sentences about the future of your country. Use *will*, *won't*, *might (not)* and *may (not)*.

1 _____
2 _____
3 _____
4 _____
5 _____
6 _____

First conditional; unless in first conditional sentences

→ SB p.61

7 ★☆☆ Circle the correct words.

0 If I *see* / *'ll see* her again, I'll tell her to phone you.
1 We won't go on holiday if Dad *is* / *will be* still ill.
2 If you *won't* / *don't* talk about it, nobody will know.
3 *Will* / *Do* they want to come if they hear about the party?
4 If they don't help, their parents *will be* / *are* angry.
5 If you think carefully, I'm sure you *find* / *'ll find* a nice present for her.
6 There won't be many people at the match if the weather *gets* / *will get* worse.
7 If you *won't* / *don't* keep in touch with your friends, they'll lose interest in you.

8 ★★☆ Match the parts of the sentences.

0 I'll take the train — d
1 Will they come for lunch
2 If you don't tell Tasha about the situation,
3 I won't phone you
4 If they don't want to come to your party,
5 She'll only buy the phone
6 If people hear how much the tickets are,
7 Unless the teacher gives us really difficult homework,

a I'll finish it before seven o'clock.
b you'll have to accept their decision.
c a lot of them won't go.
d unless Dad gives me a lift.
e if it isn't too expensive.
f how will she know?
g unless I change my plans.
h if we invite them?

9 ★★☆ Complete the text. Use the correct form of the verbs in the list.

be | be | go | invite | miss | not let | not pass

Dear Diary,
Not a great day today. Had a test in French. Unless I'm totally wrong, my result ⁰ __won't be__ very good. If I ¹_____ , I don't know what I'll do. My parents ²_____ me go to the cinema with Brandon tomorrow unless I pass. If I tell Brandon I can't go to the cinema with him, he ³_____ someone else. If he ⁴_____ with someone else, I ⁵_____ a film I'd love to see. But what if I wait and tell my parents later? Well, who knows how they'll react? I think that unless I come up with a brilliant idea, I ⁶_____ in trouble whatever I do. Well, one thing's for sure: next time I'll prepare better for my French test.

10 ★★★ Write first conditional questions. Then match them with the answers.

0 rain / what / you do
  If it rains, what will you do?
  _____

1 watch TV tonight / what / you / watch
  _____
  _____

2 what / you / buy / get / birthday money
  _____
  _____

3 feel hungry / at break / what / you / eat
  _____
  _____

4 what / you / do / not pass / the exam
  _____
  _____

5 what / you / do / lose / your phone
  _____
  _____

a I'll ask my mum for a new one.
b That won't happen!
c Nothing. I think I'll save the money.
d I'll stay at home.
e I'll watch a film.
f A sandwich or some biscuits.

11 ★★★ Answer three of the questions in Exercise 10 about you.

GET IT RIGHT!

First conditional tenses

Learners sometimes use *will* instead of the present tense in the first conditional.

✓ I will be pleased if they **like** it.
✗ I will be pleased if they ~~will~~ like it.

Correct the sentences.

0 I'll let you know if we'll be late.
  I'll let you know if we're late.

1 If we have some help, there isn't a problem.
  _____

2 I will wear a coat if it will be cold.
  _____

3 They'll understand if you'll explain it.
  _____

4 Will he go if the meeting will be at 7.00?
  _____

5 If it won't rain, they'll have a picnic.
  _____

PRONUNCIATION
/f/, /v/ and /b/ consonant sounds
Go to page 119.

VOCABULARY
The environment → SB p.58

1 ★☆☆ Write the words under the photos.

> flood | litter | melting ice | pollution
> recycling | rubbish | ~~smog~~

1 ___smog___ , _____

2 _____

3 _____

4 _____ , _____ , _____

2 ★★☆ Match the parts of the sentences.

0 Many people think we need stricter — g
1 Water bottles are an example of ☐
2 If global warming continues, many glaciers ☐
3 Some parts of the world don't get enough rain, ☐
4 Many animals, birds and insects will become extinct ☐
5 Recycling paper means ☐
6 This river's water is very clean – there doesn't seem ☐
7 To help the environment, we should avoid ☐

a while others have frequent floods.
b will melt. This will be bad for our planet.
c to be any pollution here.
d single-use plastics.
e wasting natural resources, such as electricity.
f if we don't do something to protect them.
g laws to protect the environment.
h we don't need to cut down so many trees.

Verbs to talk about energy → SB p.61

3 ★★☆ Circle the correct option: A, B or C.

0 If you reuse something, ___
  A you throw it away.
  B you charge it.
  C you use it again.
1 Switching the lights off ___
  A destroys forests.
  B saves energy.
  C wastes energy.
2 It's better to disconnect electrical appliances from their ___
  A litter.
  B power source.
  C standby.
3 Having a long shower ___ a lot of water.
  A wastes
  B saves
  C recycles
4 If you ___ electronic gadgets on standby, you waste electricity.
  A save
  B disconnect
  C leave
5 You should disconnect your phone as soon as it is ___ .
  A charged
  B wasted
  C reused
6 You shouldn't ___ plastic, paper, glass or metal. Recycle it!
  A throw away
  B reuse
  C disconnect

4 ★★★ Answer the questions.

1 What do you think is the biggest threat to our environment and why?
_____
_____

2 How do you feel when you see someone throw litter away in the street?
_____
_____

3 Have you ever told somebody not to waste paper / plastic / water / energy? How did they react?
_____
_____

4 What positive examples do you know of people caring for the environment?
_____
_____

REFERENCE

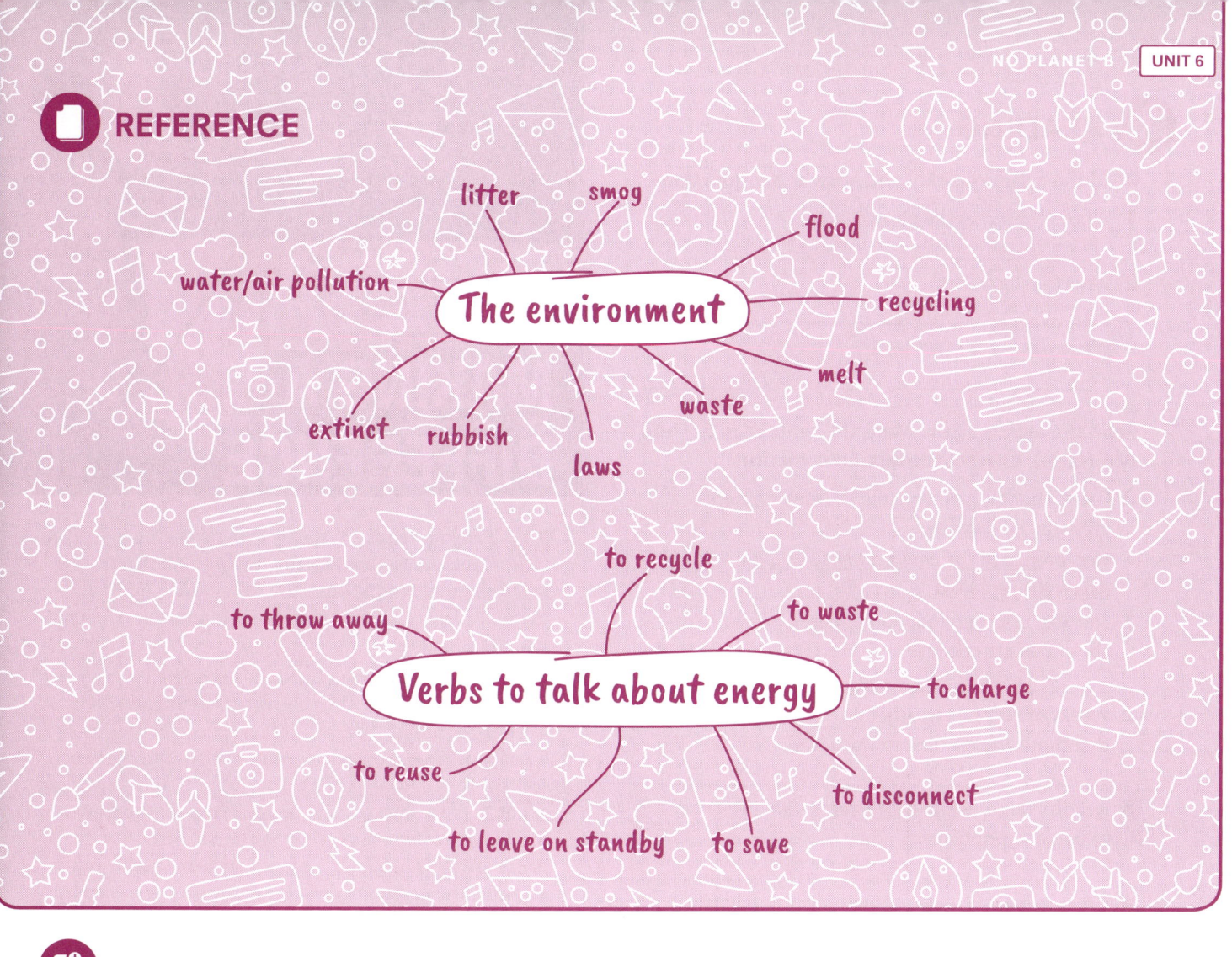

VOCABULARY *EXTRA*

1 Match the words with the definitions.

0 **generate** energy — d
1 **upcycle** furniture
2 **damage** the environment
3 **store** energy
4 **preserve** the environment
5 **reduce** energy

a keep to use later
b use less
c make sure it keeps existing
d produce
e have a bad effect on
f make nicer using old materials

2 Complete the sentences with the correct form of the verbs in the list.

~~damage~~ | generate | preserve | reduce | store | upcycle

0 The environment is being ____*damaged*____ by the amount of energy we all use.
1 We have _____ an old sofa, and it has changed the look of the whole living room!
2 We must try harder to _____ the environment, or some animal species will disappear soon.
3 _____ energy from the sun or wind will help us to prevent climate change.
4 By _____ our energy consumption, we can help the environment.
5 Governments need to think of ways to _____ the energy that solar power produces.

3 Think of an item of furniture in your house that you would like to upcycle. What would you do to it? Write sentences.

_____
_____
_____

READING

1 Read the article quickly and answer the questions.

1 Who is the girl in the photo?

2 Where is she from?

3 What was her first protest?

2 Read the article again. Mark the sentences T (true) or F (false). Correct the false information.

0 Greta Thunberg's interest in the environment only started recently. **F**
Her interest in the environment started when she was eight years old.

1 She was surprised that adults were very worried about climate change. ☐

2 Weeks of very hot weather proved to Greta that there was no time to waste. ☐

3 It didn't take very long for Greta's Climate Strike to become popular. ☐

4 Greta believes if we do something immediately, we might be able to save the planet. ☐

5 When she speaks, she doesn't like to scare people with facts about climate change. ☐

6 Greta believes that teenagers are too young to make a difference. ☐

3 Imagine you have the chance to speak to world leaders. What are you going to speak about and why? Write a short text (50–100 words).

I am going to speak about …

4 **CRITICAL THINKING** Find a sentence, or part of a sentence, in each paragraph that sums up the writer's ideas.

Paragraph 1
Here's an example of a young person who has made a lot of people pay attention.

Paragraph 2

Paragraph 3

Paragraph 4

Paragraph 5

GRETA: MAKING A DIFFERENCE

1 Imagine you feel strongly about something and you want to talk about it. You might think that no one will want to hear what you have to say. Well, here's an example of a young person who has made a lot of people pay attention.

2 Greta Thunberg's a teenager from Sweden. She was eight years old when she first heard about global warming at school. She was very worried about what she heard, but what shocked her most was that adults didn't seem to think it was serious. They weren't doing anything about it. From then on, she couldn't stop thinking about the danger of climate change. She persuaded her parents to change their lifestyle: the family became vegan and started growing their own vegetables. They travelled by train instead of plane and changed to solar energy in their home.

3 The summer of 2018 was particularly hot in Europe with more extreme weather than usual. Greta knew it was time for action. When workers have strikes, they refuse to work because they want better pay. When Greta had a Climate Strike, she refused to go to school because she wanted a better world. She wanted everyone to understand two things: climate change was real and it was serious. One Friday, instead of going to school, she cycled to the Swedish Parliament. She sat alone all the first day, but the next day, people started joining her protest after reading her posters about global warming. This small protest led to the first of many global Climate Strikes in December 2018, by more than 20,000 students in over 270 cities round the world.

4 Greta, now known internationally, began travelling around Europe to speak at important meetings. Her message is always very clear: unless you do something now, you will destroy our future. She told world leaders at a conference in Switzerland: 'I don't want you to feel hopeful. I want you to panic […] And then I want you to act.' At a United Nations climate change meeting in Poland, she said: 'The year 2078, I will celebrate my 75th birthday. If I have children, maybe they will spend that day with me. Maybe they will ask me about you. Maybe they will ask why you didn't do anything while there still was time to act.'

5 Greta's actions have made adults and young people take action around the world. She has already won many international awards and she might win more. Greta Thunberg has shown that young people can make a difference if they're brave enough to talk about the things they believe in.

DEVELOPING Writing

NO PLANET B — UNIT 6

An article about an issue

1 **INPUT** Read the extracts quickly and match them with the titles.

1 Climate change ☐   2 The problem with pollution ☐   3 Deforestation ☐   4 Not enough water ☐

A In conclusion, if the level of the oceans keeps rising, many small islands will disappear. People and animals will die. Unfortunately, this really will all happen unless we change the way we live. So please join me and write to organisations and politicians to ask them to support the environment. ☐

B In many parts of the world, people don't have enough water. When people can't find enough water or use water that is clean, they will catch diseases more easily. This is a big problem in hot and tropical countries. In this essay, I will explain what we can do to make sure that people all around the world have enough water. ☐

C We need to make sure that there are enough trains and buses so that people can travel on public transport. We also need to encourage people to walk and cycle more and use their cars less because this will mean that we will have less pollution in our towns and cities. ☐

D That is why we must introduce new laws to protect forests and rainforests. Big companies earn millions from selling wood, so they should give some of the money they earn to save rainforests. If they don't do this, they should have to pay a fine, and the people who own these companies should go to prison. ☐

2 Write (B) beginning, (M) middle or (C) conclusion next to each extract.

3 **ANALYSE** Read the phrases 0–6 and put them in the correct column.

0 Millions of trees are cut down every year.
1 Unless people do something now, it might be too late.
2 We must encourage people to stop driving their cars.
3 Every year, we lose large areas of forest.
4 Some people can't find clean water to drink or wash in.
5 If we don't reduce pollution now, climate change will get worse.
6 First, we need to learn about how many countries will lose land through climate change.

Description of a problem	Say what will happen	Suggested action
0		

4 Match each sentence with the extract it could come from. Then complete the sentences with the linking words in the list.

> that is why | if | unless | so | ~~because~~

0 These animals are endangered _because_ the ocean levels are rising. **A**
1 Every year, more trees are cut down. _____ we need to take some real action now. ☐
2 Climate change will continue _____ we all change the way we live now. ☐
3 We need to build more wells _____ that everyone can drink fresh, clean water. ☐
4 We need to let people know what will happen _____ everybody uses their car all the time. ☐

✎ WRITING TIP: an article about an issue

- Give your article a title.
- Make sure your article has a beginning, a middle and a conclusion.
- Use linking words to connect your arguments.
- Describe the issue clearly and simply.
- Explain the possible future results.
- Suggest ways we can help.

5 **PLAN** You are going to write an article about a global environmental issue. Plan your article and make notes. Use the Writing tip to help you.

- Choose a global environmental issue.
- Describe the problem.
- Explain what will or might happen if nothing changes.
- Make suggestions to solve it.
- Use the Writing tip to help you.

6 **PRODUCE** Write an article in about 200 words. Use your plan from Exercise 5.

LISTENING

1 🔊 6.03 Listen to the conversations and match them with the photos.

A ☐

B ☐

C ☐

2 🔊 6.03 Listen again. Circle the correct answers.

0 Why is Amelia excited?
  A She's going to visit a nature area.
  B She's going to finish her project.
  C Her class is going on a trip to the zoo.

1 What's Toby's opinion of the decision?
  A He doesn't think it's a good idea.
  B He isn't very enthusiastic.
  C He's surprised and can't believe it.

2 What are the friends going to do?
  A work in a friend's garden
  B make a place cleaner and nicer
  C go for a walk by the river

DIALOGUE

3 🔊 6.03 Match the sentences. Then listen again to check.

1 Well, to be honest, we didn't win. ☐
2 Come on, Toby! Aren't you pleased? ☐
3 We haven't got any lessons today. ☐
4 Nobody said no, so there'll be about ten of us. ☐
5 We're going to clean all the rubbish out of the river. ☐

a Wow! That's incredible!
b What a great idea! I'll definitely be there.
c Well, sort of.
d What do you mean? Of course we did.
e Oh really? How come?

4 Complete the phrases with the missing vowels.

0 Wh _a_ t _a_ gr _e_ _a_ t id _e_ _a_ !
1 Th __ t's __ m __ z __ ng!
2 Th __ t s __ __ nds __ xc __ t __ ng!
3 W __ w!
4 __ h, r __ __ lly?
5 H __ w __ xc __ t __ ng!
6 C __ __ l!
7 __ ncr __ d __ bl __ !

5 Write two short conversations about people telling their friends some exciting news.

Train to TH!NK

Recognising different text types

6 Read the extracts and write the text types. Check your answers using page 60 of the Student's Book.

0 Hi Jay, Gr8 you'll come over to my place on Sunday. Got some cool videos to show you. Love, B
   Text message

1 Pop in and check out our vegetables – grown by local farmers and brought to you daily by us.
   _____

2 Monday: another cool day at school. Science project interesting, working with Lisa. Tomorrow athletics competition.
   _____

3 He opened his eyes. He had no idea where he was, but he knew the place was dangerous.
   _____

4 Joel, please feed the cat. Food's in the fridge. See you tonight, Mum
   _____

5 A spokesman for SpaceLive said to reporters on Tuesday that the company was thinking of sending plants to the moon.
   _____

B1 Preliminary for Schools

WRITING
Part 1: Email

1. **You must answer this question. Write your answer in about 100 words.**

   Read this email from your English-speaking friend, Riley, and the notes you have made.

   Riley
   riley@thinkmail.com

   Hi!

   I'm going to an animal park with my family on Saturday. I know you're interested in animals and there's one free place in our car. Would you like to come with us? — **Yes!**

   There's a new African Bird Area in the park and we're going to visit The Butterfly Zone, too. You're interested in birds and butterflies, aren't you? — **Birds: no. Butterflies: yes.**

   There's a big café in the park or we could have a picnic on the grass by the giraffes, if the weather is nice. Do you like sandwiches, or would you prefer something else? — **Yes, but no meat.**

   If you can come, we would probably pick you up around ten o'clock. Is that OK? — **Tennis lesson finishes at 10.**

   Riley

   Write your email to Riley, using all the notes.

   SUGGESTED PLAN:
   - Thank your friend for the invitation.
   - Accept and explain why.
   - Say you don't like birds, but you like butterflies, and why.
   - Say you like sandwiches, but that you don't eat meat.
   - Say you have a tennis lesson until 10 and ask if that is OK.
   - Finish with a friendly phrase.

EXAM GUIDE: WRITING PART 1

In B1 Preliminary for Schools Writing Part 1, you have to write an answer to an email. There are four notes and you must include <u>all</u> of these in your answer.
- Read the instructions carefully.
- Then read the email and the notes.
- Make a plan before you start writing.
- Remember to answer all the questions, not just one or two.
- Remember who you're writing to and use appropriate language (formal or informal).

CONSOLIDATION

🎧 LISTENING

1 🔊 6.04 Listen to the conversation. Tick (✓) A, B or C.

1 Who chose the name of the band?
  A Alice ☐
  B Joe ☐
  C Ben ☐
2 What instrument does Joe play in the band?
  A keyboard ☐
  B guitar ☐
  C drums ☐
3 What instrument does Tamsin play?
  A trumpet ☐
  B saxophone ☐
  C violin ☐

2 🔊 6.04 Listen again and answer the questions.

0 Why is the band called The Green Warriors?
  to show that they care about the environment
1 What does Ben do in the band?
  _____
2 What do Jessica and Lucy play in the band?
  _____
3 How long has Tamsin been playing the saxophone?
  _____
4 Where does the band practise?
  _____

Ⓖ GRAMMAR

3 (Circle) the correct words.

I've ⁰worked /(been working) at the local nature reserve for three months. I spend half my time at the reserve and half my time visiting schools. I've ¹already visited / been visiting about 20 schools in the local area. I think it's very important to talk to teenagers. If they ²don't / won't learn how to love the environment, there ³isn't / won't be much future for our world. One of the projects I've ⁴worked / been working on for the last few months is trying to stop the local council from building hundreds of new houses. Unless we ⁵do / don't do something to stop it, it ⁶will / won't cause serious problems for the local wildlife because they want to build them on an important site for many rare birds. I've ⁷already written / been writing about 30 letters to the local politician, but so far he hasn't ⁸replied / been replying to me.

4 Complete the sentences with the correct present perfect simple or continuous form of the verbs.

0 Jane Cooper ___has been___ (be) a famous writer for a long time.
1 She _____ (write) over 30 novels now.
2 She _____ (write) novels for many years.
3 She _____ (make) a lot of money.
4 Thousands of people _____ (send) her letters.
5 She _____ (reply) to all of them!
6 Since last month, she _____ (think) about her next novel.
7 But she still _____ (not decide) what the new novel will be about.

🅰🇿 VOCABULARY

5 Match the parts of the sentences.

0 Marty James started writing   g
1 He started   ☐
2 They played their first   ☐
3 The band entered   ☐
4 And they won   ☐
5 For their prize they got the chance ☐
6 The song was   ☐
7 It soon entered   ☐
8 Next month the band are going   ☐

a a talent show.
b to record an album.
c downloaded over 200,000 times.
d on a national tour.
e gig in the school hall.
f the competition.
g songs when he was 12.
h a band a year later.
i the pop charts.

6 Read the pamphlet and complete the words. The first letters are given.

THREE SIMPLE WAYS TO MAKE A DIFFERENCE:

› ⁰S_ave_____ your plastic bags and ¹r_____ them next time you go shopping – don't ²t_____ them ³a_____ .

› ⁴R_____ your rubbish – sort out the plastic from the paper and the glass.

› ⁵D _____ electronics at night. Don't leave them on ⁶s_____ . It just ⁷w_____ power.

UNITS 5 & 6

DIALOGUE

7 🔊 6.05 **Complete the conversation with the phrases in the list. There is one phrase you don't need. Then listen and check.**

> How exciting! | I can't wait. | I'm just a bit upset.
> If you say so | No way. | So, what's the matter?
> There's no point in | ~~What a great idea!~~
> What's up, Jennie?

Jennie Have you heard the news?
Ronan What news?
Jennie We're having a school concert to raise money for the Clean Up Our Air campaign.
Ronan ⁰ *What a great idea!*
Jennie And our band's playing.
Ronan ¹ _____
Jennie Isn't it? ² _____
[Two days later]
Ronan ³ _____ You don't look very happy.
Jennie It's nothing. ⁴ _____
Ronan ⁵ _____
Jennie Remember the school concert I told you about the other day? Well, it's been cancelled.
Ronan ⁶ _____
Jennie Yes, it's true. The headteacher decided it wasn't a good idea.
Ronan It's not right. We've got to do something. I'm going to talk to him now.
Jennie ⁷ _____ trying to change his mind. It's not happening!

READING

8 Read the article. Mark the sentences T (true) or F (false). Correct the false information.

0 Kashy Keegan became famous when he wrote his song *This Is My Dream*. **F**
Kashy became famous five years later.

1 Five years after he wrote *This Is My Dream*, Kashy decided to put it online. ☐
_____

2 A Hong Kong TV station wanted to use this song to advertise their shows. ☐
_____

3 Kashy contacted the TV station and asked to perform in Hong Kong. ☐
_____

4 People in Hong Kong thought Kashy was famous in his home country. ☐
_____

Kashy Keegan always wanted to be a pop star and spent years trying to make it happen. In 2007, when he was 22, he wrote what he felt would finally be his big hit, a song called *This Is My Dream*, but it never happened. As the years passed, he started to give up on his musical career. In 2012, he decided to upload the song to a music-sharing website. He hoped someone might like it.

A few months later, he received an email from Universal Music in Hong Kong. They were starting a new TV channel and they wanted to use *This Is My Dream* as the theme tune to one of their shows. Kashy was really excited and made a deal for $5,000.

When the TV station invited Kashy to Hong Kong, hundreds of fans were waiting for him at the airport. Everyone thought he was a big star in the UK, so he explained that back home, no one knew who he was. A little later, Kashy was singing the song live to more than 30,000 screaming fans. After the show, he gave interviews and signed autographs. The next day, he was in all the newspapers and the song went to number one in the charts.

Kashy's pop dream was finally happening! In 2016, he recorded *This is my Dream* in Chinese and released the video on his Vevo channel. He became one of the first European musicians to write and sing a song in Chinese.

WRITING

9 Write a short text (about 120–150 words) about your favourite song. Include the following information:

- who the song is by
- when it first came out
- how popular it became
- what the song is about
- why you like it

PRONUNCIATION

UNIT 1
Sentence stress

1 Complete the sentences with the correct words from the list. Circle the stressed word in each sentence.

> brilliant idea | a joke | to be famous one
> changed forever | dangerous places | definitely do
> fantastic time | is for living | car accident
> help you | never heard | the new café

0 That's a _____brilliant idea_____ !
1 Can I _____ ?
2 Then one day, her life _____ .
3 I know. Let's go to _____ !
4 We should _____ it!
5 We had a _____ .
6 She travels to some of the most _____ to take photos.
7 They're going _____ day.
8 It was just _____ !
9 Then my aunt had a terrible _____ .
10 I've _____ him complain.
11 'Life _____ ,' she said.

2 🔊 1.02 Listen, check and repeat.

UNIT 2
Word stress

1 Write the verbs from the list in the correct columns.

> believe | concentrate | forget | guess | know
> recognise | remember | suppose | think

1 One syllable	2 Two syllables	3 Three syllables
		concentrate

2 🔊 2.01 Listen, check and repeat.

3 Which syllable is stressed? Write the verbs in the correct columns.

> believe | concentrate | consider | discuss
> explain | imagine | listen | motivate
> recognise | remember | study | wonder

Oo	oO	Ooo	oOo
	believe		

4 🔊 2.02 Listen, check and repeat.

UNIT 3
Words ending with schwa /ə/

1 Complete the sentences with the comparative forms of the adjectives in the list.

> early | funny | good | old
> quiet | slow | tall | tidy

0 My sister's a lot ___tidier___ than me. Her bedroom is always clean.
1 There's too much noise here – let's go somewhere _____ .
2 He's very clever and much _____ at Maths than me.
3 Mum has to go to work at 8 o'clock; she gets up _____ than the rest of us.
4 My brother's 1.72 metres. He's _____ than me.
5 Jake's fourteen and his sister's ten. He's _____ than her.
6 You're driving too fast. Could you please go a little _____ ?
7 This comedy show is much _____ than the one we saw last week.

2 🔊 3.01 Listen, check and repeat.

PRONUNCIATION

3 Write the comparatives from Exercise 1 in the correct columns. <u>Underline</u> the stressed syllable. Remember that the final syllable 'er' is never stressed. It has the schwa /ə/ sound.

Two syllables	Three syllables
<u>bett</u>er	<u>ear</u>lier

4 🔊 3.02 Listen, check and repeat.

UNIT 4
The short /ʌ/ vowel sound

1 (Circle) the word in each line that doesn't have the /ʌ/ sound (e.g. the sound in *son*, *one* and *done*).

	A	B	C	D
0	son	one	done	(dog)
1	fun	won	home	come
2	shout	young	much	tongue
3	enough	cousin	you	love
4	must	mother	nose	doesn't
5	trouble	jump	other	note
6	love	stuff	funny	ground
7	put	wonder	under	nothing
8	could	some	lovely	brother
9	Sunday	Monday	over	cover
10	none	use	monkey	another
11	good	blood	touch	couple

2 🔊 4.01 Listen, check and repeat.

UNIT 5
Strong and weak forms of *been* /biːn/ and /bɪn/

1 Match the statements (1–6) with the responses (a–g).

0 Have you <u>been</u> to London? — *e*
1 Where have you been? You're covered in dirt! ___
2 You look ill. ___
3 You need to go to the director's office, now. ___
4 Look at your face. It's so red! Where have you been? ___
5 How long has it been since you saw John? ___
6 The girls are tired. ___

a I know. I've been to the doctor's.
b I've been working in the garden.
c It's been a long time – more than three months.
d They've been playing football.
e Yes, I have. I've been going there every summer since I was ten.
f I've been at the beach all day. I forgot my sun cream.
g I've already been.

2 🔊 5.01 Listen, check and repeat.

3 (Circle) the strong forms of *been* /biːn/ and <u>underline</u> the weak forms of *been* /bɪn/.

4 🔊 5.01 Listen again, check and repeat.

UNIT 6
/f/, /v/ and /b/ consonant sounds

1 🔊 6.01 Listen and (circle) the word you hear.

0 a (few)	b view	3 a ferry	b very
1 a fast	b vast	4 a leaf	b leave
2 a fan	b van	5 a off	b of

2 🔊 6.01 Listen again, check and repeat.

3 (Circle) the correct words to complete the sentences.

0 They went out in Bill's dad's (boat) / *vote*.
1 That's a *berry* / *very* good idea.
2 She wants to be a *vet* / *bet* when she's older.
3 I wore my *best* / *vest* clothes to the party.
4 He drives a white *van* / *ban* for his job.

4 🔊 6.02 Listen, check and repeat.

GRAMMAR REFERENCE

UNIT 1
Present perfect with *just*, *already* and *yet*

We often use the present perfect with the words *just* / *already* / *yet*.

1 We use *just* before the past participle to say that something happened a short time ago.

   *They've **just** come back from their holiday.*

2 We use *already* at the end of a sentence or before the past participle to show surprise, or to emphasise that something has been done, or finished, sooner than expected.

   *Have you finished **already**?*
   *No food, thanks – I've **already** eaten.*

3 We use *yet* at the end of negative sentences and questions to emphasise that something hasn't happened but probably will in the future.

   *Have you finished your homework **yet**?*
   *I haven't played that game **yet** (but I will).*

Present perfect vs. past simple

1 We use the past simple to talk about events which are complete and finished, or 'before now', at the time of speaking.

   *I **saw** you in town yesterday. Who **were** you with?*

2 We use the present perfect to connect the past and 'now' (at the time of speaking).

   *I **haven't seen** you this week. Where **have** you **been**?*

UNIT 2
Present perfect with *for* and *since*

1 We can use the present perfect to talk about something that began in the past and continues to be true in the present.

   *We**'ve lived** here for ten years. (= and we still live here)*
   *She**'s played** in a band since 2018. (= and she still plays in it)*

2 We talk about the time between when something started and now with *for* or *since*.

   - We use the word *for* when we mention a period of time from the past until now.
     ***for** half an hour / **for** three months / **for** ages*
   - We use the word *since* when we mention a point in time in the past.
     ***since** six o'clock / **since** 2012 / **since** last weekend*

a, *an*, *the* or no article

1 We use *a*, *an* before a singular, countable noun to talk about something for the first time in a conversation.

   *Look – there's **a** horse in the garden!*
   *Do you want **an** apple?*

   We also use *a* / *an* when we are not talking about a specific thing.

   *I haven't got **a** computer.*

2 We use *the* before a noun when it is clear which thing(s) or person/people we are talking about.

   ***The** apples in our garden are delicious.*
   *Have you got **the** book? (= the book we were talking about before)*
   ***The** woman next door is really friendly.*

   We also use *the* when there is only one thing that exists.

   *Look at **the** moon!*

3 We use no article (zero article) before plural countable nouns, and before uncountable nouns, when we are talking about things in general.

   ***Cars** are expensive.*
   ***Love** is the most important thing.*

UNIT 3
Comparative and superlative adjectives (review)

1 When we want to compare two things, or two groups of things, we use a comparative form + *than*.

   *My sister is **older than** me.*
   *My old phone was **more expensive than** my new one.*
   *The film is **better than** the book.*

2 With short adjectives, we normally add *-er*.
  With longer adjectives (more than two syllables), we normally don't change the adjective – we put *more* in front of it.

  hot ➜ hot**ter**   short ➜ short**er**   clever ➜ clever**er**
  interesting ➜ **more** interesting   exciting ➜ **more** exciting

3 Some adjectives are irregular – they have a different comparative form.

  good ➜ better   bad ➜ worse   far ➜ further

(not) as … as

When we want to say that two things are the same (or not the same) we can use *(not) as* + adjective + *as*.

She's **as tall as** her mother now.
This question is**n't as easy as** the last one.

Making a comparison stronger or weaker

We can make a comparison stronger or weaker by using *much / far*, *a lot* or *a little / a bit*. These words come before the comparison.

His computer is **far better** than mine.
His bike was **much more expensive** than mine.
He lives **a little further** from school than I do.

Adverbs and comparative adverbs

1 We use adverbs to describe verbs — they say how an action is or was performed.

  She shouted **angrily**.   Run **quickly**!
  They got to the theatre **early**.

  We can also use adverbs before adjectives.

  It was **really** cold on Sunday.
  The coffee was **incredibly** hot, so I couldn't drink it.

2 Most adverbs are formed by adjective + *-ly*.

  slow ➜ slow**ly**   nice ➜ nice**ly**

  If the adjective ends in *-le*, we drop the *-e* and add *-y*.

  incredible ➜ incredib**ly**   possible ➜ possib**ly**

  If the adjective ends in consonant + *-y*, we change the *-y* to *-i* and add *-ly*.

  angry ➜ angr**ily**   lucky ➜ luck**ily**   hungry ➜ hungr**ily**

3 Some adverbs are irregular – they don't have an *-ly* ending.

  good ➜ well   fast ➜ fast   hard ➜ hard
  early ➜ early   late ➜ late

4 To compare adverbs, we use the same rules as we do when we compare adjectives. With short adverbs, we add *-er* or *-r*, and *than* after the adverb.

  I worked **hard**, but Sue worked **harder than** me!

5 With longer adverbs, we use *more* (+ adverb) + *than*.

  She does things **more easily than** me.

6 To compare the adverb *well*, we use *better … than*.
  To compare the adverb *far*, we use *further … than*.

  He cooks **better than** me.
  London to Mumbai is **further than** London to New York.

UNIT 4
Indefinite pronouns

1 We can use the words *every / some / no / any* together with *one / thing / where* to make compound nouns.

  everyone = all the people
  everything = all the things
  everywhere = all the places
  someone = a person, but we don't know who
  something = a thing, but we don't know which
  somewhere = a place, but we don't know where
  no one = none of the people
  nothing = none of the things
  nowhere = none of the places
  anyone = any person / any of the people
  anything = any of the things
  anywhere = any of the places

2 These words are all singular.

  Something smells nice. **No one's** here. **Nothing was** found. **Everywhere was** full. **Someone has** opened my desk.

3 We don't use negatives with *nothing* and *no one*. We use *anything* or *anyone* instead.

  I **don't** know **anyone** here.
  (NOT I ~~don't know no one~~ here.)

all (some / none / any) of them

With other nouns and pronouns, we use *all of / some of / none of* + plural or uncountable noun/pronoun.

All of them are yours.   **Some of** the teachers are really nice.
None of my friends called me yesterday.
Do **any of** you know the answer?

should(n't), had better, ought to

1 *Should*, *had ('d) better* and *ought to* are all used to give advice.

2 *Should* and *ought to* both mean 'I think it's (not) a good idea for you/me/him (etc.) to do this'.

  You **should do** more exercise. (= I think it is a good idea for you to do more exercise.)
  She **shouldn't talk** in class. (= I think it is not a good idea for her to talk in class.)
  We **ought to** leave now. (= I think it is a good idea for us to leave now.)

3 The meaning of *had better* is often stronger. The speaker wants to say that there are negative consequences if the person ignores the advice.

I'd **better run**. (or I'll be late)
You'd **better not talk** in class. (or the teacher will be angry)

4 *Should*, *had better* and *ought to* are all followed by the infinitive of another verb.

You **should be** more careful.
I **ought to eat** more fruit.
We'**d better hurry** or we'll be late.

5 *Should* and *had better* form the negative by adding *not* afterwards.

They **shouldn't** be so rude.
We'**d better not** stay out late.

We make *ought to* negative by putting *not* after *ought* (but we don't use this form very often).

You **ought not to** make so much noise.

UNIT 5
Present perfect continuous

1 The present perfect continuous is formed with the present tense of *have* + *been* + the *-ing* form of the verb.

I'**ve been reading** since breakfast.
Have you **been sitting** here all day?

2 Sentences with the present perfect always connect the present and the past. We often use the present perfect continuous to talk about activities which started in the past and are still continuing now.

She'**s been running** for an hour. (= She started running an hour ago, and she is still running.)

3 We also use the present perfect continuous to talk about actions with a result in the present. These actions may or may not be complete.

I'm tired because I'**ve been working**.
Jack's feeling ill because he **hasn't been eating** well.

4 We also use the present perfect continuous to talk about actions which began in the past and continue to the present, but perhaps we are not doing the action at the time of speaking.

We'**ve been studying** Spanish for six months.
(= We started studying six months ago, and we are still studying, but we're not studying at this exact moment.)

Present perfect simple vs. present perfect continuous

1 We use the present perfect simple to show that an action is finished, or to focus on what (and how much) we have completed in a period of time.

I'**ve written** an email.
I'**ve written** twelve emails this morning.

2 We use the present perfect continuous to show that an action is still going on, or to focus on how long something has been in progress.

I'**ve been reading** this book for two days.
I'**ve been reading** detective stories for years.

Compare the sentences:

She'**s been writing** books for many years.
She'**s written** over twenty books.

UNIT 6
will (not), *may (not)*, *might (not)* for prediction

1 We can use the modal verb *will* ('*ll*) or *will not* (*won't*) to make predictions about the future.

Don't worry about the exam – it **won't be** difficult.

2 We use *might/might not* or *may/may not* to make less certain predictions about the future.

It **might rain** this afternoon – if it does, then I **may not** go the match.

First conditional / *unless* in first conditional sentences

1 We use the first conditional to talk about possible actions / situations in the future, and their (possible) results.

If I finish my homework, I'**ll go** out.

2 We often make conditional sentences by using *if* + subject + present simple in the *if* clause, and *will*/*won't* / *might*/*might not* in the main clause.

If I **have** time this afternoon, I'**ll go** for a walk.
We **might go** out tonight **if** there's nothing good on TV.

3 We can also use the word *unless* in conditional sentences – it means *if not*.

She **won't come unless** you **ask** her. (= She won't come if you don't ask her.)

4 There are two clauses in these sentences. We can put the main clause first, or the *if/unless* clause first. When the *if/unless* clause comes first, there is *a comma (,)* after it.

Unless you tell me, I won't know what to do.
I won't know what to do **unless** you tell me.

IRREGULAR VERBS

Base form	Past simple	Past participle
be	was / were	been
beat	beat	beaten
become	became	become
begin	began	begun
break	broke	broken
bring	brought	brought
build	built	built
buy	bought	bought
can	could	–
catch	caught	caught
choose	chose	chosen
come	came	come
cost	cost	cost
cut	cut	cut
do	did	done
draw	drew	drawn
drink	drank	drunk
drive	drove	driven
eat	ate	eaten
fall	fell	fallen
feel	felt	felt
fight	fought	fought
find	found	found
fly	flew	flown
forget	forgot	forgotten
get	got	got
give	gave	given
go	went	gone
grow	grew	grown
hang	hung	hung
have	had	had
hear	heard	heard
hit	hit	hit
hold	held	held
hurt	hurt	hurt
keep	kept	kept
know	knew	known
lead	led	led

Base form	Past simple	Past participle
leave	left	left
lend	lent	lent
let	let	let
lie	lay	lain
light	lit	lit
lose	lost	lost
make	made	made
mean	meant	meant
meet	met	met
pay	paid	paid
put	put	put
read /riːd/	read /red/	read /red/
ride	rode	ridden
ring	rang	rung
rise	rose	risen
run	ran	run
say	said	said
see	saw	seen
sell	sold	sold
send	sent	sent
set	set	set
shoot	shot	shot
show	showed	shown
sing	sang	sung
sit	sat	sat
sleep	slept	slept
speak	spoke	spoken
spend	spent	spent
stand	stood	stood
steal	stole	stolen
strike	struck	struck
swim	swam	swum
take	took	taken
teach	taught	taught
tell	told	told
think	thought	thought
throw	threw	thrown
understand	understood	understood
wake	woke	woken
wear	wore	worn
win	won	won
write	wrote	written

ACKNOWLEDGEMENTS

The authors and publishers acknowledge the following sources of copyright material and are grateful for the permissions granted. While every effort has been made, it has not always been possible to identify the sources of all the material used, or to trace all copyright holders. If any omissions are brought to our notice, we will be happy to include the appropriate acknowledgements on reprinting and in the next update to the digital edition, as applicable.

Key: U = Unit.

Photography

All the photographs are sourced from Getty Images.

U0: Jose Luis Pelaez Inc/DigitalVision; Louis Turner/Cultura; **U1**: Jef De Puydt/500px; Ariel Skelley/The Image Bank; SDI Productions/E+; Maskot; JB Lacroix/WireImage; **U2**: elenaleonova/E+; Andreas Speich/EyeEm; Gabriele Grassl/iStock/Getty Images Plus; csy302/iStock/Getty Images Plus; Photo by Bhaskar Dutta/Moment; gldburger/iStock/Getty Images Plus; GIPhotoStock/Cultura; Valerie Loiseleux/E+; biriberg/E+; Abdul Mukmin Abdullah/EyeEm; frentusha/iStock/Getty Images Plus; Vladimir Godnik; ciricvelibor/E+; SDI Productions/E+; mediaphotos/iStock/Getty Images Plus; PeopleImages/E+; Letizia Le Fur/ONOKY; Klaus Vedfelt/DigitalVision; **U3**: Caiaimage; kali9/E+; AntonioGuillem/iStock/Getty Images Plus; filo/E+; luismmolina/E+; ISerg/iStock/Getty Images Plus; Zoonar RF; 4x6/DigitalVision Vectors; Prakasit Khuansuwan/EyeEm; **U4**: Robert Daly/OJO Images; franz12/iStock/Getty Images Plus; domin_domin/E+; Yobro10/iStock/Getty Images Plus; Bloom Productions/Stone; JBryson/iStock/Getty Images Plus; Juanmonino/E+; Juanmonino/iStock/Getty Images Plus; H. Armstrong Roberts/Retrofile RF; **U5**: Dorling Kindersley/Getty Images; RapidEye/E+; sdigital/iStock/Getty Images Plus; adventtr/iStock/Getty Images Plus; J-Elgaard/iStock/Getty Images Plus; Suljo/iStock/Getty Images Plus; Nerthuz/iStock/Getty Images Plus; Tetra Images; shironosov/iStock/Getty Images Plus; momcilog/E+; Hero Images; Mark Horton/WireImage; Amanda Edwards/WireImage; William Perugini/Image Source; **U6**: rmitsch/E+; KEENPRESS/Stone; On-Air/iStock/Getty Images Plus; Peter Dazeley/Photographer's Choice RF; Spencer Platt/Getty Images News; Kristian Bell/Moment; urbazon/E+; whitemay/E+; James Emmerson/robertharding; Caspar Benson; Ignacio Palacios/Stone; South China Morning Post.

Illustrations

Dusan Lakicevic (Beehive Illustration) pp. 5, 15, 46; Adam Linley (Beehive Illustration) pp. 21, 42; Mark Ruffle pp. 4, 17; Ben Scruton (Meiklejohn) pp. 10, 29, 37, 54; Szilvia Szakall (Beehive Illustration) pp. 8, 34.

Audio

Audio Produced by Leon Chambers